The End of Intelligence

The End of Intelligence

Espionage and State Power in the Information Age

David Tucker

Stanford Security Studies

An Imprint of Stanford University Press

Stanford, California

Stanford University Press
Stanford, California

Library of Congress Cataloging-in-Publication Data

Tucker, David, author
    The end of intelligence : espionage and state power in the
information age / David Tucker.
        p. cm.
    Includes bibliographical references and index.
    ISBN 978-0-8047-9042-0 (cloth : alk. paper) —
    ISBN 978-0-8047-9265-3 (pbk. : alk. paper)
    1. Intelligence service. 2. Espionage. 3. Information society—
Political aspects. 4. Information technology—Political aspects.
5. Power (Social sciences). I. Title.
JF1525.I6T83   2014
    327.12—dc23

                                                        2014010112

    ISBN 978-0-8047-9269-1 (electronic)

Printed in the United States of America on acid-free, archival-quality
paper. Typeset at Stanford University Press in 10/14 Minion.

To ELLEN, NATHAN, *and* SARAH
for revealing the beauty in chance events

Contents

An executive who understands the problem of intelligence,
who grasps the limitations and contributions of men of knowledge,
is more likely to temper power with wisdom.
—Harold L. Wilensky

We are prone to overestimate how much we understand about the world
and to underestimate the role of chance in events.
—Daniel Kahneman

It is because chance plays so large a role in the outcome of our actions
that a standard of goodness or badness beyond results
has always recommended itself to men of superior virtue.
—Harry V. Jaffa

Introduction

We live in the information age, as everyone now knows. Our increasing ability to collect, store, and manipulate information is revolutionizing everything we do, from how we shop to how we wage war, threatening both the power of the nation-state and the privacy of its citizens.[1] These claims may be true, but one of the most insightful accounts of our information age reminds us that there have been others, and ours perhaps less revolutionary than its predecessors. The advent of literacy, and then of printing, produced changes arguably more significant than any we are living through now.[2] Some question whether information technology will even transform economic life to the degree of previous technologies.[3] Of course, for such questions, we should probably reserve the answer Zhou Enlai supposedly gave two hundred years after the French Revolution when asked about its significance: it is too soon to say.

While we wait for answers to ripen in the bosom of time, we might address the issue of the information revolution in a narrower way. Espionage is a form of information collection. If we examine how the information revolution is affecting espionage and intelligence more broadly, we might come to understand something of that revolution's power and scope. Since information is a kind of intelligence, intelligence agencies are in some sense the paradigmatic government agencies of the information age and intelligence its paradigmatic activity. Of all government agencies, only intelligence agencies exist solely to collect and analyze information. And these agencies face particular challenges as the "tsunami of information" sweeps over the world, spreading access to information and the ability to analyze it and changing what is known and how it is known.[4]

Examining espionage is a way of testing claims made about the power of information to change not just one set of organizations but our lives as well. For example, it will reveal something about the fate of both secrecy and privacy, the former traditionally considered essential for government, the latter for liberal

1

citizenship. Espionage is a particularly good candidate for this task because it is reputed to be the world's second oldest profession. It thus seems to be somehow an elemental part of human life or to be a response to some basic human necessity. Espionage remains a pre-eminently human business in the midst of a sweeping technical revolution. We know that the information revolution has changed the oldest profession. What has it done to espionage? And what does the fate of espionage tell us about our own fate in the information revolution?

Although espionage is not just a state activity,[5] it has always been closely associated with that form of power. The state has been inseparable from the collection, storage, and manipulation of information. Espionage has long been a part of the state's information system. In discussing the fate of espionage in the information age, we are at the same time, to some degree, discussing the fate of state power.

The discussion that follows focuses on the experience of the United States. Many questions have been raised about the quality of America's intelligence services. In particular, the failures of its espionage have been examined and debated in detail. Prior to 9/11, the United States had few if any human sources that could report on al Qaeda, and before the invasion of Iraq, no human sources who could inform the United States on the status of Saddam Hussein's weapons programs. Both the attack on 9/11 and the misjudgments about Iraq, and all its consequences, are thought to be in no small measure the result of deficiencies in America's espionage capabilities. On the other hand, espionage played a decisive role in the killing of Osama bin Laden and in the killing or capturing of other notorious terrorists, as well as many less well known. So, American espionage has had its successes and failures. On balance, it seems representative of modern espionage, even if perhaps somewhat less effective than the operations of other countries. In any case, the discussion also draws on evidence from ancient China, Rome, and Greece, as well as modern Europe and the Middle East.

Most discussions of intelligence suggest that we need to be better at it, but they also suggest that we need more analysis, probably less espionage and certainly less covert action.[6] The analysis presented here reaches a somewhat different conclusion: we could do with much less analysis, at least as it has been institutionalized in American intelligence, but cannot do without espionage and covert action. Although problematic, the latter two instruments of statecraft are necessary. Understanding their problems may make their necessary use more effective. This study does not focus on the issue of intelligence reform, however. It considers, instead, the notion of reformative public policy analysis itself as an expression of the essential spirit of our information age. A recent book on the problems of American intelligence exemplifies the standard public policy approach. Although it pays lip service to the inevitable limitations and hence failures of intelligence, it argues repeatedly that past reforms have not succeeded or gone far enough because despite them, intelligence failed (for example, the 9/11 attacks or Iraq WMD).[7] The assumption is that policy analysis and resulting reforms must lead to an absence of failures; if there are failures, then the analysis was faulty or the reforms did not go far enough. Such an approach gives no serious consideration to the limits of information gathering and analysis, to the limits of human knowledge. Of course, not all public policy analysis is blind to the limits of such analysis or to the limits of intelligence itself.[8] But even these more clear sighted examples remain within the genre, analytical in method and ameliorative in intent, even if more prudent in their hopes. The following discussion of espionage and intelligence joins them by questioning such analysis and reform but aims also to question at least some of the assumptions behind such ameliorative analysis, assumptions that are central to the modern information age.

The argument unfolds as follows. Chapter One explains the connections between information, intelligence, and state power. It explains how espionage fits within this web of connections. It argues that there are differences between the ancient understanding of intelligence and the modern understanding, which emerged in the sixteenth and seventeenth centuries. In part, the chapter uses the work of Jean-Baptiste Colbert and Francis Bacon to explain the differences. Bacon is particularly important, since he was a philosopher, a statesman, and a spymaster. Using philosophy and history to illuminate espionage and the power of the state is not unprecedented.[9] The analysis offered here treats espionage and state power generally, however, rather than as practiced in one time and place, and therefore aims to address its subjects most broadly. From the historical and theoretical considerations of Chapter One, we turn in Chapter Two to an examination of espionage. This examination provides the first test of the claims made on behalf of modern information and knowledge. Espionage requires a thorough understanding of the wellsprings of human action, and, we argue, it is these that prove most recalcitrant to Bacon's program. The chapter also provides the understanding of espionage necessary to assess the claims of the information revolution considered in the rest of the book. Those claims are addressed by examining in successive chapters counterintelligence and covert action; intelligence in warfare; intelligence in irregular warfare; and the power of information inside espionage organizations. The conclusion summarizes what these chapters reveal, emphasizing that the light with which we guide ourselves is dimmer than many suspect but that we are likely to make our way more steadily if we acknowledge the obscurity in which we move. In the end, it reaches the entirely ineffective conclusion that "a standard of goodness or badness beyond results," rather than knowledge, is the key to power. Throughout, the analysis is undertaken in the hopeful spirit of the CIA's motto, an ancient thought for a modern intelligence organization: "Know the truth, and the truth shall set you free."

I began this book while on a sabbatical from the Naval Postgraduate School, Monterey, California. I completed it with the help of a grant from the Earhart Foundation. I would like to thank both institutions for their support. The Ashbrook Center, Ashland University, Ashland, Ohio, offered me a place to work during the sabbatical, making it possible. I would like to thank Peter Schramm, the former director of the center, and Roger Beckett, the current director, for their help, the staff of the center for their support, and the faculty of the History and Political Science Department at Ashland for their hospitality. Edith Foster, of that Department, helped with some classical sources on intelligence. While at the Postgraduate School I learned a good deal from a succession of officers with whom I had the privilege to work in class and on theses. Christopher J. Lamb offered valuable criticism of an earlier version of Chapter Four. Ellen Tucker read and commented on all of the chapters. Sarah Tucker provided research assistance. Anonymous reviewers for Stanford University Press offered many helpful comments and suggestions. In addition, over the years I have benefited from conversations with several individuals who must remain unnamed. One person I may name is the aforementioned Peter Schramm, from whom I have learned more than I like to admit, even if it is less than he hoped to teach. In accordance with my obligations, I submitted this manuscript for a security review. The reviewers requested changes, which I made. I am grateful for all of this assistance. The views expressed are not those of any of these institutions or individuals, but the author's solely.

1   Intelligence, Information, Power

Intelligence is important because it is information; information is important because, like knowledge, it is power. Consider some examples.

In 1673, Louis XIV declared that he had a right to the revenues of any vacant bishopric in France and that he alone had the right to appoint bishops. This declaration revived and extended a royal prerogative that had been debated for centuries. A few bishops objected to Louis's assertion and extension of these prerogatives. The pope supported the dissenting bishops. The debate turned not on abstract claims of right but on the legal standing of Louis's claim. Legal standing in turn depended on laws, charters, deeds, letters—a mass of legal and historical documents. On one side were the pope's canon lawyers and librarians; on the other, Louis's archivists and advisers. Force was always the ultimate resort, but for many reasons a legal battle was preferable. So Jean Baptiste Colbert, Louis's principal adviser, dispatched an assistant to collect documents from episcopal offices and archives. Analyzing this information, and other information already in the royal archives, Colbert prepared a report for Louis in 1675 justifying the assertion of Louis's right. This report became the basis for royal policy, as well as the principal weapon in the struggle, conducted both in the court of public opinion and the private offices of lawyers, with recalcitrant French clergy and the pope. Ultimately, Louis prevailed.[1]

In this case, information was a power that substituted for physical force. Information could also make the use of physical force possible, however. Warfare in the late seventeenth and eighteenth centuries, as it had for centuries, strained the finances of the state. In fact, wars were fought less often to a decision than to financial exhaustion, with treaties setting in place what arms had managed to achieve, until the antagonists could replenish their funds and fight again. Thus the state that could most efficiently refinance itself had a military advantage because it could dictate the initial action of the next war. In its contest with the France of Louis XIV and his immediate successor, Britain was at the beginning the weaker power but had the advantage of a financial system that allowed it to extract resources more efficiently and effectively from the British population. This was an important reason why it was able to contend with French power and, by the middle of the eighteenth century, defeat it.

The effectiveness of the British financial system derived in large part from an efficient method for gathering and analyzing information. A principal source of British state revenue was the excise tax, a tax on goods produced, bought and sold within Great Britain. To collect this tax, of course, the government had to know what was produced and sold and for how much. The British developed a special information system to track this activity, recruiting only the most competent administrators to do this. In other parts of the government administration one might get a job because of one's name or connections—but not in the Excise Department. The British filled excise positions through competitive examinations that tested mathematical ability, and not just simple matters of addition and subtraction. Those who passed the test and entered the service became what we would now call civil servants, long-term specialized employees of the state whose job it was to collect, store, and analyze detailed information on the minutiae of British economic activity. Gathering that information—how many heads of cheese or casks of port in a shop in Bristol, for example—required that the British develop and regularize unprecedented powers of government inspection. The excise system had its own system of inspectors, enforcement officers, and administrative courts to implement and administer the information system. So intrusive was this power that William Blackstone, certainly not a radical critic of Britain's constitutional system, wrote in his *Commentaries on the Laws of England* that the excise system was "hardly compatible with the temper of a free nation."[2]

An internal taxation system is not the only way that information can affect military power, of course. It may have a more direct effect. When Caesar decided to invade Britain, he sought to gather information about this unknown island. Among other things, he wanted to know what its topography might be, how many tribes it contained, how they fought, what kind of weapons they used. He also wanted to know the character of the people. The more Caesar knew about the island and its inhabitants, the better he could prepare for his expedition and the more likely that it would succeed. Seeking this knowledge, Caesar consulted traders, who knew little, and his Gallic allies, who knew less. Undeterred, he pressed on. When his forces went ashore in Britain, they were surprised at the resistance they met. The Britons had anticipated the attack. In questioning traders, Caesar had indicated his interest, and some of the traders had informed the Britons. Caesar avoided defeat because of the skill and valor of his soldiers—at a critical moment, the eagle-bearer of the Tenth Legion, rather than lose the eagle in disgrace, cried out to his comrades and charged alone through the surf at the enemy, drawing his legion and then others behind him. Critical as well was Caesar's ability to inform himself of what was happening in the battle and to respond. His means of gathering information as the battle progressed being all but nonexistent, he was dependent entirely on his ability to see and analyze the battle as it unfolded before him.[3]

Caesar's experience invading Britain shows the disadvantage a military force can labor under if it lacks relevant information. For example, not having learned much about Britain's harbors, Caesar's flotilla had to move about the coast in view of British forces before he found a place where he could disembark his troops. This gave the information advantage to the Britons, who watched as Caesar chose his landing site. On the other hand, despite his lack of intelligence, Caesar prevailed. His generalship and the overall quality of the Roman army overcame intelligence deficiencies. Caesar's approach in this instance exemplifies the idea that as long as the Romans continued on the strategic offensive, expanding their empire, thinking themselves invincible, intelligence was less important to them; it became essential when they had reached the limits of their empire, sensed the vulnerability at their borders, and in effect adopted a defensive strategic outlook.[4] The invasion of Britain was in effect an ongoing reconnaissance in force. Conquest was a form of intelligence gathering, rather than something made possible or facilitated by intelligence. Caesar sought information on Britain after he had already decided to invade.

The role of intelligence when an empire reaches its limits and takes on a more defensive outlook is evident in the way the British used intelligence on the northwest frontier of India. In this area, men called Political Officers dealt with the tribes. They lived, for example, among the tribes in Waziristan, learned tribal languages, and accumulated a good deal of knowledge about the tribes and how to deal with them. They understood which were the most influential tribes, those whose support of British policy would carry others along. They met with tribal leaders separately or in jirgas, assemblies in which decisions were (and are) taken by consensus. In each case, they had to know enough about the leaders to persuade them to act in accordance with British interests. They persuaded using the language, images, and sayings of tribal rhetoric but beyond that by understanding what the tribes and their leaders valued. They knew whom to praise and whom to insult, how and when. They also dispensed money, the British adopting the Roman custom of dealing with tribes by paying allowances that turned the tribes into clients, at least for a time. Political Officers were not uniformly knowledgeable and long-serving, but when they were, they were often effective. The British stationed forces near the tribal areas, but an effective Political Officer could limit the risk and expense of their use. At the outbreak of World War I, a Political Officer persuaded the British government to increase the allowance of a key tribe in Waziristan, which ensured its support and the support of neighboring tribes during the war. This allowed the British to send to more important theaters troops that might otherwise have been needed on the frontier.[5] Information or intelligence in this case was what is now called a force-multiplier. Knowledge of the tribes allowed the British to remain in control on the frontier and put more forces on the front in Europe.

Political officers succeeded by using their knowledge of the tribes to build influence over them. This influence was a source of power. It was also openly developed and exercised. Usually when one speaks of intelligence and influence, one implies clandestine tactics. For example, during World War II, an Italian airline flew from Brazil to Italy, in defiance of the British embargo of Europe. The flight carried personnel, gold, industrial material, and information from German agents in Brazil to Italy, where such cargo and information could make it to Germany. How could these flights be stopped? The Special Operations Executive, which carried out sabotage and other clandestine operations for the British, suggested blowing up the plane or otherwise physically disabling it. MI6, the British foreign intelligence organization, pointed out that this would only temporarily stop the flights and, since the British would be the most obvious suspects, would certainly damage British relations with Brazil. MI6 offered an alternative: through its human sources, it would obtain some of the airline's official stationery and forge on it a letter supposedly from the head of the airline in Italy to his manager in Brazil criticizing and insulting the Brazilian head of state. MI6 was given permission to conduct the operation. Leaked to the Brazilian head of state through an unwitting Allied embassy, the letter had its intended effect. The flights were shut down.[6]

This influence operation from World War II brought together several different kinds of information to produce a desired result. For example, the operation required the technical knowledge needed to forge a letter, as well as the no less important but certainly vaguer sense of how the Brazilian head of state would respond to it. In this case, knowledge allowed the British to get the president of Brazil to do something he would not have otherwise done, a simple definition of power. Often, however, intelligence is used not to gain power but to prevent suffering, particularly that caused by an unpleasant surprise, thus countering the power of uncertainty in human affairs. Consider a simple example drawn from World War I.

As the war in Europe settled into bloody stalemate, it became a matter of launching or repelling offensives against entrenched positions. Where an offensive would occur was uncertain. If one side could reduce this uncertainty and prepare in advance for an offensive, it would be more likely to repel it. British intelligence realized that it would be able to understand German offensive plans by noting the movement of troops by rail. By observing the length of trains and the equipment they carried, the British could determine which units were moving. By observing the rail lines the trains moved on, the British could determine where these units were going, and hence, where the Germans planned to attack. To gather this information, the British established and ran train-watching networks behind German lines. In one case, they recruited Luxembourgeois who could return to their home country. Some of these individuals in turn recruited others. Communicating with their British handlers in Paris by inserting coded messages in newspapers and by letter through Switzerland, the train watchers provided a stream of information that allowed the British and their Allies to anticipate German military action.[7] The information the train watchers supplied reduced British uncertainty, increasing British power.

A more complicated example of the relationship of intelligence to uncertainty comes from the Cold War case of an American source, Colonel Ryszard Kukliński, a Polish military officer who worked with the Central Intelligence Agency (CIA) from 1972 until 1981. During these years, Kukliński gave the agency more than forty thousand pages of documents on Soviet war plans, wartime command and control, and advanced weapon systems. Kukliński also was a key source of information during the Solidarity crisis, which culminated in the suppression of the Solidarity workers' movement and the imposition of martial law in December 1981. By that time, Kukliński had been in the United States for five weeks, having signaled the CIA that he had fallen under suspicion and that he and his family needed to be brought to safety.[8]

The documents that Kukliński provided allowed the U.S. government to understand Soviet plans and intentions for military operations and technology. This spared resources that would have been spent countering threats that did not in fact exist, allowing their use on those that did. This increased American power in several ways. Kukliński's information helped NATO identify key targets that it would need to attack in the event of war, reducing NATO's uncertainty about how to fight. Kukliński also revealed Soviet deception efforts, allowing NATO to maximize the power of its military capabilities: it would not waste effort on less important targets. In addition, Kukliński's information on Soviet/Warsaw Pact war plans and ways of mobilizing reduced uncertainty about Soviet intentions. Knowing what the Soviets would do if they were preparing for war improved the ability of the United States to extract accurate warnings from Soviet military activity. This made the United States less likely to misread Soviet training activity, for example, and overreact, thus bringing on a war neither side intended.

As noted, Kukliński also reported on the events surrounding the imposition of martial law in Poland. Here the issue of uncertainty gets more complicated, not to say uncertain. The analysts and policy-makers who read Kukliński's information understood it in light of what they already knew. They were convinced that not the Poles but the Soviets would impose martial law, because the Soviets had done so in Hungary in 1956 and Czechoslovakia in 1968. Kukliński's firsthand information and, according to one analyst, in retrospect, the run of events leading up to the imposition of martial law, contradicted the view of the analysts and policy-makers. Nonetheless, the United States was surprised when the Poles themselves imposed martial law. In fact, the erroneous view of the analysts and policy-makers may well have encouraged the Poles to do so. Focused on the Soviet Union, the United States did little if anything to indicate to the Polish government that imposing martial law would be costly. Consequently, the government may have thought it had an implicit "green light" to go ahead with the suppression of Solidarity.[9]

That the Polish government thought it had a "green light" draws support from the consequences of Kukliński's departure for the United States. He had fallen under suspicion in part because a Soviet intelligence source in the Vatican told the KGB that the Americans had the plan for the imposition of martial law. The KGB passed this information on to the Polish intelligence service. The Vatican had the plan, or at least some details of it, because once the United States received it from Kukliński, it informed the Vatican in hopes that Polish pope John Paul II could influence the Polish government not to impose martial law. Kukliński, who was involved in planning for martial law, was one of the few people with access to the complete plan. The sudden departure of Kukliński and his family removed any doubt that he was the one who had given the plan to the United States. Thus, both the Soviets and the Poles knew that the United States knew the plan for martial law and knew, furthermore, that the United States was aware that they knew that the United States knew. Although this situation may sound like a parody of the world of intelligence as a refracting hall of mirrors, it was actually a situation of unusual clarity in international relations in which intelligence work in principle removed ambiguity and uncertainty for both sides in a conflict. Given this unusual transparency, it was not unreasonable for the Soviets and Poles to conclude that the lack of a red light for the Poles from the United States was in fact an implicit green light. Surely, the Soviet and Polish leaders must have thought, the actions of the Americans must be based on the unusual degree of knowledge they had. In fact, as we have noted, American actions were based not on what Kukliński revealed but on what past events suggested. The fact that preconceptions prevailed over Kukliński's information on the suppression of Solidarity demonstrates the limitations of even the best intelligence.[10] It reminds us that whatever may be true of knowledge and power, there is no necessary connection between intelligence and power.

Although the examples we have just presented illustrate something about the connection between intelligence and power, there is a good deal that remains unclear or assumed. For example, we have assumed that information, knowledge, and intelligence are roughly synonymous. Is that true, or do these terms differ in some important ways? On the other side of the equation, can power be defined in different ways, changing our understanding of the role of information and intelligence in relation to state power? Addressing these questions in the following pages, we will consider a number of issues beyond knowledge and power, including gender, secrecy, privacy, the modern state, science, liberalism, and war. The discussion becomes so broad because intelligence, as an object we seek, is a kind of knowledge, and human life, because it is beset by uncertainty, is essentially a quest for knowledge. We could begin this broad interconnected discussion at almost any point, but perhaps the best place to begin is by contrasting two different ways of conceiving of intelligence, which, not altogether arbitrarily, we designate the ancient and the modern understandings.

Ancient Intelligence

Our brief discussion of Caesar operating in Gaul and Britain has given us a sense of what ancient intelligence was like. In the Roman version, it was connected directly to military operations and based almost entirely on what we would today call open sources. Ancient military planning was simple, little more than the intention to attack some place. Hence, there were no elaborate plans to steal. Nor, typically, were there technological breakthroughs to discover. Only in the East, and only for part of its existence, did the Roman Empire face enemies of sufficient sophistication that spying on them would provide an advantage. "There was no need to deal in the intricacies of balance-of-power politics," a historian has written. "Rome confronted no consistent high intensity threats. Parthia was the only exception, and," he notes, "Parthia was actually more a target than a threat."[11] In these circumstances, tactical skill and courage, of the kind displayed by the eagle bearer of the Tenth Legion, were more important for Roman success than intelligence.

To rest with this assessment would display a modern liberal bias that intelligence is a foreign rather than a domestic issue. In fact, for the Romans, as for most ancient regimes, the most important intelligence was domestic. Compared with the length of its borders and the size of its population, the Roman Empire had a small army that could not both police the empire and protect it from foreign enemies. Roman intelligence, therefore, focused on enemies internal to the empire, on revealing their secret conspiracies, so the army could focus on those external to it. Even in domestic matters, however, intelligence was less important for security than the cultivation of a sense of loyalty and a feeling of being Roman among the empire's heterogeneous population.

The Romans, of course, were not the only ancient people to seek intelligence on their enemies. The Bible reports that as he prepared to invade Canaan, Moses sought to gain knowledge about the land and its inhabitants, just as Caesar sought to gain knowledge of Britain. When Joshua took over from Moses, he sent spies into Jericho before attacking. The spies found a safe house of sorts, lodging with a prostitute, the second oldest getting help from the oldest profession.[12] In describing the operations of the Israelites, the Bible appears to report common practice among ancient peoples. After all, it does not take divine inspiration to realize the advantage of knowing something about the enemy one is going to fight. The Greeks conducted such intelligence operations to satisfy their minimal intelligence requirements. Like the Romans, they used traitors, prisoners, travelers, merchants, and prostitutes as sources. Ambassadors, although not permanently resident in other countries, and other sorts of emissaries and messengers were sources of intelligence as well. Also like the Romans, the Greeks understood the importance of domestic intelligence. When associated with military operations, ancient intelligence gathering is most often best described as reconnaissance rather than espionage, and those who carried it out as scouts rather than spies—but such activities and personnel appear to be coeval with conflict, as conflict seems coeval with humanity.[13]

These first uses of knowledge or intelligence to enhance power are straightforward, even elemental. All living things exist in environments not under their control, hence marked by uncertainty. Drought, plague, or predators make continued existence pre-eminently uncertain. Knowledge reduces uncertainty; ignorance means greater danger. Forewarned is forearmed. All organisms, therefore, need to collect information in order to survive and prosper. Some of this information is given (the word "data" comes from Latin *dare*, to give). A plant must take what is given—water and sunlight, for example. It has no ability to move from place to place. Moving from place to place, an animal lives in a more complicated environment. Correspondingly, it is not restricted merely to using data. It can to some degree interpret what is given: what sounds or sights indicate a threat; when it should flee. Some animals have only a very limited ability to interpret; others can do more. The more freedom an organism has, the more it can change its location and circumstances; the more varied its circumstances, the more and more various are the dangers it may encounter. The more freedom an organism has, therefore, in order to preserve itself and thrive, the more it needs to make sense of or interpret the data it is given, the raw basic facts or even sense data on its environment it collects. Information, making sense of their environment, was essential to humans as they hunted and gathered, as it would be when they farmed and traded. In a sense, humans are always hunters and gatherers. In accounts of early warfare, we encounter packs of humans on the prowl, driven by scarcity or want. This was as true when Caesar invaded Britain as it had been when the Carians and Phoenicians raided in the eastern Mediterranean.[14] In this light, the Punic Wars between Rome and Carthage were fought by two of the ancient world's most effective hunters and gatherers, the Carthaginians being descendants of Phoenicians.

No matter the kind or complexity of their activity, humans face uncertainty. It is coeval with or identical to their freedom. Freedom means that human actions may result in either benefit or harm. Risk, the chance that the result might be harm, is inherent in uncertainty. Humans seek to reduce risk and uncertainty. They have done so in various ways, including prayer, superstition, magic, insurance, probability theory, prudence, derivatives, fire departments, technology, science, and philosophical detachment. In nineteenth-century

Great Britain, as science and technology began to transform human life, not least by supporting great engineering works, the workmen carrying them out still "consulted the position of the stars" before they went to their dangerous work.[15] In doing so, they were dealing with the uncertainties of their livelihoods and lives, even as the engineering works they were building were meant to reduce that uncertainty. Consulting the stars and the other techniques of dealing with uncertainty just mentioned are more or less failed ways of compensating for the fact that we do not control our environment. Intelligence, ancient or modern, is another such technique.

The need for intelligence and espionage arises out of elemental human needs. The foundation of espionage, indeed, is the human body. The body is visible but it is private, in the sense that its goods cannot be shared without being diminished. The soul is invisible but it is public, in the sense that its goods, such as an idea, can be shared without being diminished. The goods of the body are a source of conflict, then, in a way that the goods of the soul are not. Cannot the goods of the soul, such as religion, be a source of conflict? They have been, but would they be if they were not connected to the goods of the body? In service to the body, the soul is a source of conflict. Intentions are thoughts, but they arise because of the needs of the body. Because bodily things cannot be shared without being diminished, intentions that arise from the needs of the body often threaten others. We see what people do but we cannot see what they think. While they may act in a way that suggests they are friendly, they may be entertaining unfriendly thoughts. How are we to know? This problem is often expressed in the world of political science and security studies as the problem of the difference between capabilities and intentions.[16] We are more likely to suffer an unpleasant surprise when we forget this difference. It is important to know what people do, but it is above all important to know what they think. Visible bodily actions may provide cover for unfriendly invisible thoughts. Although not heeded in every case, Kukliński's information helped make the United States more secure by revealing Soviet intentions as well as capabilities. If men were angels, entirely spiritual beings, not only would they not need government,[17] they would also not need espionage.

Perhaps the most important ancient reflections on intelligence are those of Sun Tzu, a Chinese general, who wrote during what is called the warring states period (ca. 450–250 BCE). At this time, the area we now know as China was divided into a number of separate political entities that battled continuously for supremacy. It should not surprise us, therefore, that Sun Tzu argued that war was essential to the state, its successful conduct the difference between survival and ruin. To this premise, Sun Tzu added another, that secret operations were essential in war, leaving his readers to complete the argument by concluding that spying is essential to the state. In addition to stating his premises, Sun Tzu remarked that all warfare was based on deception, that warfare and human affairs generally were variable, that it was critical to know the enemy's plans, and, matter of factly, that one purpose of intelligence gathering was to set up assassinations. In the matter of knowing the enemy's plans, Sun Tzu rejected as useless "spirits, . . . gods, . . . analogy with past events, [and] . . . calculations," time-tested devices for dealing with uncertainty that the Romans used to supplement their intelligence,[18] and Americans to analyze it. According to Sun Tzu, "[K]nowledge of enemy plans . . . must be obtained from men who know the enemy situation." War is essential to the state, and espionage, human intelligence, is essential to war.[19] But even good intelligence from a man who knows the enemy situation can be trumped by analogy with past events, as we saw in the Kukliński case.

A situation of warring states was not, of course, unique to China in the two or three centuries of Chinese history designated by that phrase. It prevailed in ancient Greece, as the city-states continuously fought and competed for supremacy. In Plato's *Laws*, in a private conversation, an old statesman explained the peculiarities of his city's customs by noting that the lawgiver who established them understood, as the many do not, that "for everyone throughout the whole of life an endless war exists against all cities. . . . For what most humans call peace he [the lawgiver] held to be only a name; in fact, for everyone there always exists by nature an undeclared war among all cities."[20] In this war of all against all, the noble Greeks were not averse to using deception, even if they were unwilling to speak or write about it as openly as Sun Tzu.[21] "Warring states" is also, of course, a good description of politics in Renaissance Italy or modern Europe. From reflection on such situations, analysts have devised a theory of international relations known as realism. These theorists see states as competing for power and survival without benefit of any arbiter other than this unrelenting competition. Competition is the *ultimo ratio*, a slogan that Louis XIV had imprinted on his cannon. Surrounded by potential enemies who individually or together are powerful enough to destroy them, states are driven by the uncertainty of others' intentions into a relentless pursuit of power. This is their principal purpose, to which all others are subordinate. To achieve it, they will "lie, cheat and use brute force." There are seldom if ever status quo or satiated powers in this view. All states compete ceaselessly for power. They do not do so mindlessly, however. They calculate the possibility of gain or loss in a particular situation and act accordingly. They do miscalculate, however, because they are deceived by their opponents or fail to properly assess their military strength and resolve.[22] Providing information to avoid such failures is the role of intelligence. Its principal task is to discover the harmful intentions of enemies, which because they are harmful are kept secret. Intelligence may also assist with lying, cheating, and brute force, especially when it is to the advantage of a state to keep its use of such means secret.

Considering the examples of ancient times, Renaissance Italy, and modern Europe, we see that the ancient view of intelligence might be better called the original view or even, accepting the guidance of the old statesman in the *Laws*, the natural view. In any event, it is important to note that as a way of understanding intelligence or the conditions that make it important, the ancient view of intelligence did not come to an end with the years BCE. It is a perennial way of thinking about the role of information or knowledge in international relations, if not human life more generally. A striking example of the persistence of the ancient view of intelligence comes to us from Alexander Orlov.

Orlov worked for Soviet intelligence during the civil war that followed the Russian revolution, organizing guerrilla warfare and sabotage against the revolution's enemies, and in Spain during the civil war there, organizing the assassination of Trotskyites and other enemies of the revolution. He defected when Stalin's purges threatened his own life, ending up in the United States, where he lived for fifteen years under an assumed name, apparently without the knowledge of U.S. officials. In 1953 he published a book on Stalin's crimes, and in 1963, *The Handbook of Intelligence and Guerrilla Warfare.* In his *Handbook,* Orlov (one of many names he used during his life) took for granted that life, and both domestic and international politics, was by nature an undeclared war. Intelligence was, therefore, of utmost importance. He argued that America was surprised at Pearl Harbor because it did not take intelligence seriously. Americans had viewed the broad oceans as "impregnable defenses," reducing their sense of threat and thus of the need for intelligence. But the atomic age had put an end to that. Americans now needed good intelligence. By intelligence, Orlov meant secrets, preferably in documents, although a good informant would do. The work of intelligence was to steal these secret documents, documents that were secret because they revealed the plans and intentions of enemies. According to Orlov, this was the core idea of Russian intelligence: stealing secret documents. Americans, on the other hand, preferred unclassified or open sources and got 80 to 90 percent of their "intelligence" from this kind of research. Orlov was contemptuous of this approach. Research was women's work, he wrote. "According to the views of Russian officers, it takes a man to do the creative and highly dangerous work of underground intelligence on foreign soil." If one gathered open source data, Orlov wondered, how was one to know what data was important? This question did not arise if one stole secrets. Go after what your enemy has hidden, Orlov argued. If he was hiding it, it must be important. He quoted approvingly Stalin's statement to his intelligence analysts: "Don't tell me what you think, give me the facts and the source!" Orlov emphasized this point by quoting General MacArthur's testimony to Congress on the surprise he suffered in Korea when the Chinese sent their forces into the war. In his defense, MacArthur said (Orlov quoted the general's words) there were "no means or methods" that could have predicted such an attack except spying, getting someone inside the enemy camp to get the information. Precisely so, commented Orlov. That was the heart of the intelligence business,[23] as Sun Tzu understood, we would add.

Although they agree on most things, Orlov and Sun Tzu differ in one way. Orlov emphasized stealing documents, whereas Sun Tzu focused more on verbal intelligence. This difference reflects the more complicated nature of modern war and statecraft. To move vast armies about and coordinate the efforts of large bureaucracies require written plans unnecessary to the simpler warfighting of centuries ago. Yet this difference is small compared with the more fundamental points on which Sun Tzu and Orlov agree. They both see political life as war; both see the intentions of others as uncertain but presumptively hostile and the principal target of intelligence operations, and human intelligence or espionage as the principal means for gaining knowledge of others' secret, because hostile, intentions. The purpose of intelligence is to collect information that will reveal the plans of the enemy and allow one's leaders to better guide the state through a hostile world.

Modern Intelligence

That Orlov and Sun Tzu are in agreement on fundamentals becomes even clearer when we contrast ancient with modern intelligence. Perhaps the best source for understanding modern intelligence, certainly its American version, is a book by Sherman Kent, *Strategic Intelligence for American World Policy* (originally published in 1949).[24] Kent was a member of the intelligence analysis staff in the Office of Strategic Services (OSS) during World War II and a founder of the intelligence analytical community in the United States during the CIA's early years. Kent's book and his writings published in the CIA's in-house journal, *Studies in Intelligence,* were for a time probably the most influential writings on intelligence in the United States, and they remain important. In 2000, the CIA named its analytical training school after Kent. Kent is still cited as "the paragon of intelligence analysts" in award-winning books.[25] Kent was a Yale University history professor before he went into government service. Reading his remark that he knew "of no formula for evil that is any surer than sloppy research unfootnoted,"[26] we know we are in a world different from Sun Tzu's and Orlov's. But the difference is not, or not only, that Kent was an academic and Sun Tzu and Orlov military men. The difference runs deeper. Modern intelligence is broader than ancient intelligence both in its temporal orientation and its scope. Most important, modern intelligence claims superiority because of its methodology.

The difference in temporal orientation is evident in Kent's distinction between what he called descriptive and speculative intelligence. The former kind of intelligence deals with the past or the present: with things that are unchanging, such as geography and topography; things that change slowly, such as demography; and transient things such as governments and economic conditions.[27] Descriptive intelligence would also include data about a country's armed forces. Lots of descriptive data is available about any given country and most of it is not secret. Kent called speculative intelligence that which dealt with the future, with what the leaders of another nation might do or what the climate might be like, and hence at best with probabilities. The distinction that Kent made between the two kinds of intelligence distinguishes ancient and modern intelligence. Ancient intelligence was concerned primarily with what Kent calls descriptive intelligence. Caesar and Moses wanted this kind of intelligence as they prepared for operations in Britain and Canaan. Ancient intelligence also sought information on the intentions or plans of enemies, but in ancient warfare such intentions and plans were part of the current situation and thus part of what Kent called descriptive intelligence. Ancient intelligence, in the spirit of Stalin, provided the source and the facts, but not speculation or estimates of future conditions.

The difference in scope between ancient and modern intelligence appears in the opening lines of Kent's book: "Intelligence means knowledge. If it cannot be stretched to mean all knowledge, at least it means an amazing bulk and assortment of knowledge."[28] Ancient intelligence focused on human enemies, foreign or domestic. As the opening statement of his book and the explanation above of descriptive intelligence indicates, Kent believed that intelligence as synonymous with knowledge should address virtually anything that concerned human well-being in modern industrial societies. Assessments of global warming, for example, would be something that Kent, if still alive, would consider an appropriate task for a nation's intelligence service. For Kent, the job of intelligence is not so much to report on the decision-making of the other side as it is to guide the decision-making of its own side.

The most important difference between ancient and modern intelligence—its methodology—emerges as it becomes clear that Kent had something specific in mind when he spoke of knowledge. He meant the social sciences, which "very largely constitute the subject matter" of intelligence.[29] Knowledge, hence intelligence, resulted from following the methodology of the social sciences. In his book, Kent provided an analysis of that methodology specifically designed for the world of intelligence. In summary form, its steps are:

1. Noticing a problem
2. Analyzing the problem to discover any relevance to the United States and its policy-makers
3. Collecting data relevant to the problem
4. Evaluating the data to determine its validity
5. Studying the data to determine its meaning—that is, framing hypotheses that make sense of the data
6. Collecting more data to test the hypotheses
7. Presenting the hypothesis that appears most true.[30]

This is indeed a recognizable version of modern scientific method. One immediate difference between ancient and modern intelligence is that nowhere in his account of methodology does Kent mention secrets. In fact, Kent minimized the importance of secrets, emphasizing what is openly available,[31] as Orlov said Americans did. In common usage, "intelligence" is a synonym for secrets, and so, for example, one could say that Colonel Kukliński passed intelligence to the CIA. But that is not what Kent meant by "intelligence." For Kent, intelligence is not necessarily secrets but rather knowledge that results from research, from following the methodology of the social sciences. No one, according to Kent, collects intelligence. Collection "without its accompanying research, will produce spotty and superficial information."[32] Research is not just one part of the intelligence business. It *is* the intelligence business, according to Kent. In modern intelligence, social science methodology replaces collecting secrets as the key activity.

In Kent's account, social science methodology is a process that moves from data (step 3, above) to meaning (step 5) and then to knowledge or intelligence (steps 6 and 7). Meaning is first hypothetical (step 5) but when tested and confirmed becomes knowledge. Research "is a systematic endeavor to get firm meaning out of impressions."[33] In formulating the steps to knowledge in this way, Kent articulated what has become a standard way of understanding the connections between data, information, and knowledge.[34] In this now standard language, data plus meaning is information and information plus analysis (what Kent called "research") is intelligence.

An example may make this formulation clearer: will Russia impose martial law on Poland? This was a problem clearly relevant to the United States (steps 1 and 2). Lots of data about Poland was available, but only some of it relevant to deciding if Russia would impose martial law. Data on life expectancy reveals a good deal about what is going on in a country but would not necessarily reveal much about whether the Soviet Union was going to suppress the Solidarity movement. The location and movement of Russian and Warsaw Pact forces were likely to reveal more. But the location and movement of the troops were part of an annual and publicly announced training exercise. The exercise could obviously be a screen to hide preparations for martial law. Again, lots of data might be available on the exercises, Warsaw Pact command and control, the kinds and numbers of troops in the exercise, when it occurred, and a host of other things. In addition, there were the reports coming in from Kukliński that the Polish government was planning to suppress Solidarity. Intercepts of secret communications, the visit to Warsaw of high-ranking Soviet generals, as well as the public statements of officials in Moscow and Warsaw Pact capitals would also be data to consider. All of this data would need to be collected and validated (steps 3 and 4). For example, by the time he was reporting on events surrounding the Solidarity movement, Kukliński had established himself as a reliable source.

So far, all we have is a mass of data. It is not yet information, and certainly not intelligence, the stuff upon which policy-makers should depend when making their decisions. The next step, step 5, then, is to discover what Kent calls the "inherent meaning" of the data that will make it information. For Kent, the meaning of the data is the hypothesis that makes the best sense of it. For all the things one sees happening in and around the Solidarity movement, what are the possible explanations? Each of these possible explanations gives a different sense or meaning to the data. For instance, one might hypothesize that a Russian invasion will suppress Solidarity. With this hypothesis in mind, the training exercise becomes cover to put Russian troops in position to move against the workers' movement. The hypothesis also makes sense, let us say, of unusual patterns or types of communications or the unusually large number of internal security forces joining the exercise. The hypothesis seems reasonable. It seems to explain or make sense of much of the data. But how much confidence can we have in it? To find out, we collect other relevant data and see if the hypothesis can explain them (step 6). Most often, no single hypothesis will explain all the data, but the one that explains the most or is least contradicted by the data is the one most likely to be true. This is the hypothesis that the intelligence analysts present to decision-makers (step 7).

Kent's claim that intelligence is research and not stealing secrets—that modern intelligence is superior to ancient intelligence—rests on the strength of his research methodology. Central to this methodology is discovering meaning in data or formulating hypotheses that make sense of the data. Kent wrote little about this key component of his methodology. He did say three things, however: (1) formulating hypotheses ideally occurs at step 5 but in fact occurs at different times, even before data collection; (2) "what is desired is a large number of possible interpretations of the data, a large number of inferences, or concepts, which are broadly based and productive of still other concepts"; (3) second-rate minds, no matter how many of them are brought together in an organization, are unlikely to produce the requisite quantity and quality of hypotheses.[35] The second claim is sound, perhaps commonsensical. The larger the number of possible hypotheses, the more likely we are to find one that explains the data and generates other good explanations. The first and third claims are problematic, however, and cast doubt on Kent's claims for his method and understanding of intelligence.

The first claim acknowledges that formulating hypotheses may precede collecting data. Proceeding in this order would appear to be the antithesis of the scientific method, as Kent implied by writing that "one would be pleased to think that they [hypotheses] appeared at this, the respectable [step] 5." If hypothesizing occurs before data selection it might suggest a bias in the selection. Might we not deem relevant only the data that fits our pre-existing hypothesis?

Indeed, it seems inevitable that human beings, not just intelligence analysts, must be selective—that is, prejudiced in their use of data. When confronted with a complex event like the emergence and possible suppression of Solidarity, how do we know what data is relevant? We noted that demographic data like life expectancy would not be relevant to the issue of suppressing Solidarity, but of course it could be. Falling life expectancy or rising infant mortality rates might indicate a failing society. If the Soviet leaders thought their prospects worsening over time, then Solidarity might appear a greater threat than it would otherwise. If additional information shows the Soviet leaders to be risk-takers (they had recently decided to invade Afghanistan), then one might see falling life expectancy as a key bit of data, implying that the risk-taking Soviet leadership would act before its position deteriorated further. Hypotheses, then, do not just give meaning to data, they establish what we consider relevant data in the first place. In this modern conception, data is never something simply given to us. All that we refer to as data is inevitably dependent upon some pre-existing understanding or intention or hypothesis.[36] Kent was aware of this problem but chose not to discuss it.[37] Instead, he proceeded in his presentation as if forming hypotheses occurs after data collection, at step 5, and then discussed step 6. After formulating hypotheses, one should collect more data to test "the more promising hypotheses, to confirm or deny them." Again, we note, as Kent did not, that the data collected to test the hypothesis is made relevant by the hypothesis.

As Kent seems to have acknowledged, humans engage in almost precognitive sense-making. For example, they interpret what is in front of them based on past experience. Proponents of the scientific method seek to overcome this problem with more rigorous application of the method, peer review, and other measures. The larger and related problem with Kent's approach appears, however, if we consider his third claim, that second-rate minds will not do. Kent made this claim because hypothesis formulation is essential to his methodology, but there is no methodology for hypothesis formulation. It depends on human intuition. Kent noted that men like Darwin and Freud relied on facts that "were there for everyone," but only these men framed the hypotheses that so advanced human understanding. He commented that "the great discoveries of the race are the result of rigorous, agile, and profound thinking." Kent did not at this point further describe or analyze this thinking, which is essential to his conception of intelligence. In a passage a few pages earlier, however, he made a revealing comment. Considering there how problems come to the attention of an intelligence agency, he noted that one way is through collectors, or "surveillance" in Kent's terminology. Collectors become aware of something unusual. He then asked, "How can [collection] be sure of putting the finger on the three things per week out of the thousands it observes and the millions that happen which are really of potential moment?" Kent argued that even collection required research to guide it, and this passage illustrates why. A collector is faced with lots of data. How does he know what data is relevant? This is a version of the problem faced by the analyst who must make sense or information out of the data that is in front of him by formulating hypotheses. The collector we now see faces the same problem. The solution, Kent wrote, was to find someone "wise in the subject" and "*pray* that their mysterious inner selves are of the kind which produce hypotheses of national importance."[38]

This is a remarkable admission from Kent. He did not discard intuition as "invariably a false friend," but he certainly thought social science more reliable than intuition and presented social science as intuition's authoritative guide.[39] Yet, if we consider together what Kent wrote about collectors making sense of the data they encounter and the analogous act of formulating hypotheses in the scientific method, we see that at the heart of the intelligence enterprise as Kent understood it lies a mystery: the ability of the wise to make sense of or give meaning to the data they confront. Appropriately, when confronted with a mystery, Kent, like the ancients he hoped to supersede, offered prayer as a way of dealing with the problem. Those committed to intelligence analysis as a rigorous, scientific approach to problem solving might respond, as noted above, that Kent's method, and all intelligence and scientific method, is intended to overcome this problem. Kent himself put his faith, so to speak, in the methods of social science.[40] Method makes up for human deficiency, as all exponents of method since Francis Bacon have argued. It is method and not genius that gets results. But method cannot overcome the problem indicated by Kent's description of how to make sense of data or come up with good hypotheses. The movement from data to information relies on hypothesis, which in turn relies on intuition. To argue that method, which relies on intuition, can overcome the lack of intuition, is to move in an infinite regress or a vicious circle (method ensures intuition; intuition ensures method). Neither motion gets us anywhere.

Kent himself avoided this futile motion because he did not argue that more application of the scientific method could solve the method's problem. (As we will see, others address the problem by appealing to the results of the method.) Ultimately the scientific method that Kent espoused depends on human insight that is not reducible to that method, as Kent implicitly acknowledged when he argued that the intelligence business had to recruit "its professional staff from among the nation's most gifted people."[41] Without putting too fine a point on it, this did not happen or happen often enough. But even if it had, it would only have highlighted another problem with Kent's understanding of intelligence. Kent argued that intelligence as social science was to replace the less reliable intuition of decision-makers; but if social science, like all human cognition, rests on intuition, a mysterious inner process of sense-making, how is it superior to the intuition of the decision-maker? Kent acknowledged that social science was more problematic than natural science. "The social sciences have by no means yet attained the precision of the natural sciences; they may never do so." But he believed they had come a long way, far enough that they represented "a block of wisdom on humanity" that formed a solid ground for intelligence analysis, even the estimative sort of analysis that tried to establish what would happen in the future. More than sixty years after the first publication of his book, however, its readers may wonder if Kent did not place too much faith in social science. We have no reason to believe, for example, that social science can be predictive, even if it—or at least simple algorithms—do better on average than "expert" opinion. If intelligence as social science relies on something like intuition and cannot be predictive, how is it an advance on the intuition of the experienced statesman?[42] In fact, the results of social science, we might argue, are likely to be inferior to the statesman's intuition, which, unlike the intuition of the finest academic minds in the country, will have been tutored by long experience in affairs of state. No one—"expert," statesman, or analyst—or no method can predict the future, but who is more likely to judge correctly what needs to be done in a given situation, the kind for example that Caesar faced, as his legionnaires struggled in the surf with the Britons, victory or defeat hanging in the balance? Not every decision is so critical, of course. Still, we have no reason to believe that the judgment of the analyst will be superior to the statesman's and some reason to believe it will be inferior. If the intuition at the heart of modern intelligence is inferior to the statesman's intuition, then we are led back toward the ancient view of intelligence, the view that the job of intelligence is only to collect and present secrets, so that leaders may better judge what to do. The problem with Kent's understanding of intelligence is one reason why the ancient understanding persists.

We will return to the issue of intuition or judgment in subsequent chapters, but here we may note that the ancient understanding of intelligence is not without its own problems. If your enemy knows that your intelligence operation is guided by what you declare secret and hide, then it may well create and hide secrets that are false in hopes that you will steal them and be misled.[43] To avoid being misled, you will need to analyze the documents you steal and the circumstances in which you steal them. To do this, whether you realize it or not, you will need to formulate and test hypotheses. You will be driven back toward what Kent called research, even if it is women's work. An advocate of ancient intelligence might insist that the research will be based only on those stolen documents, but why must this be the case? Could not open source information shed light on the analysis of secret documents? Can secrets be entirely separate from what is not secret? Must there not be some correspondence between what is secret and what is open? An invasion cannot occur without moving troops. Their movement is often unavoidably open information and reveals something about the hidden intentions of the enemy. It is true that the more something is in the future, the less we see evidence of it in the present, and the less we see a correspondence between the secret and the open world. Intentions may be so undeveloped that nothing in the open or physical world corresponds to them. The closer an intention comes to realization, however, the more indication of it should we see. We would have had early warning of the invasion of Korea, one of the examples that Orlov cited to show the need to steal secrets, if we had had a source in the meeting when Chinese leaders first raised the possibility. Yet, in fact, there were open indications that the Chinese were going to invade long before they did. Open sources offer valuable information on their own as well as when used to corroborate stolen information. More important, whether we use open or secret sources, research or analysis is unavoidable. Since both the ancient and the modern approach to intelligence rest ultimately on intuition, we might prefer the ancient view, as it more forthrightly accepts this dependence—or because the intuition it relies on, that of the statesman rather than the social scientist, seems more likely to steer us through our dangerous world. Yet if the ultimate way to secure ourselves is to increase our power, then the relative merit of the two approaches changes. We should not let Kent's horror of sloppy footnoting mislead us into thinking that his approach was overly academic and hopelessly ivory-tower. Or, rather, the fact that it was academic and hoped to imitate social science research should not lead us to conclude that it could not also serve state power as or more effectively than Orlov's tough-guy approach. Kent's view of intelligence in fact continued a long-term historical relationship between scholarship or knowledge and state power. Colbert's use of scholarship to increase the power of the French state at the expense of the church, discussed in the opening of this chapter, long predates Kent's appeal to social science. A fuller assessment of the relative merit of ancient and modern intelligence requires that we consider more broadly the relationship between knowledge, power, and the state.

Knowledge and State Power

Kent came to government from the academy, a road well traveled by the time he took it. Indeed, literacy, numeracy, and the state are probably roughly coeval; literacy and numeracy were originally technologies of state power, with scribes the first information specialists, allowing governments to keep the accounts essential to controlling their domains and extracting revenue. This is one of the first ways that states made their domains "legible,"[44] a process Colbert developed to a high degree with the aid of his clerks. The British revenue system was a later example of the same process, with the place of the ancient scribes taken by university-trained civil servants. The term "statistics" originally referred to quantitative information important to the state. Another term for such information or its analysis was "political arithmetic." On the basis of such information gathering, states were able to extend their control over and build their power from the activities of their subjects and citizens. Michael Mann has called this kind of state power infrastructural, by which he means power that penetrates civil society. According to Mann, "[T]here is no hiding from the infrastructural reach of the state."[45]

Scholars and scribes have always been important to the infrastructural power of the state. Louis XIV and his minister Colbert, for example, benefited from the revival of learning and scholarship we call the Renaissance. This revival had another effect on state power as well. It changed how it was understood. By making available a sense of the past different from the Christian tradition, Renaissance learning helped to revive the idea of secular government. Furthermore, it allowed history to teach the art of wielding power in such a government. The histories and tracts Humanists wrote taught princes how to gain power, form alliances, deal with opponents, and control the multitude.[46] The revival of secular learning also informed the broader debate about the limit and control of state power. If, for whatever reason, one was not willing to seek justification for government in the will of God, where was one to seek it? As a historical matter, this question arose as even the pretense of a Christian empire (for example, the Holy Roman Empire) in Europe became impossible to maintain. One answer to the question was to seek justification in the necessities of governing itself. This is the tradition of raison d'état, or reason of state, often associated with the writings of the Roman historian Tacitus. Not Christian precepts or ethics, but the needs of the state, maintaining its existence and increasing its power, should determine what governments do.[47]

The term "reason of state" appeared about the mid-sixteenth century in Italy and became widely used in political writing throughout Europe in the decades following.[48] It is often associated with Cardinal Richelieu (1585–1642), a principal advisor to Louis XIII. Reason of state was contrasted with written law.[49] Where the reach or authority of written law ended, reason of state began. For example, an assassination might be forbidden by law but required to preserve the state. The necessity of preserving the state became the justification for acting beyond or against the written law. All students of politics had recognized the limitations of the written law. For one thing, no written laws could cover all the situations that made up human affairs. Life is simply too variable. Something then was needed to guide human action in those instances when the written laws failed. In the Christian tradition, those looking for guidance beyond the written law could appeal to the laws of God or natural law or God's providence. Reason of state was a non-Christian alternative to such ideas. Many writers considered it to be synonymous with the interest of the ruler, while others considered this bad reason of state.[50] Good reason of state was acting in accord with the common good or limiting one's actions to what justice would allow. Some writers, resisting the non-Christian character of reason of state, argued that it should be guided by piety or the law of God. Yet even those who argued that reason of state was compatible with traditional or Christian notions of justice found themselves discussing devices recommended by Machiavelli, who was regularly accused of atheism. Generally, certainly by the time of Richelieu, reason of state was most commonly associated with the interest of the state, whatever needed to be done to preserve or increase its power.

Reason of state was thus the early modern version of the realism we have associated with ancient intelligence. As Sun Tzu might have predicted, among the warring states of early modern Europe, espionage became commonplace as monarchs battled foreign and domestic enemies. Bernadino de Mendoza, Spanish ambassador from Philip II to the court of Elizabeth I, ran agents in the Queen's court and plotted with Catholics to overthrow her and place the Catholic Mary Queen of Scots on the throne. His plotting uncovered by Sir Francis

Walsingham's counterintelligence operations, de Mendoza was expelled from the court but carried on his ambassadorial and espionage activities at the court of the French king, Henry IV, where he funded and helped organized what would today be called covert or political actions (such as riots, assassinations) in furtherance of Spanish policy. Walsingham not only ran counterintelligence for Elizabeth, he also conducted foreign intelligence operations throughout Europe. For example, his agents kept the court well informed about the preparations of the Spanish Armada. So prevalent in early modern Europe was espionage that it inspired an extensive array of thinking and writing about its necessity and practice.[51] The revival of ancient learning, then, contributed to the revival and justification of the ancient understanding of intelligence.

If reason of state came to prevail in Europe, its sway did not go uncontested. Eventually a compelling alternative developed, which also held that knowledge could serve state power, but understood knowledge and intelligence differently. This is the ultimate source of Kent's view of intelligence. The alternative to reason of state emerged, we might say, not from considering how states acted but how they should act. Consider the confrontation between the United States and the Soviet Union called the Cold War, or more particularly that part of it concerned with Poland in the early 1980s. Because of their espionage, the United States and the Soviet Union knew a good deal about what each other knew and what each wanted in that confrontation. If the two states had shared information more openly, could they not have resolved their differences peacefully and at lower cost? The problem was that the Soviet Union and the United States were such different sorts of states, with such different objectives, that they could not trust each other enough to share information. The problem, then, was the kind of states involved in international politics. If states were focused above all on the well-being of their citizens, and not increasing their power at the expense of others, then they could cooperate in pursuing that objective, for example through trade and economic growth that benefited all.

Something like this was the view of Thomas Jefferson. He acknowledged that Europe had been locked for centuries in the grip of the realism of power politics. He also acknowledged self-preservation as a natural law that states were justified in obeying. Furthermore, he knew that human affairs were so variable that a statesman might have to break laws and treaties and otherwise engage in ungentlemanly conduct. When he himself faced such necessities, Jefferson violated written laws and proposed what can only be called Machiavellian schemes to ensure the survival and well-being of the United States. Yet he believed that human beings and the states in which they lived were not restricted to power politics. If all states were democratic, devoted to the well-being of their citizens, then power politics and war itself might cease. America had the chance to bring about such a world because, as Orlov and many others have noted, America was separated from the warring states of Eurasia by two wide oceans. This unique and privileged position was the leverage point from which the world of warring states and power politics might be shifted in a more benign direction. The example of America would persuade the world that there was a better way. It would promote a revolution that would change politics forever and thus change forever the relations of states. Indeed, as the spreading revolution led states to become more alike, it might eventually lead to a kind of world government or at least to a kind of universal citizenship.[52]

The Jeffersonian view of international relations is what Kent had in mind when he spoke of himself as a member of what he called the liberal tradition.[53] Kent believed that states should have two broad purposes or policies, one positive, the other defensive. The positive policy aimed to bring about "a better world order and a higher degree of national prosperity."[54] To the degree that the better world order was one in which trade was free, these two positive goals were one and the same. The defensive policy was "necessarily undertaken to counter those policies of other states which are inimical to our national aspirations" for a better world order and greater prosperity. The positive policy is the real policy of states or at least those that are part of the liberal tradition. It is the real policy because it is the one that is a state's "own self-initiated policy."[55] It is the only one liberal states would need to pursue, if they did not face illiberal enemies. In the liberal tradition, knowledge should increase state power so that liberal states can better deal with their illiberal competitors, but ultimately so that all states and peoples may benefit.

Kent's view of intelligence, with its disparagement of espionage, fits easily with the liberal tradition. Liberals dislike espionage and intelligence because secrecy is incompatible with the openness necessary to build trust, which is enhanced and made possible by information sharing. Liberalism promotes sharing knowledge to increase knowledge (science, technology), which benefits all, and to help states avoid or manage crises. In a world consisting of states and people holding liberal views, there would be no need for secrets, at least state secrets, and no need for espionage. Everyone would live by open agreements openly arrived at, in the words of Woodrow Wilson. Prior to the emergence of such a world and to encourage it, one should act as much as possible as if it already existed. Thus a member of the liberal tradition like Kent would downplay the importance of espionage, use it only reluctantly, and one might think, half-heartedly. In this view, espionage is merely a concession to the fact that illiberal states still exist.[56] The liberal tradition is liberal, in a sense, because it hopes to free mankind from the necessity of espionage and everything that has made espionage necessary. From the viewpoint of ancient intelligence, this would require a revolution in human affairs and a revolutionary change in human nature. What power could bring about that revolution and how would it do so? To understand the answer to those questions, we need to better understand liberalism's nemesis, secrecy.

Secrecy

The aim of the liberal revolution was to make secrecy unnecessary, or to free human life from the power of secrecy. Another way to put this is to say that liberalism was the antithesis of reason of state, and reason of state in its origins was intimately connected with secrets of state.[57] It is not hard to see why. In the first place, as we have seen in several of the examples that opened this chapter, knowing something that your opponent does not know can give you an advantage. Hiding one's intentions or the motives for one's actions, using dissimulation or deception, which depends on secrecy, is clearly advantageous for a prince or government amid warring states. Writers in the Tacitean tradition quoted a reputed saying of Louis XI: "[W]ho can't feign, can't rein."[58] In chapter 18 of the *Prince*, appealing to the necessity of maintaining rule, Machiavelli argued that "a prudent lord" did not need to keep his word and should not, when doing so would harm him, but indicated that it might also harm the Prince to be known as someone who did not keep his word. Therefore, a Prince should learn to hide his faithlessness and appear to be "merciful, faithful, humane, honest, and religious," especially the latter. There is advantage in appearing to be good, as most people understand that term. (But human affairs are so variable that on occasion it is useful to do a great act of evil publicly.) There are several reasons why appearing to be good is advantageous. For one thing, it might promote trust between the ruler and the people: if the lord is merciful, and the like, he may be thought to be ruling according to some notion of justice, according to the common good, and not merely his own good. In this case, others would be more inclined to accept his rule. (This was the reason that the Romans promoted the idea of Romanitas, or Romanness, and its benefits among those they conquered.) In addition, a point that Machiavelli does not make, a ruler who has a sense of honor as that is typically understood may well feel shame at the terrible things that he must do as a ruler. He will want to keep those shameful acts secret. In this connection, it is worth noting, that in its early years, the British intelligence service, later known as MI6, met resistance in Britain in part because its activities were considered incompatible with those of gentlemen.[59] During World War I, a gentlewoman of Luxembourg resisted British efforts to persuade her to become a train watcher in her home town simply because spying was not compatible with her sense of honor.[60] It is testimony to the brutalizing effects of the twentieth century if such qualms now seem quaint.

In early modern Europe, before the rise of liberalism, secrecy was synonymous with advantage and greater power. Therefore, it is not too much of an exaggeration to say that everything was secret. Human beings lived their lives within three overlapping realms of secrecy: *arcana naturae*, *arcana dei*, and *arcana imperii*: secrets of nature, God, and political power.[61] Each of these realms had its particular expert or guardian: kings and their ministers in politics; priests in religion; and philosophers, who were often clerics, in nature. Supreme among them were priests, as God was supreme in nature and human affairs, and supreme among priests was the pope.[62] The vast majority of people were to have no access to these secret realms, while the masters of politics and religion were to know everything about the people, so that they could better direct them. Priests heard confessions, and no one had what we have come to recognize as a right to privacy.

The masters of secret knowledge justified their authority in various ways. If the world or nature is God's creation, then it is in a way his revelation and shares in the ultimate mysteriousness of God. Nature, then, has secrets impenetrable by human intelligence. Only those to whom God has revealed what is hidden will know the truth. Similarly in politics, if the king rules by divine right, then there is no reason to believe that anyone not so touched by God's hand could understand the mysteries of ruling. The belief that secrets and hidden knowledge were fundamental led to a tradition of esotericism, the view that only those initiated into the secrets, as opposed to the common people, should know the truth.[63] This view had an heuristic effect. It encouraged people to study, to seek learning, and thus increased and helped preserve learning. It also had a less noble effect. It served to keep alive the tradition of dealing with uncertainty and risk through the use of amulets and spells, secret knowledge to manipulate secret powers.[64]

Many defenders of the various *arcana* criticized the hucksters who dealt in amulets and charms for discrediting the notion of secret knowledge. But the tradition was compromised in more fundamental ways. For one thing, kings and their ministers did not accept the supremacy of the pope and fought with the pope and his priests for centuries.[65] The dispute between Louis XIV and the bishops was just one late example. The causes of these disputes were hardly secret or mysterious. Rather, they were all too evidently struggles for very earthly power. But the greatest threat to the authority of secrecy came from the philosophers, or, as they came to be called, the scientists. In the theory of secrecy, scientists were under the control of priests (for example, Galileo's prosecution), or under the control of increasingly independent secular rulers, especially when the philosophers examined politics. Because they had neither physical nor spiritual power, the philosophers were at a disadvantage when it came to preserving their activity against the power of the church and the state. Eventually, they sought allies among the people, the only other such disadvantaged group. What they promised the people in exchange for their support was increased power over politics and nature. The scientists and their propagandists (such as Tom Paine) in effect declared the kings and priests no different from the hucksters selling magic potions. Through their research and its dissemination, philosophers would expose the so-called secret knowledge of priests and kings as fraudulent and thus not to be feared, casting light into the obscured realms these charlatans guarded, allowing the common people to see and decide for themselves. The philosophers also promised that their techniques and practices would truly increase power over nature, to ease human suffering and improve life, making magic unnecessary. What we might call the foreign policy of the philosophers (building alliances to fight stronger powers) ultimately made the philosophers or scientists very powerful, as, with their aid, their allies, the people, dethroned kings and replaced them as sovereigns. The scientists' reward has been large grants of research dollars by the representatives of the people and an acceptance of the right of scientists to delve into any secrets they wish to investigate. The extent of the scientists' power is evident in the claim of someone like Kent that a version of their knowledge, social science, can stand in judgment of the decisions of politicians. It is also evident in the accepted claim of scientists and their supporters that nothing should limit their research, not even serious potential danger to the people, whose safety and happiness were the original justification for the independence of the scientists.[66]

The alliance between the people and the philosophers/scientists, which is the basis of the liberal tradition to which Kent appealed,[67] dethroned not only kings but secrecy as well, and necessarily at the same time. The liberals did not declare politics, nature, and religion open books but rather books that could be pried open through human endeavor, using the right method. No special divine revelation was necessary to understand these realms. Thus the liberal tradition held a presumption against secrecy in politics, nature, and religion, and a presumption in favor of privacy for scientists and the people. This was a historical reversal of great consequence. Yet, much as the theory of secrecy undermined itself, so has what we might call the theory of privacy. Privacy is, after all, a kind of secrecy. Both are a withholding of information, the former voluntary, the latter compulsory.[68] Thus the methods and motive (increased power) that pried open secrecy can work against privacy as well and are now doing so. So great is the wealth to be gained by extracting information from the private lives of people, and so powerful and available the technology to do so, that privacy now seems threatened.[69] What first invaded the sacred secrecy of monarchs now threatens the sacred privacy of citizens. How far the invasion of privacy will go, we do not know. But it is clear that the rout of secrecy has been extensive. So few, if any, are the justifiable political secrets and so great the power of information-making and manipulation to expose them, and so great the advantages of openness held to be, that some have begun to ask whether secrecy has or should come to an end.[70] And if transparency replaces secrecy, perhaps we are finally tending toward the world that liberalism first hoped to bring into existence. Of course, if intelligence consists, as in the ancient view, in the collection and analysis of secrets, and secrets have come to an end, then intelligence has as well.

We will return to issues of secrecy, privacy, openness, and intelligence, particularly espionage, in Chapters Two and Three. But it should now be clear that it would be wrong to see the opposition between ancient and modern intelligence, between Orlov and Kent, as based on a disagreement over the importance of power, with Orlov representing those who believe that power is the essence of politics and indeed human life, and Kent representing those who disparage power. This view has some plausibility, because the liberal tradition to which Kent claimed allegiance sought to limit the power of the state, which the revival of the ancient view of intelligence in early modern Europe sought to increase. Thus it may seem that ancient intelligence values power in a way that modern intelligence does not. Yet, in fact, power is more important for Kent than for Orlov. As we noted, the liberal tradition had revolutionary ambitions.

It aimed to overcome the necessities that all before the liberal tradition held to characterize human life, even if they were reluctant to talk about them. We noted that Jefferson thought the United States could be a fulcrum upon which to lever human affairs and the entire world into liberalism. Such leveraging would require vast power. Where was this power, at the heart of the liberal tradition and essential to its success, to come from? According to those fomenting the revolution, the revolutionary power of knowledge (that is, science) would drive the liberal revolution. To understand modern intelligence and its relation to the modern state, then, we need to consider the source of its power.

Power

Jean-Baptiste Colbert collected, organized, and analyzed information because it increased his power and the power of the king he served. Colbert collected information on "bishoprics and abbeys, the military and the nobility, magistrates and the quality of justice, finances and tax collection, the estates of the crown, natural resources, navigable rivers, commerce, industry, horse-breeding farms, and counterfeit coinage." Parish priests were to keep records of baptisms, marriages, and burials on a yearly basis and turn them over to the government. All of this information described the resources of the state, which could not be put to use unless this information was collected, stored, and made accessible to the state. (Jefferson's only book, *Notes on the State of Virginia,* was in part a similar effort.)[71] But Colbert did more than increase the infrastructural power of Louis's regime. Colbert collected personal information on every member of every parlement (regional legislative and judicial bodies) in the country. He amassed the most information on the most important parlement, the Parlement of Paris. Colbert's purpose in having this information ready to hand was to understand the members of the parlements, what they hoped for or desired, what moved them, what they had done, what they hoped to keep hidden, so that he could influence, pressure, or undermine anyone who might oppose the king.[72]

In Colbert's use of information to exploit resources or coerce people, there was nothing new. Indeed, Colbert's informational activities would have been recognizable to an ancient scribe and his pharaonic master. There was nothing revolutionary in Colbert's system, nothing recognizably liberal. Colbert wanted to make France and its people legible to the king; kingship was not to be legible to the people. The court was to have information superiority. It was to maintain its secrets; the people were to be transparent. The liberal revolution reversed all of this. Government became public, open; the people gained a right to privacy. What accounts for the difference between Colbert and the liberal tradition Kent was proud to be a member of?

Oddly, as we will see, perhaps the best answer to this question appears in Thomas Hobbes's *Leviathan*. Hobbes there wrote that "the power of a man (to take it universally), is his present means to obtain some future apparent good."[73] There are other ways to define power, but Hobbes's definition recommends itself to the student of intelligence for three reasons. First, a close connection exists between the world as Hobbes described it and the warring states environment in which intelligence has typically been deemed most important. This environment exists when states compete against each other with no higher authority to control them. According to Hobbes, this is man's natural state or condition. By nature individuals, just like states, compete with each other because there is no higher authority to control them. In the absence of such authority and in the presence of inevitable scarcity, this competition leads to a war of all against all. To confirm the accuracy of his description of man's natural condition, Hobbes himself pointed to the analogy with warring states.[74] This fundamental sympathy between Hobbes's understanding of man's condition and the circumstance in which intelligence is most valuable explains why those concerned with intelligence and strategy tend to understand power as Hobbes did. Michael Herman, for example, based his notion of "intelligence power" on the idea that power is the "capacity to produce effects that are more advantageous than would otherwise have been the case."[75] That is essentially Hobbes's definition of power.

Second, finding man's condition to be one of continual war and thus, famously, "solitary, poor, nasty, brutish, and short," Hobbes strove to devise a way for man to escape his natural condition and the supremacy of secrets of state, religion, and nature. Hobbes was one of the philosophers we spoke of above, who sought an alliance with the people based on attacking the three realms of secrets that ruled them. He sought to set men free from the uncomfortable circumstances in which they found themselves by, for example, openly explaining what politics and human life more generally were really like. For Hobbes, this liberation came through subjection to the Leviathan,[76] the sovereign power of the state. Later liberal thinkers contrived ways to avoid this fate, while retaining the objective of freeing men from the control of secrecy. Hobbes was one of the founders of the liberalism that Kent espoused. The world peace and prosperity that Kent argued was the principal objective of policy, and thus the principal objective of modern intelligence, was a comprehensive refuge from the war and poverty that Hobbes argued was mankind's lot by nature. In the mid-twentieth century version of liberalism, this world peace was considered preparatory to world government,[77] a Leviathan on a scale that Hobbes did not imagine. Hobbes's understanding of power was integral to his escape plan, his liberalism, and thus integral to, even if now forgotten by, modern intelligence.

The third reason to use Hobbes's definition of power is the connection between knowledge and power that was part of his liberalism. *Leviathan* appeared in 1651, fourteen years before Colbert took office as the Controller General of finances, but it presented a new understanding of power not present in any of Colbert's activities. That new understanding of power, which was to propel men out of their nasty natural predicament, depended on a new understanding of knowledge, what we now call science. The understanding of science that Hobbes presented followed the argument of Francis Bacon, for whom Hobbes served for a time as an amanuensis. Science thus conceived came to have a critical role in state power and in the intelligence that serves that power. For example, as we have discussed, the social science that Kent made the essence of intelligence was modeled on the methods of the physical sciences. Bacon, Hobbes, and others in the seventeenth century developed this new method and new understanding of science or knowledge.

In *Leviathan*, Hobbes defined science as "the knowledge of consequences, and dependence of one fact upon another, by which, out of that we can presently do, we know how to do something else when we will." If power is the means to some apparent good, as Hobbes argued, then science is the knowledge of those means. As knowledge of means, knowledge is the key to power or power itself, "because when we see how any thing comes about, upon what causes, and by what manner, when the like causes come into our power, we see how to make it produce the like effects."[78] Hobbes was here paraphrasing Bacon. In the *Novum Organum Scientiarum,* or New Instrument of Science (1620), Bacon had written that "human knowledge and human power meet in one; for where the cause is not known the effect cannot be produced. Nature to be commanded must be obeyed; and that which in contemplation is as the cause is in operation as the rule."[79] Command of nature, power over nature, comes from understanding natural causes. Once the causes are in our understanding, they are in our power. We can use them to produce the effect we desire. We then have the means to any future good, Hobbes's definition of power. This approach promised great benefits, including the prolongation of life and the mitigation of pain. These benefits were what the scientists promised in their proposed alliance with the people. Bacon himself hoped that the science he proposed would receive the support of Her (then) Majesty's government. The mutual support of science and political power ultimately came to pass, for example, as it became U.S. government policy to support science in order to improve national health and increase employment, national wealth, and military power.[80]

Although Bacon's focus on science was new, his understanding of the relationship between science and power was similar in an important way to Colbert's. Colbert wanted to know what had moved members of the parlements in the past, so that he could move them as he wanted in the future. Bacon and Hobbes wanted to know what had moved things in the past, so that they might move them as they wanted in the future. The manipulation of individuals was not new, of course, but coeval with human life. It is what is sometimes referred to as the art of low politics, another one of the techniques by which men strive to overcome uncertainty. The effort to make knowledge or science manipulate nature, on the other hand, was new. As an effort to manipulate, we might say, the new view of science applied the low arts of politics to the high act of understanding. Walsingham used torture to get information with which he protected Elizabeth. Bacon argued that it was necessary to vex nature to make it reveal its secrets.[81] This was new and shocking, as the political advice of Machiavelli was shocking, because in the tradition of secrets that both Bacon and Hobbes attacked, "nothing could be more perverse than to seek to know 'high things' by means of the low."[82]

Bacon acknowledged the charge that he was turning something traditionally thought to be high to low ends. In the *Novum Organum*, he imagined someone objecting that he was altering the goal of science and directing it toward what was neither true nor best. Contemplating the truth, the critics would contend, according to Bacon, is the true goal of science and something loftier than "utility and magnitude of works." Bacon's focus on the ordinary, on the matter out of which things were made, on observations of natural processes, would simply drag the mind down to earth, "withdrawing it from the serene tranquility of abstract wisdom, a condition far more heavenly." Bacon accepted the critics' description of what he was doing but denied that there was anything wrong with it. He was turning, he wrote, from the foolish fancies and imaginings of the philosophers' systems to the facts, to things as they really are. "Truth therefore and utility are here the very same things: and works themselves are of greater value as pledges of truth than as contributing to the comforts of life."[83] Critics would be wrong to contrast noble truth to base utility as the goal of science. In fact, there was no difference. In fact, utility was the measure of truth.

Bacon's contemporaries objected to what he did and found it shocking,[84] because he was overturning traditional learning. This is sometimes understood to mean that Bacon emphasized empiricism, the careful observation, patient collecting, and cataloging of data, while the tradition emphasized theoretical formulations. But the tradition that Bacon overturned also insisted on careful observation and collection of data, as Aristotle's biological studies make clear. Bacon's real departure was not in collecting data or focusing on its importance but in his method of making sense of it or turning it into information. As Bacon said in distinguishing his new method from the old, "[T]he evidence of the sense . . . I retain. But the mental operation that follows the act of sense I for the most part reject."[85] What Bacon meant by the mental operation that follows the act of sense was what the tradition, following Aristotle, claimed was the ability of the human mind to grasp the nature of something. According to this tradition, as we look at things, we are able to grasp what the individual things have in common, which we express in speech with common nouns such as "chair" and "dog." Indeed, our ability to understand and speak intelligibly, according to the tradition, depends on this ability of the human mind to grasp the natures of things from how they look to us. Both the thing itself and the human mind are informed by this common nature. In this sense, for the Aristotelian tradition, the truth of things is on the surface of things, how they look to us.

By the time of Bacon and Hobbes, Aristotle's teaching had devolved into a system of jargon, the now infamous doctrines of the so-called schoolmen. Hobbes ridiculed this doctrine in the opening chapter of *Leviathan*. After offering his own account of the senses, Hobbes noted that "the Philosophy-schools" in all the universities in Christendom offered a different account based on Aristotle. "For the cause of *understanding* . . . they say the thing understood sendeth forth *intelligible species*, that is, an *intelligible being seen*, which coming into the understanding, makes us Understand."[86] Bacon and Hobbes understood the Aristotelian view to equate being seen with being known, or being and knowing. While in the Aristotelian tradition this emphasis on appearances signified the openness and intelligibility of the world, it also was in a sense the beginning and the end of knowledge. "Intelligible species" were the basis of speech, and science or knowledge was all about understanding them. Aristotelian science did not produce works, as Bacon and Hobbes argued. It did not intend to. It was then, according to its seventeenth-century critics, merely a surface or superficial understanding of things, productive only of endless discussion—of benefit to none but those engaged in it. For Bacon and Hobbes, and now for virtually all of us, as a result of their ridicule and the ridicule of others, the talk of the schoolmen has become, as Hobbes put it, mere insignificant speech.

The ridicule of Bacon and Hobbes was in a sense not unearned. For one thing, the Aristotelian approach, based on an ability to apprehend essences and "quiddities," bred not only the jargon of the schoolmen but also in certain respects the practices of magicians and alchemists and talk of "occult powers." But going beyond all this, to the texts of Aristotle, raises other problems. The sections in *De Anima* in which Aristotle explains thinking (3.4–8), especially that aspect which grasps the nature of things, are obscure and difficult.[87] More important, if we look at things, it is not evident that we come to understand what they have in common—their shared nature—or can truly grasp them as a species. For example, a group of naturalists associated with Galileo collected an astounding assortment of specimens, corresponding with other naturalists across Europe and seeking samples of what was being found in the New World.[88] Their purpose was to catalog and classify all of nature. In carrying out this work, they came to see, as others had before, that there were many monstrosities or sports of nature, individual entities that were in effect caricatures of more commonly experienced things. They also came across fossils, earlier, different versions of the kinds of things that existed in their world. Finally, even among the individual entities that made up the currently existing kinds, they discovered numerous differences. When they looked at the surface of things, they increasingly came to believe that they saw not "intelligible species" but only individuals. When they looked below the surface of things, dissecting them and observing with microscopes, they found what appeared to be geometrical shapes. Looking at these shapes and thinking about them mathematically, however, reduced individual entities to varying combinations of these geometrical shapes.

Again, the naturalists associated with Galileo were not the first to note the blurred lines between kinds or species. (The Aristotelians were aware of the variance in individuals of the same species, but in a science consisting of speech the "intelligible species" inevitably had more importance.) Nor were they the first to conclude that our minds do not extract from the surface of things an "intelligible species." Among the schoolmen, those espousing this view were called Nominalists. They held that abstract nouns, "chair" and "dog," were not intelligible essences but merely the names of things. The significance of the naturalists was twofold, however. First, apparently under the influence of Galileo, they came to see the possibilities of using geometry or mathematics generally to understand the homogenous shapes they observed beneath the surface of things and thus to understand nature, even living things, through mathematics, something that Bacon did not appreciate.[89] They were thus stepping over the threshold into the reductionist approach to nature, which in the terminology we have used, means turning from the intelligible whole, the individual starfish or wolf, as it exists and as we grasp it mentally, to the data or elements which compose it. Over time, science captured and formulated this data increasingly in mathematical terms, which removed human understanding even further from the immediately intelligible.[90] Second, the blurred boundaries between kinds or species that the naturalists discovered as they cataloged and classified led them toward the view that it was the differences of things, not their similarities, that are most defining. This view led in turn to the conclusion that the world consisted of unique things, which, as unique, could not be understood as they were in the Aristotelian tradition. Not having anything in common, individual entities or beings do not allow the mind to grasp a common nature or to know anything. How are we to understand things then? How do we know if we know something? Although the naturalists around Galileo did not form this view, at least explicitly, it came to be held that if we cannot know what a thing *is*, we can at least know what it *does*. This is what Bacon and Hobbes wanted to learn by studying past examples of cause and effect. Thus, in the Baconian tradition, to know is not to grasp the intelligible whole or "species" but to know the effects we can produce. The only way to know what these effects might be is for humans to experiment and see exactly what the results or effects are, what they can make with something. In this sense, what humans can know (that is, effects) depends on what they can make. If in the Aristotelian tradition being and knowing are identical, in the Baconian tradition making and knowing are identical. Or, in other words, efficient causation, producing effects, replaced final causation, the preeminent kind of causation in the Aristotelian tradition. Knowledge is power (the ability to produce an effect or apparent good we want) ultimately, according to Bacon, because there is nothing else it can be. Knowledge means the ability to produce a desired result; power is producing the desired result. The result becomes the standard by which everything is judged. Moreover, if a thing has no essence, there is no limit to the effects that it might be able to produce and, hence, no limit to human power. Human power might increase to the degree that it would be sufficient to propel mankind out of the violent penury of its natural condition into the world of peace and prosperity espoused by liberalism. As one leading mid-twentieth-century liberal put it, "[M]odern science, when devoted whole-heatedly to the general welfare, has in it potentialities of which we do not dream."[91]

The Limits of Intelligence and the Need for Espionage

Kent was not the only person to place modern intelligence in the liberal tradition. Consider, for example, the views of Vannevar Bush, who made the Hobbesian foundation of modern intelligence more apparent than did Kent. Bush had headed the U.S. government's Office of Scientific Research and Development during World War II and authored the report that launched the U.S. government into widespread support of science. In a book published the same year in which Kent originally published his book on intelligence, Bush wrote of science providing "security against the ravages of nature or of man"; of the need "to order our lives in the light of the terrors of nature and of man, whatever their form may be"; and of the "hazardous world, beset by the perils of harsh nature and the greater perils of harsh men." Given his sense of what the world was like, it was no wonder that Bush, like Kent, argued for what he called "scientific intelligence . . . using modern methods" to deal with its uncertainties and threats.[92] Kent also saw modern intelligence as a way of dealing with uncertainty, since it was to inform America's grand strategy and "in the perfect grand strategy nothing that happens can have been unexpected." Modern intelligence will do away with surprise as it puts an end to uncertainty. Moreover, we should recall, the purpose of grand strategy was not just national security but a better world. Building a better world, replacing the natural world with one of our own contrivance, was the liberal expression of the Baconian aspiration to complete command over nature or the universe. As Bacon wrote, control over all causes and effects and hence over everything that happened would put an end to fortune or the uncertainty that plagued human life. Bush spoke of men molding the whole earth in the pattern of human freedom and creating one world under law.[93]

What are we to make of the arguments and aspirations of men like Kent and Bush? Is modern intelligence, scientific intelligence, as they conceived it, possible? To recapitulate, we have seen at least two reasons to doubt that it is. We saw that humans have a tendency to hypothesize about the present based on the past that leads them to misunderstand the present. In the spirit of Kent, a number of methodological suggestions have been made to overcome this problem, but none seems likely to work. First, reasoning by analogy from the past, using experience-derived assumptions, is one necessary way that humans make "sense of a complex and contradictory world." We cannot simply stop doing it. Besides, most often this approach works. Yet it does mean that we will be surprised by the extraordinary event or human action. Encouraging "thinking outside the box" so as not to be surprised by the extraordinary will mean being wrong more often in the ordinary cases.[94] The problem posed by the extraordinary is a reminder of the uncertainty of the world and thus the limits of methods, which are designed to deal with the ordinary. This problem could only be overcome if it were possible for liberalism to remove uncertainty from the world, but if it is true that uncertainty and human freedom have the same source, one might certainly wonder if the benefit would be worth the cost.

As we also saw, the social science methodology espoused by Kent has a fatal flaw. The methodology is supposed to improve on or guide intuition but is itself dependent on intuition. Kent tacitly acknowledged such difficulties by writing, somewhat like a good Aristotelian, that he would not go below the surface of things into the depths of epistemology. The problems on the surface of scientific methodology, however, are sufficient to make us doubt that this methodology, no matter how useful to analysts,[95] can do what Kent and others hoped it would. There are unavoidable limits to what methodology and scientific intelligence can accomplish.

Indicative of these limits is the failure of social science to attain the success at prediction enjoyed by natural science. In his aspirations for social science, Kent was much like Bacon. In the *Novum Organum*, Bacon argued that his method applied not just to natural philosophy but to all sciences, including ethics and politics, and to this end advised making "a history and tables of discovery for anger, fear, shame and the like."[96] Human nature, however, has so far proved recalcitrant to Bacon's or any modern scientific method. Perhaps, despite all the evidence to the contrary, in time human action will be so thoroughly understood that scientists will be able to predict what men will do. Yet it may be that we should accept the judgment of one student of uncertainty, who, having turned his learning into great works (that is, lots of money) should have authority with moderns. His judgment is that "the true source of uncertainty lies in the intentions of others."[97] If this is true, then there is an essential uncertainty about things and, therefore, also an essential secrecy about them. The great liberal campaign against secrecy cannot make the human will transparent.

Humans form intentions freely. This is the source of uncertainty. As long as the human will remains opaque, we will need ways to deal with it. To do so, we could resort to any number of the techniques humans have developed over the centuries, but perhaps it would be most useful to rely on seasoned judgment or prudence, the human ability to assess correctly what to do in the face of the uncertain world in which we live. We should rely on prudence for the solidly modern reason that having evolved amid the war of all against all, humans have become equipped with the capacity, not evenly distributed, to assess the most important phenomenon in their world—other human beings. Such assessments, however, to be worthwhile, must be well informed. The irreducible need for prudence leads, therefore, to the irreducible need for information gathering, for intelligence. As it is the intentions of others that are the greatest source of uncertainty, the intelligence that can provide information on those often secret intentions is most important. The irreducible need for prudence points to the irreducible need for espionage. This conclusion depends on the reliability of seasoned judgment, particularly experienced judgments about human beings. This is one of the issues we take up in the next chapter.

2   Espionage

So powerful is the liberal tradition of which Kent spoke that it has reduced the once great realms of secrecy—the secrets of nature, God, and political power—so that only in a small area of government activity does secrecy exist with the sanction of law enforced by the power of the state. And this small area—intelligence—both as an activity and as a protected body of information, is under constant political and technological pressure: revelations that the government is secretly collecting information on the cell phone use of citizens cause a backlash, while private and public means of surveillance make secret activities more difficult to carry out. Can secrecy survive the liberal tradition and its technological power? In what follows, we address this question by considering espionage as a test case. This is an important test because as we have seen, espionage has long been a part of the state's information system, longer than either intelligence analysis or the technical collection of information. Given the connection between information, particularly secret information, and power, in discussing the fate of espionage in the information age, we are at the same time, to some degree, discussing the fate of state power. The discussion returns us to the issue of intuition, as we examine the role of judgment in espionage, causing us to revisit Kent's claims about the relative merits of intuition and scientific method. In discussing espionage, we use historical examples ranging over centuries. This is useful because it builds confidence that we are discussing permanent, fundamental aspects of the business. The presence of regularities in espionage will be an issue, as we shall see, and these, if they exist, are most likely to appear in historical perspective. Having established the basics, we touch in this chapter on how information technology may affect them and continue that discussion in the next chapter.

Espionage

Although its workings can become complex, in its essence espionage is simple: one human being tries to get another to share information that the first wants to know and the other should not reveal. For an example of both the simplicity and complexity, consider the activities of Jean-Baptiste Van Male, Spanish envoy to the English court from 1615 to 1629, a period that coincided with the final years of Francis Bacon's life. In 1620, Van Male heard rumors in the court that the British had intercepted letters from a Spanish military leader engaged in the conquest of the Palatinate. This campaign was part of what we now call the Thirty Years' War, a fierce religious struggle between Catholics and Protestants, in which Spain and England were on opposite sides. As the chronicler of Van Male's activities notes, Van Male immediately realized the significance of the rumor, and "he began at once to take all possible steps to find out about the matter."[1]

The steps that Van Male took included espionage, since, like many diplomats of the time, Van Male engaged in this ancient profession as well as in diplomacy. By 1620 he had been in England five years, developing extensive sources of information. His official position allowed him to learn some things, of course, but he also had informants and agents, the former people who volunteered information, the latter people whom he paid. With the aid of these various sources of information, Van Male was able to identify the man who was supposed to decipher the Spanish letters. He approached "Vincentio," as he referred to him in his dispatches, "made friends with him and gained his confidence." Vincentio showed Van Male the letters; Van Male encouraged him not to decipher them. At the same time, Van Male consulted with his superiors in Brussels (then under Spanish control), telling them what he had discovered, seeking guidance, suggesting courses of action, and, like his fellow spies before and since, more funds to carry them out.

The funds were more slow in coming than the guidance. Both were necessary because Van Male had discovered from Vincentio that he had worked for the Spanish before, spending time in an English prison as a result. Van Male wanted to recruit him but needed more money to do so. Van Male pressed on, meeting secretly with Vincentio, but Vincentio was under pressure from the English to decipher the letters and Van Male was unable to fully counter that pressure. His task then switched to discovering how the English would react to the deciphered contents, a task his other sources were able to assist him with.

Van Male's chronicler presents Van Male's approach to Vincentio as a fairly simple matter (Van Male sought out Vincentio and befriended him), and in a sense it was. We all make friends. What could be simpler than that? It does not take much imagination, however, to see the difficulties Van Male operated under. Finding Vincentio may not have been that difficult. Presumably, there were a limited number of deciphering experts; Van Male was well informed. But having identified his target, Van Male needed to make a careful approach, so that Vincentio would not report Van Male's contact. It turned out that Vincentio had Spanish sympathies, or at least was willing to work with the Spanish, but Van Male did not know that when he first approached him. Or perhaps he did. Some of the informants and agents that Van Male used to locate Vincentio may have been able to provide information about him, including his past work for the Spanish, that would have guided Van Male in his first meeting.

It is also worthwhile to think about the first meeting. No matter how much Van Male knew of Vincentio, in the first meeting Van Male would have to start developing some sense of what Vincentio was like, whether he had any motivations that Van Male could use to get Vincentio to do what Van Male wanted him to do. Van Male needed in this first meeting to build some influence over him. Perhaps because of his Spanish sympathies (were they religiously based? Was Vincentio a hidden English Catholic?) or his desire for money, Vincentio proved susceptible to Van Male's persuasion. He did not quickly decipher the messages for his English masters.

Van Male's reports make clear his initial success, but they also point to other problems he faced. How did he know that the letters Vincentio claimed to have were in fact the letters of the Spanish official fighting in the Palatinate? How could he be sure that Vincentio could actually decipher them? Van Male was successful enough in building influence with Vincentio that Vincentio gave Van Male the letters. But, of course, they were enciphered, and Van Male could not read the cipher. Van Male made copies and sent them to Brussels. To test Vincentio's ability to decipher, Brussels sent a test letter, which Vincentio deciphered and Van Male returned to Brussels. Brussels confirmed that the letters Vincentio gave Van Male matched copies they had, but they were not impressed with Vincentio's ability to decipher. They sent another test, which Vincentio declined to take unless he was paid more money. By this time, the deciphered letters were in the hands of the English, but if Vincentio was not in fact an adept at deciphering, what were the English reading?

In addition to the complexities of the Vincentio case, Van Male was dealing at the same time with other espionage matters. For example, Van Male learned from his sources that a French count named Delormes had arrived at court with a secret weapon that was supposed to be able to destroy an enemy's cannon. Van Male set out to recruit a servant of the count's to find out more. He was subsequently able to report that the count's demonstrations to the court had proved unsatisfactory. As Van Male conducted his espionage, he had to consider the counterespionage activities of the English, as well as conduct some of his own. Slow responses from Brussels made him question the security of his communications. Had someone intercepted his letters? Had they opened and deciphered them before sending them on their way again? If he could recruit agents from the personal staffs of diplomats and officials, why could not the English or others do the same with members of his staff? Van Male was aware that the English were attempting such things, because his sources reported it. On one occasion, he discovered and reported to Brussels on the activities of the British envoy William Trumbull, who had letters of credit for Antwerp, the funds intended for espionage work against Spanish interests.

Some Aspects of Espionage

This brief account of some of the activities of a diplomat-spy in the early-seventeenth-century English court reveals some of the basics of espionage, such as cover, assessing and gaining influence over a source, vetting the source, counterespionage or the security of a secret relationship, and the risks involved in espionage. If we consider these aspects of espionage in a bit more detail, making allowances for the more bureaucratic age in which we live, we will be able to evaluate the place of espionage in our current information age. We will also learn some things that will help us understand the role of espionage in war and in irregular warfare, subjects we address in subsequent chapters. Finally, with some understanding of espionage, we will be ready to consider in Chapter Six the difficulties that an intelligence agency has in understanding its own activities.[2]

To carry out his work as a spy, Van Male had to have a legitimate reason for being at court. He did, of course: he was a Spanish envoy. Holding that official position allowed him to carry on his other duty, running espionage operations. In Van Males's case, as was the practice at the time, his job included both diplomacy and spying. His open job and his cover job were closely related and supported each other. They were not perfectly compatible, however. As a diplomat, what reason did Van Males have to seek out the cipher expert Vincentio, someone known to be working for the court he was accredited to? Even if cover is very good, carrying out espionage activities is likely to create anomalies that could alert a counterespionage service. Maintaining perfect cover will ensue the security of espionage work, but largely because none will be going on.

Cover for espionage activity allows the human intelligence officer to do his job, which is getting information from human sources. This is a risky business. For example, as we noted in the case of Van Male and Vincentio, the potential source may report the intelligence officer to the authorities, or the source may be trying to fool the intelligence officer, perhaps at the direction of the counterespionage service. To deal with such problems, and increase the security of espionage operations, over time, the process of acquiring human sources for intelligence work has crystallized into something called the recruitment cycle, which is said to consist of spotting, developing, assessing, and recruiting a human source. Spotting is what Van Male did in locating Vincentio. More generally, it is locating the people who can answer the questions the officer wants answered. Locating the people with the relevant information might be difficult in some cases, but it seems likely that the more difficult step will be developing and assessing the people the officer locates. Assessing the potential source means determining what his or her motivations might be and if they suggest that a recruitment might work. Developing a source means establishing a relationship in which the source's motivations become clear and through which it might be possible to make the potential source an actual source. If we think about any human relationship, we realize immediately that assessing a target's motivations is unlikely to be a perfectly clear checklist sort of activity. It must entail a great deal of uncertainty, especially if the intelligence officer and potential source do not share a native language or sociocultural background.

If the purpose of the recruitment cycle is to reduce the risks and uncertainty of espionage, yet its central activity is the effort to assess often obscure, unstable, and conflicting human motivations, one might think that it would be better to deal with the uncertainty by using coercion. Would not force be a more sure way to get information one wanted, rather than trying to understand and manipulate the vagaries of the human heart? Resorting to force would be to apply Machiavelli's advice about Fortune,[3] or Bacon's about nature to espionage. Among those who have practiced espionage, views on the role of coercion in recruitment vary, even it seems within a single account of recruiting. Victor Cherkashin was a Soviet officer who recruited Aldridge Ames, a CIA officer who gave up the names of a number of Soviet agents working for the U.S. government. Cherkashin recruited Ames by turning Ames's effort to do a one-time cash for information exchange into an officer-agent relationship that did enormous damage to the United States. In his memoir, Cherkashin wrote that trust was critical in recruiting, and that it turned out to be so with Ames in particular. Yet he also recounts numerous examples in which his intelligence service, the KGB, used derogatory information that it held on individuals in order to extort their cooperation. As we saw in the previous chapter, this was a technique that Jean-Baptiste Colbert would have recognized. For the KGB, most often the derogatory information consisted of pictures of the target having sex with one of the women who worked for Cherkashin or other KGB officers. The derogatory information also included involvement in illegal money changing activity, again engineered by the KGB, and information from its extensive files that connected a naturalized American citizen serving as an official overseas to pro-Nazi activity during World War II.[4] This sort of extortion is what most people have in mind when they think of "exploiting vulnerabilities" or coercion in recruitment. It is hard to tell how often the KGB used these techniques, but it long had the reputation for doing so.[5] It is also hard to see how such techniques are compatible with the notion, put forward by Cherkashin, that trust is critical in recruitment. According to Cherkashin, no coercive methods were used with Ames. Cherkashin established trust with Ames by showing that he was concerned above all with Ames's safety.

Issues similar to those raised in Cherkashin's account emerge in Dewey Clarridge's memoir. Clarridge, a high-ranking officer in the Central Intelligence Agency (CIA) famous for his role in the Iran-Contra scandal and more recent efforts running a private-sector information-gathering service, wrote that it was important to establish trust with the target if a recruitment was to succeed, but he also argued that it was critical for the officer to dominate the target. Clarridge dismissed the notion that a target accepts recruitment. According to Clarridge, the officer imposes himself and the recruitment on the target. We might not normally think of trust and domination as going together easily in a relationship. What Clarridge wrote about leadership, referring to his brief stay in the army, suggests a way they might. Clarridge argued that a leader in the military gets his men to follow him into life-threatening situations through the force of his personality and their belief that his competence will minimize the danger as much as possible.[6] Similarly, Clarridge seems to be saying, the officer succeeds at recruiting because the agent comes to trust that the officer will be able to keep him safe, or as safe as possible, in the dangerous work he is about to undertake. The officer's professional competence, manifest in his self-confidence, concern for the security of the target, and knowledge of how to maintain that security, builds trust in the target as their relationship develops. Domination, we might say, perhaps putting Clarridge's terminology in the best possible light, is shorthand for the self-confident competence that a target comes to rely on. In any case, it is not coercion as practiced by Cherkashin and the KGB.

Clarridge's account of a recruitment he made does not seem to bear out what he says about the importance of domination.[7] On one tour, Clarridge chanced to bump into a couple who were part of the foreign commercial service of a Warsaw Pact country. The husband became a target for recruitment because it turned out that a relative of his wife's was on the military staff in their country. Clarridge doggedly pursued the husband for five years and through tours in two different cities. Clarridge did in a sense impose himself on the target, inviting him to dinner and arranging numerous "chance" encounters. After establishing some rapport with the target, Clarridge, in part through his wife's discussions with the target's wife, learned that the couple was disaffected with the communist regime in their country and interested in creating a better life for themselves and their children. This was the target's vulnerability. At one point, wishing to suggest a way that the target might improve his circumstances, Clarridge suggested that the target could help him understand what was going on in his country, a certain quid pro quo implicit in the suggestion. The target argued that he did not know anything that would be of interest. Clarridge continued the pursuit. At one point, the target needed Clarridge's help, which Clarridge provided skillfully. After some more contact, and further encouragement from Clarridge, the target agreed to provide information and Clarridge completed the recruitment.

Did Clarridge coerce the target in this case? Not at all. Did he impose himself on the target? He did. He stalked him. He did not, however, impose recruitment on the target. Instead, Clarridge relentlessly pursued the target, making increasingly clear to him that Clarridge could help him, if he helped Clarridge. It seems likely that when the target did need Clarridge's help, the competence that Clarridge showed in providing it helped make the target believe he could trust Clarridge in the dangerous business of being a spy in a police state. To put this in perhaps overly rational terms, Clarridge's conduct increasingly lowered the target's view of the cost of being a spy (the risk of being caught) until the target's motivation to receive the benefits of spying loomed larger than those costs. In a recruitment, the target's motivations or reasons for wanting to spy are at least as important as the encouragement or commanding presence of the officer.

As Cherkashin's account indicates, coercion makes the target's motivations irrelevant. If you can force someone to be an agent, you do not need to worry about his messy motivations. Coercion, however, has significant disadvantages. As one early practitioner of modern espionage put it, "[An] agent moved only by fear of punishment . . . is in no frame of mind to exploit his own skills or possibilities to the fullest."[8] Moved only by the force applied to him, so to speak, through the coercion of the officer, the agent will not be a self-mover. Such an agent will lack initiative, a critical requirement for an effective agent. Just as important, he will be unreliable. Forced into being an agent, he will seek to break the grip of coercion. He may even volunteer to work for his country's counterintelligence service. A coerced agent is a security problem waiting to happen. The more that security is a concern, the less useful is coercion. (A counterintelligence service might use coercion on its own turf to recruit because it faces minimal security problems in that case.) For these reasons, although there are circumstances, as we will note below, in which coercion might be employed, it is generally not a desirable basis for an officer-agent relationship. The best basis, although hard to determine, changeable, and never perhaps completely certain, is the target's motivations.

It may be worthwhile at this point to address briefly the use of torture in interrogations. This issue is the same in principle as the issue of coercion in relations between an officer and a possible source. Coercion may get some information out of a source, just as inflicting pain will get information out of the target of an interrogation. In this sense, torture "works." Sir Francis Walsingham's torturers extracted enough information from Francis Throckmorton to destroy his plot to kill Elizabeth I. The Royal Ulster Constabulary was able to coerce information from IRA suspects.[9] (It will not always work; Jean Moulin, a leader of the French Resistance, reportedly resisted the Gestapo's torture.) But the point of recruiting a source or interrogating a suspect is to get the maximum information from him. To get this maximum, the agent or the suspect must willingly reveal information. He must take the initiative, so to speak, and actively seek to help the officer or interrogator. More of importance is to be learned by sympathetic openness than by slapping someone around. Thus, both recruitment and interrogation aim at winning the willing not coerced cooperation of the target. In this sense, torture does not work.

Willing cooperation comes from understanding and appealing to the motives of a possible agent. What might these be? Cherkashin believes they are sex and money, mostly money. Ironically for a loyal servant of the Soviet system, Cherkashin in his memoir expressed a faith in the power of money that perhaps only a caricatured capitalist could match. He wrote that all agents talk about wanting to help promote world peace (all potential agents present themselves as liberals, apparently), but that this was just fluffy rationalization. They want money. Interestingly, Clarridge remarked at the end of his account of the recruitment of the Warsaw Pact commercial official that his motivation ultimately was probably money, although Clarridge remained unsure what motivated the agent. While money is surely a motivation, it is not the only one or necessarily the principal one, or even always present. (In Cherkashin's operations the desire for sex was not so much a motive for recruitment as an opportunity for coercion.) Other motivations include patriotism, self-protection, a desire to be involved in something grander than the agent's simple daily life, self-importance, revenge or spite, and ambition. A target may feel that his cooperation with a foreign power will ultimately benefit his country. This was apparently a large part of the motivation of Ryszard Jerzy Kukliński, the Polish officer who, as discussed in Chapter One, worked with the CIA.[10] Or if he fears what may happen to his country and therefore his family, the target may see cooperation as a safety net, not just for the additional money it provides, but because he hopes that it may lead somehow to a new life somewhere else. Some people simply like to be involved in the secret world, either because it makes them feel important or because it lifts them out of their mundane existence. Others may cooperate because they feel they have been slighted or harmed by those in power (Ames and many Soviet agents apparently had this motivation) or because they think cooperation will help them get ahead. They see the officer and his intelligence service as a powerful backer. Often these motivations and others combine. Non-monetary motivations may be so strong that the officer has to practically force some monetary compensation on the target. (This is the sense one has about the Kukliński case. Kukliński apparently took very little money for his work.) One reason an agent may resist taking money is that doing so changes the relationship with the officer. If the agent's relationship began with the officer who recruited him, then taking money indicates that the relationship is no longer simply a friendship.[11]

Whatever the source's motivations may be, they should become more and more apparent as the officer gets to know him or her, although this does not always happen, as just noted in the case that Clarridge described. It is also the case, of course, that the potential source is getting to know the officer as the officer is getting to know him. Some of what the case officer reveals will be real, but some may be feigned. For example, Clarridge did his best to appear sympathetic to the Eastern European official, and claimed as his own interests or hobbies that were really only the target's. The target may of course be doing the same thing, but it is up to the officer to figure that out. Sensing Van Male's interest in the letters, Vincentio may have pretended to be further along in deciphering them or better at it than he was, or may have pretended to be interested in working with Van Male. (Was collusion with the Spanish the real reason he spent time in prison?) Also, a perceptive target may well come to believe that the officer is manipulating him, but that is to a degree inevitable, part of the officer making his real intentions clear. If the manipulation is offensive or uninteresting, the target will back away. If it is intriguing or suggestive, the target will be drawn in. What the officer reveals about himself could be exploited by a hostile intelligence service. This is a risk but an unavoidable one. (It is worth noting perhaps that Cherkashin's memoir, assuming it is reliable, reveals that efforts to coerce and blackmail American and British officials and intelligence officers failed.) The interactions between an officer and a potential source, then, may be a kind of strategic game, with each responding to the other based on assessments that may be subject to dissimulation and include judgments about the assessments that the other side is making. If so, this would only increase the complexity and uncertainty of the recruitment effort.

The result of the development and assessment process, if it works, is that it becomes clearer and clearer whether or not the officer should attempt a recruitment. It may turn out that the target does not have the access to information he was thought to have (doubts arose in the development process about Vincentio) or has revealed no motives that can be used to influence him. (The target has a vote too, of course, and may decide to end the relationship.) If the target does have access and seems recruitable, then, the officer will attempt it. The accounts by Cherkashin, Clarridge, and others suggest that the officer making the attempt is more likely to be successful if he thinks through how he will present the new relationship he is offering in such a way as to make it as easy as possible for the target to accept it. In doing so, the officer is using what he has learned about the potential source during the development and assessment process.

If development and assessment have been done well, the assumption must be that there is a good probability of success, or if the recruitment does not work, a low probability of bad consequences. In addition to allowing assessment of a target, development should create some cushion of rapport and friendship that will buffer the officer from the bad effects of a rejected pitch. All recruitment attempts assume some weighing of risks and benefits. The greater the hoped for benefits, the greater the risks that might be run. On occasion, even a so-called cold pitch might be attempted. This is a recruitment attempt in which there has been little or no preparatory rapport building or perhaps even much assessment. Cherkashin recounted several of these he or people working for him attempted during his career. This is the riskiest way to try to recruit someone, but the hoped for benefits might make it appear worthwhile. (In Chapter Five, we will look at cold pitches done as part of a campaign to disrupt an organization. In this case, there may be a benefit even if the pitch fails; even a failed pitch might increase distrust in the target's organization.) Usually, however, development and assessment take place to determine if the target is worth recruiting and to create the circumstances in which a pitch is most likely to succeed at the lowest risk of negative consequences.

As this discussion makes clear, the recruitment cycle requires access and time. The officer must be able to meet with a target often enough and long enough to assess and develop him. A so-called hard target is traditionally understood to be one who is hard to get access to. Clarridge had to go to great lengths to manufacture "chance" encounters with his Warsaw Pact target, all the time keeping in mind the counterintelligence scrutiny that the target would be under. And a Warsaw Pact official was not even the hardest of the Cold War's hard targets. We should also acknowledge, however, that officials from countries with a developed sense of patriotism will also be hard targets to recruit, even if an officer can get access to them almost whenever he wants. Such access is possible, because an officer's job or cover job creates access to other people. Like all people, officers have social lives outside work, and this also creates access. This is one reason spouses can extend the range of an officer's access and his ability to assess, since spouses have their own activities and circles of friends. Clarridge makes clear that his wife was useful in the pursuit of the Eastern European hard target.

Neither an officer's work nor social activities are likely to bring him into contact with terrorists. This is the basis for the now cliched remark that intelligence officers need new kinds of cover because terrorists do not attend cocktail parties.[12] An extension of this line of thinking is the remark by a recently retired CIA officer, and others, that targeting terrorists requires intelligence officers who look and speak like members of the ethnic group from which the terrorists come.[13] This seems a reasonable claim, but it is not clear exactly what is meant by it. The same retired officer makes clear that intelligence officers like him are staff members of an intelligence organization. It is their job to manage an intelligence operation and, as their experience deepens, to manage others who are managing intelligence operations. For that reason, they are valuable commodities. In addition, they hold in their heads lots of valuable information. Why put that experience and information at risk by putting an officer inside an organization that would not hesitate to kill him or torture him to get that information? For the security of its personnel and agents, an intelligence organization would have to assume that a captured officer would give up everything he knew and would necessarily take steps to protect everyone involved in every operation the captured officer knew about. Against this great risk weighs the possible benefit of finding out about terrorist operations. But even if an officer penetrated an organization, he might find out nothing about operations or find out only what his own little cell is doing. It might take years for the officer to work his way through the organization's networks of trust deeply enough to get a more comprehensive view of the organization's operations. In addition, the way terrorist groups operate may limit the utility of having sources inside. They may not have time to communicate what they learn about an attack before it occurs.[14] It seems unlikely, then, that it would ever make sense for staff officers of intelligence agencies to try to penetrate terrorist organizations. Remote and uncertain benefits do not outweigh present and grave risks. Nor will looking like a terrorist necessarily increase contact with terrorists. What is the cover that the ethnically appropriate officer will use to reduce the risks of exposure as he tries to get close to the terrorists? If he acts like a potential terrorist, will he not highlight himself to various security services? Finally, the markers of acceptance for terrorists are likely to be religious behavior or combat in a previous struggle, or old bonds of friendship, as much as, if not more than, skin color or appropriate speech. An intelligence officer with long experience in the Middle East has noted that he kept a picture of a youth soccer team in his office. Several members of the team went on to be leaders of Hizbollah and its terrorist operations. "You don't penetrate an organization like that," he remarked.[15]

Getting access to terrorists is a problem, but it is not as great as some critics of standard intelligence operations claim. Terrorists do not live in com-

plete isolation, even if they have joined the "underground" and their operations are tightly compartmented. They have wives, brothers, sisters, parents,
uncles, cousins, friends, comrades, and former comrades, to all of whom they
talk. They may not discuss operations but they will give up information about
themselves, and those close to them are likely to know or suspect that they are
engaged in terrorist activities. Those to whom they talk, talk to their own relatives and friends.[16] These human connections form the stepping stones that an
officer may follow, or have his agent follow, to terrorists. Moreover, terrorist organizations have a political purpose; this distinguishes them from criminal organizations. Because they are political, they must reach outside their organizations.[17] In doing so, they create opportunities for others to reach inside. Again,
the officer does not need to reach directly inside. His network of contacts, at
degrees of remove from the officer, can make contact with the terrorists' network of contacts. More than the fabled six degrees may separate the officer
and the terrorist, but it will not be an infinite number and may be relatively
few. Some of these contacts may develop into what are known as access agents,
people who can spot targets and provide assessment information about them.
They may even be able to develop the target and collect operational information from him or, if the circumstances are right, arrange for a "chance" encounter between an officer and the target. This approach, based on the recruitment
cycle managed by the officer at a distance, is similar to the way intelligence
services have always operated against hard targets. In Clarridge's account of his
recruitment of the Warsaw Pact official, there appear to have been at least eight
instances in which Clarridge got important information or assistance from access agents, although in some cases the sources may have been technical rather
than human. This method is operationally effective, preserves security, and bal-
ances risks and benefits. It does take time and requires patience, but quicker,
less secure methods are not an alternative. (It is true that law enforcement officers or FBI special agents, unlike case officers, go undercover inside the organizations they are targeting. We will consider this issue in more detail shortly.)

We should note that the recruitment cycle, whether used against a hard or
"easy" target, is driven by the basic operational circumstances of the officer.
He is operating outside his home country (for example, Van Male in London)
and contrary to the laws of the country in which he is stationed, as are his
agents. If discovered, the officer's connection to his government may protect
him, although this is not always true,[18] but his agent will not have even that
protection. Security of the operation is critical, therefore. This is true not only

to protect the officer and his agent and to minimize the political damage if his operation is discovered. The information the officer and agent steal is worth much less—perhaps nothing at all—if those from whom it was stolen know that it was stolen.[19]

The purpose of the recruitment cycle is to preserve the security of the officer and his operations and agents or, better put, to manage the risks of conducting clandestine operations by ensuring that they are as secure as they can be. Development and assessment allow the officer to evaluate the access of the target and to understand his motivations and suitability to operate as an agent. The vetting that takes place in development and assessment should help prevent the officer from recruiting someone who is a fabricator of information, as it may have in the case of Vincentio, or working for another intelligence service or some other organization that intends the officer and his intelligence service harm. Developing and assessing take time. They represent a considerable investment. For this reason, intelligence services think of their agents as long-term assets. Given the time and money spent recruiting agents, it takes time for them to repay the investment, so to speak. And the officer needs to take the time to develop and assess carefully, because he is operating in hostile territory, on someone else's turf, and must do everything he can to keep his operations secure.

As noted at the outset, this account of espionage rests on historical examples, virtually all of which took place before the latest information revolution gathered force. Has that revolution changed espionage? The public evidence in this matter is slim. A recently retired officer, Henry Crumpton, has, however, provided some useful comments in his memoir.[20] He notes that technology has always assisted espionage and that espionage has enabled technical collection. For example, a human source might place a listening device in an office or home that produces intelligence or information that allows for the assessment of a target and ultimately the successful recruitment of a human source. Crumpton presents the latest technological advances as fitting into this pattern. More than that, he argues that the new information technologies have created a whole new set of targets. "[Intelligence] officers should recruit computer hackers, systems administrators, fiber-optic techs, and even the janitor if he could get you to the right data-storage area or fiber-optic cable." How this recruiting occurred, he does not report. He does say of the advent of the new digital technology that "we just needed to understand the relationship between foreign intelligence in digital form and human nature. We would exploit the relationship. That I understood. That I could do." This suggests that the new information revolution did not alter the espionage business fundamentally. It is true that so-called cyber espionage (using computers to steal information from other computers) can produce vast quantities of information, suggesting the redundancy of human espionage. Yet a human agent who works in a particular office will be best placed to know those thoughts that have not been digitized and exactly which documents are worth stealing. It may well be true, therefore, that human espionage is not redundant in the information age, but, as we will see in the next chapter, there are reasons to believe that the information age has not left human espionage unchanged.

Handling

Because agents have a long-term relationship with an intelligence service, how they are handled is important. If an agent is mishandled, he may become less productive, or cease producing at all, or fabricate information. If he is badly mishandled, he might even become hostile and willing to work with another service. The Soviet intelligence officers who handled Harry Gold, "the man who gave the Soviets the Atom Bomb," as a recent biography described him, so mishandled him that a sympathetic FBI officer was easily able to turn him.[21] Proper handling ensures that an agent will have a long term and productive career; but proper handling is difficult. The difficulties arise from two fundamental characteristics of the espionage relationship. First, the officer is supposed to direct the agent, but the agent operates on his own without the direct supervision of the officer. In addition, agents need initiative and independence because it is impossible to foresee all the possible complications as the agent goes about his business while away from the officer. This works against the idea that the officer directs the agent. As an agent gains experience, the difficulty might increase, especially if the person handling him is less experienced. The agent is likely to have his own ideas about what makes a secure operation. Second, the objectives of the officer and agent are unlikely to coincide perfectly. The officer wants information and career progress. Getting the information is the ultimate objective of the officer. The agent may want any number of things, from remuneration to recognition. Getting the information is only a means. The officer's objectives and requirements should dominate the relationship; otherwise there is no reason to have it. Fulfilling the needs that led the target to become an agent is not the purpose of the officer-agent relationship. At the same time, the officer cannot ignore the needs of the agent. Describing the situation we have just summarized, one officer acknowledged that dealing with agents was a matter of negotiation, of establishing "an agreed reconciliation of purposes."[22] Achieving this reconciliation entails some element of duplicity on both sides about motivations and objectives (not the information exchanged), but not so much or so evidently as to undermine mutual confidence. Maintaining this balance is the art of handling an agent—and probably the art of handling an intelligence officer.

If an agent is handled well, he will produce intelligence. Part of the handling is to keep him in a position or move him to a new one in which he has access to information. An agent is most secure if the intelligence he gathers comes to him in the normal course of his work. He will put himself at risk if he wanders around his organization asking friends and colleagues about what they are working on, although Ames did this for some period of time at the CIA without making himself suspect. Once the agent has the information, the trick is to get it to the officer securely. This is where the tradecraft of espionage becomes critical. An agent may be able to explain why he is in possession of classified material outside his workplace, but no cover story can explain why he was observed handing the material to a foreigner. Similarly, no cover story can explain why an officer is observed in a park with a piece of radio equipment not commercially available. The trick is not to be observed, and that trick is performed through tradecraft.

When handling an agent, the officer needs to be alert to any changes in the agent's work or life that might affect his access or security, as well as to changes in attitude or motivation that might affect the agent's willingness to work. To maintain or renegotiate as necessary the reconciliation of purposes that allows their espionage work to continue, the officer handling an agent must continue to develop and assess him. He may even need to re-recruit him or at least re-motivate him on occasion. In this sense, handling is not different from the recruitment cycle, which is itself not a one-time process but a recurring set of activities that allows successful espionage to occur.

What Do Officers Know and How Do They Know It?

As is evident from our review of the recruitment cycle, it rests on the assumption that the officer can learn and make accurate judgments about the potential source and how that source is likely to respond to a recruitment attempt and the demands of espionage. If, as Clarridge claimed, one could reliably impose recruitment on a target, then this assumption would not be so critical. The bulk of the evidence available to us suggests, however, that such imposition is not possible, at least not in the majority of cases. Recruitments, then, must result from either an officer's informed judgment about potential recruits or luck. Those who have been involved in or studied espionage acknowledge the large role played by luck, but no one seems to think success results only from luck. The officer's informed judgment and perseverance are also part of the story, and the larger part, most seem to say.[23]

Reflecting on what leads to success as a recruiter, Crumpton, the recently retired intelligence officer, argued that the critical characteristic, along with self-knowledge, is "emphatic intuition," by which he seems to mean the ability to escape one's self and effectively understand how the other sees things.[24] This emphatic intuition is what allows officers to come to know and make judgments about those they deal with. In making intuition central to recruitment, Crumpton creates a difference between espionage and analysis. Kent argued, as we have seen in the previous chapter, that intuition was not a reliable foundation for the latter. Is this a real difference? Does it point to some ability that those successful in espionage possess, that those in analysis lack, or is it unnecessary as Kent would have it? And should the answers to these questions cause us to reconsider our contrast in the preceding chapter between the relative worth of the statesman's seasoned judgment, or intuition, and the social scientist's methodical analysis?

There are two schools of thought concerning intuition, one that finds merit in it, and one that does not. The leading exponents of these two schools published a paper together in 2009, expressing not a "negotiated reconciliation" of their opposed views but a reasoned, one might say dialectical, appreciation of their shared ground.[25] At first glance, the results are not favorable to Crumpton's view. Citing previous research that corroborates the experts' dialectical conclusion, they note the poor results from the intuitive judgments of "clinical psychologists, psychiatrists, college admissions officers, personnel selectors [all professions that have at least some plausible connection to selecting recruits for espionage], and intelligence analysts." These professionals performed more poorly than livestock judges, astronomers, test pilots, chess masters, and photo analysts, among others, because of the conditions in which they operate. Intuitive judgments are likely to be sound only if those making them operate in "an environment that is sufficiently regular to be predictable" and have "an opportunity to learn these regularities through prolonged practice."[26]

Kent was right, then, to warn against the use of intuition in intelligence analysis, certainly in long-term intelligence estimates, because the long term is not sufficiently regular to be predictable. Luck and chance have a role in human life, and over longer periods of time their effects accumulate. Even in the shorter term regularities are unlikely to be sufficient to make intuition a reliable tool for, say, political analysts because they, unlike analysts examining a photo, often deal with dynamic rather than static situations.[27] However that may be, if Crumpton's claim about the importance of intuition is to stand, the dialectical conclusion of the experts requires that the operational environment of espionage possess enough regularities to be predictable and that those engaged in espionage have the opportunity to learn these regularities through prolonged practice.

The latter of these two conditions is evidently met in espionage. Like diplomats and military officers, officers in modern espionage organizations slowly advance through the ranks as they gain experience. This slow advance, making mistakes as they go and learning from these mistakes,[28] is the prolonged practice that could make intuition effective. The long process of development gives them time to notice regularities in their targets. But do these required regularities in targets and espionage more generally exist?

Considering what we have seen so far, it seems difficult to imagine more dynamic, uncertain situations than those encountered in spying. Those experienced in it mention luck as often as do critics of intuitive judgment, probably for the same reason: they appreciate the powerful and pervasive role of chance.[29] But the experts on intuitive judgment caution that regularities and uncertainty are compatible. They cite the example of bridge: "[S]kill, the ability to identify favorable bets, improves [outcomes] without guaranteeing that every attempt will succeed." They also mention warfare in this connection, which must encourage those claiming that intuition can work in espionage, since war is thought to be one of the most uncertain of human enterprises, an issue to which we return in Chapter Four.[30]

But the encouragement that comes from comparing war and espionage might well be false. In war, physical force provides regularities. It may dominate or help dominate an enemy and, to that extent, make war more predictable. Caesar in his history of the Gallic wars wrote that fortune does much in our lives but especially in war.[31] Even more so, might we conclude, does luck play a role in espionage, because unlike Caesar an officer does not have the power of the legions behind him to overcome uncertainty and impose some regularity. Still, some regularity may exist in espionage or at least in some aspects of it. As the experts on intuition agree, it is possible for some tasks in a profession to display more regularities than others. For example, in contemplating a recruitment, an officer is not predicting the productivity of the source over a twenty-year period. Intuition in this case is as likely to be as unreliable as in any intelligence estimate. Instead, the officer is really predicting how the target will respond to an appeal to motives that the officer has identified and even tested in the course of the process of developing and assessing the target. In this process and the recruitment itself, the officer will be alert to cues that provide immediate feedback on his tests and suggestions, a critical element in the experts' argument for what can produce effective intuitive judgment. To refer to Clarridge's example, he met the Eastern European target by chance and arranged other "chance" encounters with him. But in talking to him, observing him, and testing him over a period of time, he was learning the regularities in the target's responses, which allowed him to form what Crumpton referred to as an intuition about how the target would respond to the recruitment attempt.

In sum, then, to the degree that intuition plays a role in espionage, it is the result of the officer observing and learning through prolonged experience and practice about the regularities that exist, when they do, in the various tasks that make up espionage. Principally, it is the long experience with the potential recruit that occurs in the recruitment cycle that allows the officer to observe and learn about the potential recruit. Another example would be the officer's sense or intuition about the risks of the operational environment, which is the result of both his accumulated operational experience and his growing experience of the environment he is currently operating in. He is not unlike the firefighter who, alert to cues of regularities in a burning house, notices an anomaly and orders his fellow fighters to evacuate moments before it collapses. His sense that something is wrong or his intuition is "the recognition of patterns stored in memory."[32] This recognition and learning from patterns and cues is a good definition of information and how humans acquire it, similar to processes we discussed in the previous chapter. In this sense, if intuition plays an effective role in espionage and not in intelligence analysis, it is because there are more patterns or regularities in espionage than in intelligence analysis, although perhaps fewer than in warfare. Correspondingly, luck plays a greater role in the success of intuition in analysis than in espionage, but a smaller role in war than in espionage. Referring to intelligence work as an art or skill, as Crumpton does, would be correct, then, but only if we acknowledge the limit of that skill and the role of luck.

The account just offered of what an intelligence officer involved in espionage knows and how he or she knows it seems reasonable, given the available evidence. It comports well with Crumpton's emphasis on practice and experience. It also makes sense of his remarks about the importance of understanding culture. This means being alert to culturally specific cues about human behavior, which is a kind of pattern or regularity recognition. It also makes sense of what Clarridge did when he recruited the Eastern European official, rather than what he later wrote about it. Clarridge did not impose himself on the recruit. Rather, he observed the patterns in the recruit's behavior and based on that and his other operational experience formed intuitions or hunches about how to proceed in the case and how to recruit the target. There is, of course, more involved in judgment than we have discussed. For example, the experts on intuitive judgment emphasize the role that emotions, preferences, and tastes play in their own judgments and everyone else's. It is also the case that while prolonged practice is important for effective intuitive judgment, there are limits to what it can accomplish. In noting the importance of pattern recognition and picking up on cues, the account highlights traits unlikely to be evenly distributed among people. This would explain Crumpton's claim that intelligence officers are born and not just made, no matter how much practice and experience they get.[33]

The account is also incomplete because espionage is more than effective intuition. A former head of MI6, the British foreign intelligence service, offered a short list of "important truths" of espionage:

> the vital need for trust between the players and, as part and parcel of this, the constant need for the human touch in addressing people's problems and anxieties; the difficulty of sustaining this trust at long range over a severely restricted channel of communication; passionate attention to detail . . . ; and, perhaps most important of all, the ability to recognize golden opportunities and to grab them as they come—they don't come twice.[34]

These remarks broaden our view of what espionage requires but also bring us back to intuitive judgment by highlighting the importance of the ability to recognize opportunity. Recognizing opportunity presumably has the same basis as recognizing danger: knowing the regularities, one recognizes an anomaly. In one case the anomaly suggests harm, in another benefit; in one case we are alerted to danger, in the other to an opportunity. The regularities are constant, of course; it is the anomaly that comes only once in a given situation. Those with the best pattern recognition skills, who are most alert to cues, will be the ones most likely to note the anomaly and, therefore, the danger or opportunity.

Recognizing danger and opportunity in a given situation might also be a way of describing the intuition of the statesman. Kent would be right to criticize this intuition if it presumed to know the future better than an intelligence analyst or an algorithm, but if the statesman's intuition is used to judge what to do in a given situation, it would have some validity, at least in some of the tasks of statesmanship. In this view, the statesman would be like the firefighter in the burning building or Caesar as he surveys the battle before him.

Agents, Contacts, Informants, and Sources

However it comes about, the end result of the recruitment cycle is a recruitment, an agent, someone who has entered a long-term relationship in which he or she works for the espionage service and is under its control. Again, "control" does not necessarily imply coercion. Blackmail need not be involved. But to call someone an agent is to say that they do what the officer directs them to do. They work to carry out the officer's objectives. The officer can task the agent, as the professional language has it, and the agent will try to accomplish the task. Given the differences in purpose and motivation between the officer and the agent, the agent may not always accomplish the task completely, but that he or she do so is the aim of the relationship, of the negotiated reconciliation of interests between an officer and an agent. This negotiated reconciliation raises a number of issues about the integrity and reliability of espionage that we will take up in Chapter Six. For the moment, we can get a better sense of the officer-agent relationship by noting how it differs from several similar relationships: the relationships between a diplomat and his contacts, a detective and his informants, and a journalist and his sources.

A diplomat meets with his contacts, say a counterpart at a foreign ministry, to find out information that his government wants to know and to share information that his government wants the other government to know. To aid this process, because friends more readily share information, the diplomat may seek to build rapport with his contacts by taking them to lunch or inviting them to his house for dinner. He will also provide information to his counterpart when he requests it. This mutuality makes the difference with the intelligence officer apparent. The information that the diplomat deals in is not public; if it were, he would not need to collect it. It is information that a government may not want to make public, perhaps for domestic or foreign political reasons, but which it does want another government to know. It consists of the reasons a policy was adopted, or an explanation of the extent to which it will be pursued, or reassurance that it will not conflict with the interests of the diplomat's nation, or is merely an expression of a willingness to go along with another country's policy. The key point is that it serves the interest of the government to share this information. The assumption in diplomacy is that the sharing of such information will keep relations between countries steady. The purpose is to minimize the friction of international relations, so as to minimize conflict and war, or to so arrange things that if war is necessary it occurs on terms most advantageous to the diplomat's country. It does this by seeking mutual benefit, although mutual benefit is not necessarily equal benefit. When William Donovan, who was to head the Office of Strategic Services, an intelligence agency that operated during World War II, sat down for a conversation with Mussolini prior to the war, he was engaging in diplomacy, the exchange of explanations and perspectives to increase mutual understanding—not espionage.[35]

There may be instances when one party to the diplomatic exchange says things that go beyond his or her brief. If the information shared is not just personal opinion but secret controlled information, then the diplomat and counterpart are engaging in activity that is illegal, even treasonous, from the viewpoint of the counterpart's government. The diplomat has moved from activity that is peaceful because mutually beneficial to activity that is hostile because damaging to the contact's government. In this case both the diplomat and his contact are at risk, and control and security precautions would be important to ensure the safety of the contact. While a diplomat may occasionally operate beyond the limit of the mutually beneficial, intelligence officers do so habitually. They engage in activity hostile to other governments or organizations. Theirs is a world of conflict, not peace. Diplomats exchange information; intelligence officers steal it. The fundamental difference between diplomacy and espionage explains why over time the two functions were separated. In early modern Europe and for centuries after that, ambassadors carried out both diplomatic and espionage activities. Military attachés also often performed double duty. This began to change toward the end of the nineteenth century, but the German ambassador to the United States prior to World War I was directly involved in espionage and subversion operations throughout the United States.

If a hostile operating environment is something that divides diplomats and spies, it is something that unites intelligence and law enforcement officers.

When the police deal with an informant, the informant may receive something in exchange, if only not being arrested for vagrancy, but he is giving up information that will harm someone else. Similarly, an agent typically receives compensation, and his work will harm someone. Informants and agents do differ, however. An informant is often a passive collector of information. If a detective needs to find out something, he goes to someone who he thinks will have the information. He does not direct the informant to find things out, except perhaps to say "keep your eyes open." He asks what the informant may have heard on the street or seen because he sells newspapers on a certain street corner. The direction provided—the tasks levied on the informant—may go beyond merely passive observation, of course, but the assumption with an agent is that they most often or always will. In addition, the informant's usefulness may be limited to a specific case. Once that case is over, the detective may never talk to the informant again. Detective-informant relationships are not necessarily long term. Finally, what the informant is doing may be dangerous, but it is not illegal. Therefore the detective does not need to conduct a clandestine relationship with the informant. He only needs to protect the informant from being discovered by the target of the investigation. If the informant becomes a witness, then it may be necessary to protect him or her for a long time.

The description of the police-informant relationship given so far assumes that the police are trying to identify or find an individual or at most a small group, who, for example, robbed a store. The situation changes if the police are working against an organization, whether a corporation, a mafia family, a drug trafficking operation, or a terrorist group. In these cases, law enforcement is working against not only individuals but the organization. This may extend the time horizon of the operation, as the police try to figure out how the organization works and collect evidence against those running it who may not be involved directly in the commission of crimes. In this case, the police may need to keep informants in place for a long time, even directing informants who are part of the organization. An interesting example of this is the FBI's use of Mark Whitacre as an informant to investigate price fixing at Archer Daniels Midland (ADM). Whitacre carried out this role for several years, was directed by the FBI, and, within the corporation, acted clandestinely, taping meetings and working to help the FBI build its case. Again, the FBI did not need to meet clandestinely with Whitacre because their contact with him was legal, and ADM did not have a counterintelligence capability looking for someone like Whitacre. This would not be true of a terrorist organization or even some other illegal organizations, so law enforcement might have to conduct clandestine meetings with its informants when working against these organizations. In these ways, an informer would be more like an agent than the informer as we first described him. The FBI, for example, does run agents in the sense that this term is used in intelligence.

Differences remain, however, between the law enforcement and intelligence approach to using agents. Law enforcement seeks to gather information to make an arrest, to close the case. Even if it takes years to build the case, the objective is still to make the arrest and close the case. Intelligence organizations want to go on collecting information. This gives them a longer and a broader perspective on their agents than law enforcement typically has toward its informants or agents. This difference in attitude—closing the case versus continuing to collect information—has another important consequence as well. Closing the case may come at the expense of gathering important information. Reportedly, according to an FBI official, when the FBI interrogated Ramzi Yousef, they asked him only about the first World Trade Center bombing. He could have told them about al Qaeda, but he was not questioned more broadly.[36] An intelligence officer presumably would have questioned more broadly because he would not have been focused on making a case against a suspect but on getting all relevant information he could out of him. Generally speaking, we might say that law enforcement officers seek information in order to get the man, while intelligence officers seek the man in order to get information.

This difference in perspective is not accidental or trivial but results from the different selection, training, and reward processes that law enforcement and intelligence agencies use; and these in turn result from their specific tasks, closing a case and collecting intelligence. These differences fundamentally affect how the two types of organizations understand and deal with the people, the informants or agents, that provide them information. This difference also explains why the FBI has had so much trouble in transforming itself from a law enforcement agency into an intelligence agency.

Other differences exist between informants and agents. We noted that the way an intelligence officer operates, his use of the recruitment cycle, his attention to the security of his operations, reflects the fact that he is operating always in hostile territory. Discovery of his operation will have significant consequences. Therefore, we argued, officers tend to avoid coercion in dealing with agents. Police use coercion, even if it is only the threat of arrest or the promise of leniency, to get information and to get informants to work with them. They can use coercion because if the informant objects, he has nowhere to go. Will he report the police to the police? Law enforcement targets may be hostile, but law enforcement operates in a friendly environment. It operates inside the law and often with the cooperation of the public. In addition, if a law enforcement officer or his informant are in danger or might be, they can call for backup and often have it standing by. Intelligence officers may have some people to provide surveillance of a meeting site (Clarridge describes examples of this), but often they do not even have this much support. To a much greater degree than law enforcement officers, intelligence officers operate on their own.[37] Their security is entirely dependent on their ability to understand and control the agent they are meeting and their skill at keeping the meetings secret. All of this affects perceptions of risk and the way that an intelligence as opposed to a law enforcement officer deals with sources of information.

The difference in risk explains why law enforcement officers sometimes themselves operate under cover and penetrate an organization, while intelligence officers typically it seems do not. Law enforcement officers have reportedly become members of motorcycle gangs and right-wing organizations, but this has occurred inside the United States and presumably in situations in which the risks were manageable in a way they would not be overseas or with organizations that would not hesitate to kill a discovered American, or torture him for information. As a general rule, law enforcement officers might themselves penetrate a criminal organization, while a case officer would not penetrate a terrorist organization because of the risks involved in each case. Intelligence officers operate in environments and against targets that pose a level of danger that law enforcement officers encounter less frequently. And when they do encounter it, they do not or should not themselves penetrate the targeted organization. We might say, as far as intelligence officers are concerned, that any organization worth penetrating by them personally would be too dangerous to permit doing so. As we have argued, espionage seems capable of penetrating terrorist organizations using traditional techniques, making it unnecessary to run such risks.

Finally, we should contrast intelligence officers and journalists. Reporters meet people to gather information and then write reports or news stories. They cultivate sources, although most often, at least in the United States, they do not pay them for information. They flatter and cajole. They manipulate. To get the information and leaks for their stories, they take advantage in sources of a desire for revenge or a hope for fame or a taste for affecting events from behind the scenes. They might even threaten or coerce by arguing, for example, that they are going to publish no matter what, so the reluctant source should tell his or her side of the story to provide balance. The information divulged to a journalist may be damaging to individuals or the country. It may be illegal to share the information. Hence, journalists need to protect their sources. In these ways, they are like intelligence officers. They differ in significant ways. A journalist's source is a volunteer. The journalist does not control the source and may not have a long-term relationship with him or her. The negotiated reconciliation of purposes in this case is more likely to be equal or even favor the source. The information shared is more likely to serve the personal or bureaucratic interests of the source than would be the case with an intelligence source. That is the theory, at least. Journalists also want the widest possible dissemination for their information. Intelligence officers serve a very specific audience. A final difference between intelligence officers and journalists is that officers, because of their operational skill, access to other sources of information, and the power of the government they represent, are typically better at collecting information in dangerous circumstances and surviving than are journalists. Testimony to this is the greater number of journalists killed in action than intelligence officers.

Another significant difference between officers and journalists concerns the validity of the information they collect. An editor may review what the reporter writes but does not always even know who the source is. The description of the source in the published story is minimal or nonexistent, often something like "a high-ranking official." The source description does not always include a statement about the reliability of the source based on the source's reporting history. A journalist or his or her employer may require corroboration of the information by a second source, but that source's bona fides may be no better known than those of the original one, and the corroboration may not make it into the published story. Journalism is said to be the "first draft of history." The assumption is that it will be rewritten and corrected. Much different is the case with an officer's intelligence report. The source is known and vetted. He is under the control of the officer or coming under his control. Any reports submitted are reviewed before being disseminated; source descriptions and reliability ratings are considered. The intelligence report goes to analysts who place it in the context of other reporting and prepare a draft finished intelligence report. Several layers of management review these draft reports, and, if it is a "community" product, other intelligence agencies review it as well. Consumer (policymaker) response is fed back into the system, driving and refining collection requirements and future reporting. (The consumers of journalism have no direct means to affect what is collected and printed, although they clearly influence that by what they buy or do not buy.) The intelligence report is presumed to be true, although it may not be the whole truth. We know, of course, that not all processed intelligence is accurate. But the fact remains that the efforts to ensure the validity of intelligence reporting are much more extensive than the efforts to ensure the validity of journalism.

Conclusion

What we have described so far is the traditional view of espionage and the traditional activities of the people who carry it out. As we noted at the beginning, it is an activity suffused with chance events and based on the vagaries of the human heart. Although it takes skill, it is sometimes unclear whether skill or luck prevails. At most, skill works with, rather than overcomes, chance to produce the desired outcome. Espionage may produce decisively important intelligence, but it is also less reliable than other intelligence derived from orbiting satellites or the emissions of industrial smokestacks. This is one reason why informed and thoughtful students of intelligence see human intelligence operations as "more an art than a science" and consider it suspect.[38] Intended to inform the intuition of leaders and help them overcome the uncertainty they face, espionage itself is suffused with uncertainty.

The traditional view of espionage is the basis for the distinctions we have just drawn between agents, contacts, informants, and sources and between officers, diplomats, detectives, and journalists. As we have noted, there are similarities between these providers and collectors of information as well as differences. The similarities are one reason why as we face new or evolving problems, the traditional division of labor between these collectors has come into question. When reviewing the poor performance of U.S. intelligence in Afghanistan, for example, a senior military officer suggested that intelligence collectors there should operate more like journalists with regard to how they both made sense of information and disseminated it.[39] The FBI has been operating in Afghanistan to identify and target terrorists, alongside the military and the Central Intelligence Agency. We will consider such developments further. But first, having described the traditional business of espionage, we need to consider in more detail the effect on it of modern information technology.

3 Counterintelligence and Covert Action

On February 17, 2003, a man known as Abu Omar was kidnapped in Milan. He was taken to the U.S. air base at Aviano and from there flown to Egypt. Abu Omar was a militant Muslim, whom the Italian police had taped discussing various terrorist operations. He was held in Egypt and reportedly tortured. We know this and a good deal more about this case because Italian investigators uncovered its facts. Their investigation led to the indictment of thirty-five people, including high-ranking Central Intelligence Agency (CIA) and Italian security officials. Twenty-five people were ultimately convicted of crimes related to the kidnapping. The investigators unraveled the case in large part through analyzing cell phone records. A witness to the abduction reported that one person involved was on a cell phone. Using that information and the location of the kidnapping as a starting point, the investigators used software to correlate calls and identify the phones used. Since the phones provided location and time data, the investigators were able to reconstruct in detail the movements of the people involved. Some of the cell phones the investigators tracked were used to make calls to northern Virginia, where the headquarters of the CIA is located. The cell phone records also led investigators to the home of the CIA's chief of base in Milan, where they recovered additional incriminating information from the chief's personal computer, including "records of an internet search" by the chief "to find the quickest route from" Abu Omar's home to the Aviano air base.[1]

On January 19, 2010, Mahmoud al-Mabhouh was assassinated in his hotel room in Dubai. He was injected with a muscle relaxer and then smothered. The Dubai authorities were able to reconstruct many of the details of the operation that led to his assassination because of the closed circuit video cameras that recorded the movements of people at the airport and hotels in Dubai. Based on information from the videos, the authorities were able to identify passports, credit cards, and cell phones used by the team of assassins. The team did not call each other while the operation was under way, communicating instead through four numbers in Austria. They carried forged passports, using the identities of Israeli citizens who had dual citizenship in European or other countries. This circumstantial evidence pointed to Israel as the author of the attack. Israel had a motive. Al-Mabhouh was a senior military figure in Hamas, responsible for the deaths of Israelis, and had also been involved in procuring weapons for the organization.[2]

These two events raise issues about both counterintelligence and covert action in the information age, and about espionage as well, since covert action has traditionally required espionage, the use of human agents, and counterintelligence seeks to stop espionage.[3] In the information age, some have concluded, counterintelligence or detecting the work of intelligence services is much easier, and covert action, secret actions undertaken by these services, therefore, much harder, if not impossible. This supposedly is the lesson of Milan and Dubai. As a former U.S. national counterintelligence executive put it:

> In an age of surveillance and instant electronic storage and retrieval, covert espionage operations will never be the same again. The intelligence business, like everyone else, now operates in a glass house. This isn't a case of heavy-handed government surveillance. It's a case of pervasive light-handed surveillance by just about everybody, producing massive amounts of information that can be correlated with a few keystrokes or mouse clicks. Transparency has come to the intelligence business.[4]

Supporting this claim is the fact that the CIA's use of aircraft and airports to carry out renditions secretly was uncovered by nongovernmental observers using data analysis software to correlate plane tail numbers and other information.[5]

If claims like this are true, the implications would reach beyond the world of intelligence. If the advent of unavoidable transparency means the end of intelligence, and intelligence is a proxy for the information dominance of the state, the advent of transparency implies the end of that dominance and perhaps a fundamental change in the nature of the state. At the same time, of course, transparency would mean the end of privacy and imply perhaps a fundamental change to liberal citizenship. But are claims of unavoidable transparency true? Or, to the contrary, if intelligence operations can remain secret, do they point to the limits of transparency in the information age?

To answer these questions we must consider counterintelligence and covert action more thoroughly. In doing so, we will focus on those aspects of counterintelligence and covert action most relevant to the issue of intelligence in the information age, allowing us to avoid many of the details of counterintelligence that generate the "wilderness of mirrors," into which one may easily enter, never to reach clarity again.[6]

Counterintelligence

Whatever intelligence organizations do, they do either clandestinely or covertly. They act clandestinely when they hide what they do or who did it. They act covertly when they hide, not what they do and who did it, but who ordered the act. For example, when stealing secrets (for example, military plans), an intelligence service must hide the fact that it has stolen the plans, or those from whom they were stolen will simply change them. In this case the intelligence agency must hide the act and the actor (its agent). Of course, each government assumes that its enemies are trying to steal its plans; there is no need to hide that fact; but to benefit from this activity, governments must conceal their successful thefts. In contrast, if the intelligence agency interferes in the political process of another country or sabotages some infrastructure, the act itself will become known. A rally will occur or a bridge will blow up or an oil line rupture. The act will become known once it is done, but the operation itself needs to remain unknown until it reaches its culmination, or it will be stopped. In this case, the act becomes known but the agent who carried it out needs to remain hidden, as does the identity of its author, the country that sponsored the attack. If the author remains hidden, the act is covert, even when the act itself is known. Finally, if someone uses information technology to commit sabotage, both the act and the actor (for example, a computer virus) are likely to become known, but the identity of the author could remain hidden. This would again be a covert action. Traditionally, clandestine operations were those in which the act and agent were hidden; covert operations were those in which the agent, but above all, the sponsoring state, was hidden.

Whether conducting clandestine or covert operations, intelligence organizations must defend and protect their operations from the efforts of those who want to discover them. In addition, if they analyze the information they collect and turn it into polished judgments for decision-makers, intelligence organizations need to ensure that enemies do not deceive the analysts or influence their analysis and in that way deceive or influence decision-makers. For example, to the extent that Saddam Hussein was able to deceive the intelligence community over the years about his possession of weapons of mass destruction (first, that he did not have them and, second, that he did), to that extent he was able to influence decision-makers in the Bush administration. That it is easier for deception to work when it confirms established opinion does not alter the fact that in this case deception of the intelligence community helped deceive decision-makers. Beyond these defensive measures, counterintelligence may also include the offensive measures, including deception activities, that intelligence organizations take in order to mislead other intelligence organizations.

"Counterintelligence" is the name given to the measures that intelligence organizations take to protect their information from manipulation by another intelligence organization and manipulate other intelligence organizations. Not all the efforts an intelligence organization takes to ensure the integrity or validity of its information are counterintelligence. Training analysts to draw inferences properly is not counterintelligence. Training in logic is not intended primarily to defeat the manipulations of another intelligence service. Locks, fences, and guards may all protect the intelligence service, but unless they are protecting it from another intelligence service, they are security measures and not counterintelligence. What distinguishes counterintelligence from security is that counterintelligence defends against or attacks the activities of other intelligence services. As the examples just given illustrate, security and counterintelligence may overlap.

Of the two aspects of counterintelligence, defensive and offensive, the defensive is most fundamental. Offensive counterintelligence, particularly deception, has little chance of succeeding unless it can be kept hidden from its targets, and this depends on the effectiveness of defensive counterintelligence. In addition, defensive counterintelligence is most important for judging the fate of intelligence and secrecy in the information age. If the development of information technology means that a state cannot keep its intelligence operations and other secrets secure either from other states or private individuals, then the information advantage that has been essential to the state and its power has disappeared. In this way, we may say defensive counterintelligence defines the limits of transparency in the information age. For these reasons, we will begin with defensive counterintelligence or the efforts an intelligence service takes to keep its activities hidden.

Counterintelligence should be an integral part of intelligence operations from the beginning. As soon as Dewey Clarridge realized that his chance encounter with an Eastern European official had given him an opportunity to develop a relationship with the official, he began to think about ways to restrict knowledge of his contacts with him. Similarly, once Cherkashin realized that the person volunteering information might be a CIA officer (he turned out to be Aldrich Ames), he began to think about how to protect the relationship.[7] Some of the protection that intelligence organizations provide comes from the fact that they are storehouses of information. A former counterintelligence officer recounted that decade-old information held by his headquarters allowed him to identify someone as an intelligence officer from a hostile service. Using this information, the counterintelligence officer was able to protect a source by guiding him in how to avoid the identified intelligence officer. This allowed the counterintelligence officer a small victory over his opponent and is a simple illustration of how information is power.[8]

Both Cherkashin and Clarridge were dealing with highly sensitive contacts, and so were immediately concerned with their security. It is clear from their memoirs, as a moment's reflection would also suggest, that not everyone they met raised such concerns. It is also clear that a principal task, certainly when Cherkashin met the volunteer, was to confirm who he was and if he was in fact a CIA officer. Similarly, Van Male had to confirm that Vincentio had the stolen Spanish letters and if he could decipher them. Cherkashin was also acutely aware that the volunteer could have been a trap set for him by the FBI. He discussed the risks with Moscow, but the possible gain was so great, it outweighed the risk of falling into a trap. What was involved in this judgment, to use the language of the previous chapter, was not just an assessment of cues in the volunteer's behavior (they suggested he was legitimate) but also an assessment of the possible gains compared with the possible risks. Or perhaps the weighing of gain and risk was itself an example of experience-based intuitive judgment using regularities apparent to Cherkashin and the experienced officers he consulted with.

It is also clear from Cherkashin's account, as his concern about the FBI indicates, that a key consideration in his meeting with his sources was the hostility of the environment in which he was operating. How good were the local security services? How interested were they in what he was doing? Cherkashin knew that he and his fellow Soviet intelligence officers were the principal target of American counterintelligence and that Washington, DC, where he was stationed, and New York City, the location of the Soviet mission to the United

Nations, were the focal points of that counterintelligence effort. In these places he had to be particularly attentive to security in conducting his espionage activities.

However sensitive the source or hostile the environment, the greatest threats to the security of intelligence operations come not in developing sources but in conducting operations once a recruitment takes place. One old espionage hand explained this by arguing that no cover story can explain the act of communication between an officer and an agent, thus making it the most risky part of espionage.[9] If the officer and the agent never met and did not communicate with each other, then their relationship would be secure, almost perfectly so. If they did not meet or communicate, how would anyone know the agent or officer were part of a clandestine relationship? In fact, of course, they would not be; no communication means no relationship. The communication does not need to be face to face. Dewey Clarridge recruited his Warsaw Pact official outside of Eastern Europe and arranged for him to provide his information without meeting anyone when he returned home. This impersonal communication can be done in various ways, the hidden writing that Jean-Baptiste Van Male dealt with in his espionage in England in the early seventeenth century being a long-established one. Thomas Jefferson encrypted parts of the letters he wrote to James Madison and others. But in this case, it was perfectly legitimate for Jefferson to be in touch with his correspondents. He was only interested in hiding from others certain things he told them. Communications with a recruited agent must hide both the fact of the communication and what is communicated.

Technology can facilitate secure communications. This is one way in which the revolution in information technology is enhancing both secrecy and privacy. Powerful encryption is publicly available, for example. There are ways to use various forms of digital communications protected by passwords to improve security. The speed with which high-tech devices communicate and their miniaturization also reduce the risk to secure communications. None of these high-tech techniques are perfectly secure, however. Whatever their technical merits, they are still used by humans, which inevitably injects error into the system. Problems with high tech may make low-tech communication methods more appealing, especially if what the agent is communicating is not time sensitive. An agent and an officer may use old-fashioned impersonal communications, such as a dead drop. This is a location where the agent at one time leaves information and the officer at another picks it up and leaves requirements or instructions for the agent. Although the officer and the agent are at the same physical location, they are there at different times, thus minimizing the risk that their clandestine activity will be discovered, especially if both have taken steps to detect surveillance. Robert Hanssen, an FBI special agent, often described as the most damaging spy in American history, communicated securely with the Soviet and then Russian intelligence services for long periods using impersonal communications. He was finally identified reportedly only when the FBI bought information from a former KGB officer that identified Hanssen as a spy. Having identified Hanssen, the FBI placed him under surveillance and arrested him when he went to the dead drop. They then kept Hanssen's arrest secret and waited for his Russian contact to come to the drop, but he never showed up.

Because they keep the officer and the agent more separate than face-to-face meetings, impersonal communications are more secure than such meetings. If the officer and the agent are discovered together, how is that to be explained? What about the official documents found with the officer and the agent as they supposedly meet to explore their shared interest in gold coins from the late Roman Empire? While more secure, impersonal communications are more time consuming, and hence less efficient than face-to-face meetings. In addition, human beings are such that face-to-face contact, especially in such a stressful business as spying, can be a deeply felt need. It is more difficult to direct and sustain a relationship impersonally than personally. This is clear in the accounts of the espionage of Colonel Ryszard Kukliński, described in Chapter One. Kukliński was an extremely valuable source, operating in a hostile environment. Opportunities for face-to-face meetings were rare, but Kukliński sought them nonetheless, apparently as a way to overcome or deal with the isolation he faced operating as an American source in the heart of the Warsaw Pact.

This brief, incomplete account of agent communications, together with what was presented in the previous chapter about recruitment, provides the background necessary to consider the effect of information technology on the security of the officer-agent relationship, which is the heart of espionage. On balance, the business of recruiting and running an agent does not seem much dependent on new information technology. This should not be a surprise, since, as reputedly the world's second oldest profession, espionage has been around a lot longer than modern information technology. Like the only older profession, espionage may be aided by information technology, but it does not require it. In both professions, the business is fundamentally personal, not technical. Nor does counterintelligence seem to be altered fundamentally or decisively by information technology. Certainly, index cards are slower and less efficient than an electronic database as a way of managing and retrieving information. In cases where speed is of the essence, therefore, information technology might be a critical advantage in vetting someone, but these cases are likely to be few. Everything publicly available about the espionage business suggests that, generally speaking, developing and assessing someone takes time that information technology cannot help shorten.

While it may be right to conclude that espionage is not dependent on or fundamentally altered by information technology, we should not underestimate the aid that this technology can provide counterintelligence and thus the threat that it poses to intelligence operations. When CIA agents alerted the U.S. government that the Soviet Union had U.S. Army war plans, the army initiated an intensive search for the spy inside its ranks. One thing army counterintelligence did was to identify who had access to the plans over time. Tens of thousands of soldiers had. The CIA's agent reporting also gave counterintelligence knowledge of how the documents were getting to the Soviet Union. Using this information, army counterintelligence put together a profile showing the probable habits and circumstances of the spy. In the early 1980s, when this case unfolded, the limited data-processing capabilities available made sifting through all those thousands of soldiers to find those who fit the profile a nearly impossible task.[10] It would be much easier today because of advances in information technology, a clear indication of the help that now basic information capabilities give to counterintelligence.

It is important to note, however, that in the case of finding the spies turning over American war plans, identifying who might be doing it was just the beginning of the counterintelligence operation. The case was ultimately resolved by putting human agents in touch with the suspects in order to confirm that they were spying, how they were doing it, and who else might be involved. These human intelligence operations, indeed the whole case, were continuously aided by technology, including listening devices, but the human element was essential and there do not appear to be any technological developments since the 1980s that would alter that conclusion.

One reason that information technology has not fundamentally altered counterintelligence is that most of the advantage of information technology for counterintelligence comes from monitoring other information technology. It is true that if one has a Facebook page and puts personal information on it, an intelligence service can exploit that in various ways.[11] One does not need to have a Facebook page, however. If one avoids such technology, and e-mail, cell phones, and credit cards, one avoids the monitoring. This may mean that one's operations will occur more slowly or inefficiently than they might. This is a cost imposed by the so-called Panopticon, the all-seeing eye of the modern media and information age, but how high is the cost? Is one reduced, for example, to operating as inefficiently as the Viet Cong and North Vietnamese forces, who lacked the electronic sophistication of the United States? These unsophisticated forces defeated American and Vietnamese intelligence and counterintelligence, if not entirely, at least frequently, with largely low-tech or no-tech means.[12] Why is operating at an old-fashioned pace such a disadvantage? If one has a long-term perspective, it might not be considered an exorbitant or impossible cost.

The low- or no-tech, long-term approach is one that al Qaeda or some of its members have adopted. Documents recovered from Osama bin Laden's home in Pakistan after he was killed indicate that he saw as key to his continued survival avoidance of information technology. He wrote that it was possible to survive and operate even against U.S. technology as long as one "does not commit a security error." He counseled avoiding phones, computers, daytime activities, unless it was cloudy, items provided by untrusted sources (they might contain tracking devices), and even excessive contact with people, especially those not known to be trustworthy. He advised using only couriers to communicate and explained what he thought was the most secure way to do so. He acknowledged that these security measures would slow al Qaeda's work, but he had a long-term perspective and saw these measures as necessary for survival. That bin Laden survived for ten years as the most hunted man on earth suggests that his security measures were good. (How much his hiding might have been aided by Pakistan or by Pakistani officials sympathetic to him, we do not know.) When he was caught, it was reportedly because interrogation of captured al Qaeda personnel and other human sources identified one of his couriers. The courier was located reportedly because in a phone conversation with an acquaintance he made remarks indirectly revealing that he might have contact with bin Laden. Once the courier was located, he was followed until he made contact with bin Laden. He was followed, it seems, by old-fashioned methods, although perhaps not exclusively.[13]

It is important to note that the pressure put on bin Laden and his organization had a greater effect than just slowing down the pace of al Qaeda's operations. Ultimately, al Qaeda is a political organization. It wants to produce changes in this world, in the way people live and conduct their affairs. If the pressure on al Qaeda was such that it had to limit its contact with people, then it was operating under an enormous constraint on its political effectiveness. Bin Laden's tapes and recorded pronouncements carried by courier to various media outlets helped overcome this political disability (compensation by information technology for a disadvantage imposed by information technology). Having people who shared bin Laden's goals involved only in more or less legitimate political activity, and thus spared the pursuit that hounded the violent, helped as well. But a merely digital political campaign, even if it uses human surrogates, does not seem to offer much hope of success. (Bin Laden's popularity had been declining for years before he was killed.)[14] If the leader of the campaign must isolate himself in order to survive and thus must restrict his communication with his followers and surrogates, he will have problems imposing a strategy on his organization, as bin Laden did.[15] Bin Laden's approach amounts to the leaderless resistance strategy advanced by white supremacist Louis Beam, which Beam at least acknowledged was for a political movement not a brilliant strategy but a last desperate effort to survive. So while the low-tech, long-term approach may allow one to live long, it may make it hard for one to prosper. We should note, however, that espionage is not political. Unlike a political movement, it does not need to be in touch with lots of people. Thus, if an espionage activity adopts the low-tech, long-term approach, it will not suffer the disadvantages that bin Ladin suffered. It will survive, and because its objective is different, it may well prosper.

Adopting the low-tech approach does create a vulnerability, however. In many places around the world, the failure to use common information technology can itself cause suspicion. Paying cash for a large hotel bill in Milan or Dubai, for example, or for an airplane ticket rather than using a credit card, might in itself be alerting. This brings us to the two operations with which we opened this chapter. Modern life now requires the use of information technology or other technologies, such as credit cards and hotel room card keys, that are subject to information technology. The Abu Omar case, the kidnapping in Milan, suggests the vulnerability of secret operations in such an age. This suggestion is misleading, however. Those involved in the operation seem to have taken almost no precautions to hide what they were doing, so it is not a good test of the claim that information technology makes secrecy impossible.

The Mabhouh case, the assassination in Dubai, is a better test. Whoever killed Mabhouh knew that someone would find the body and that Mabhouh was important enough that his death would be investigated. They may have hoped to carry out the assassination in such a way that the death would be thought natural, which was apparently the first ruling in Dubai. But given Mabhouh's history, his death in a hotel would arouse suspicion. Once it did, an investigation would ensue. It is unlikely that those who planned the assassination did not know that there were surveillance cameras all over Dubai. The extent of such surveillance may not be common knowledge, but that it takes place is. The operation was carried out by a sophisticated service, so it is likely that it had the same video analytical capabilities as the service in Dubai, or at least understood that capability and the threat it posed to clandestine operations. Altogether, then, the service that carried out the assassination was probably not surprised that details of the operation became known, although the quantity of details and the speed of their publication might have surprised it. Presumably all of this risk of exposure was part of the brief given to the political leaders who made the decision to go ahead. We may conclude, therefore, that someone judged the cost of those operational details becoming known worth the benefit of killing Mabhouh. In reaching such a decision, the critical issues would have been first, whether the operation could be clandestine long enough for it to be carried out, and, second, whether it could be covert, carried out in such a way that the author remain hidden or plausibly deny its involvement. The judgment was made evidently that both conditions could be met, and this turned out to be the case. Rather than showing the impossibility of clandestine and covert operations in the information age, the Mabhouh case shows how possible they are. An intelligence service can maintain the clandestinity of its operations while it is carrying them out and their covert character after it has done so.

These operations are possible, however, only if one is willing to pay their cost. This has always been true, of course, but the point to grasp is that information technology is raising the cost. In the Mabhouh case, the cost included exposing a number of personnel, whose faces now being well known may find it difficult to work or even travel overseas again. But that is just one of the costs raised by operating in the Panopticon. Those involved in the operation used stolen identities. These allowed those involved to carry out the operation, as we have noted. If one of those involved had been detained for some reason, however, how well would that stolen identity have held up to scrutiny? Again, this has always been an issue, but developments in information technology have made it more salient. As one student of secrecy in the information age has noted, people are rooted in a community, and that rootedness displays itself in connections to other people, social groups, commercial entities, institutions, and organizations. All of these connections leave traces that information technology can reveal. A single piece of information on someone can lead quickly to a profile that will include a name, address, birth date, gender, value of house and annual salary (at least within a range), spending patterns, net worth, credit cards owned, car ownership, unlisted telephone numbers, e-mail addresses, and social security information.[16] People can even be identified by the characteristic way they write e-mails. If an identity is stolen, then to maintain the identity, the person using it will need to remember all the details of that identity. Even real people forget details of their past, but how much more likely is someone who is not that person not to know those details? Is the discrepancy likely to be alerting to a security service? Will the security service, even a relatively poor one, not have access to lots of information rather quickly and easily from the web or information brokers? In the movie *Argo*, the cover story for the operation it portrays is established by a magazine story, a few other props, and a phone call to an office set up for that purpose. Such contrivances seem unlikely anymore to be sufficient.

Even if more elaborate cover identity support were in place, this would not end the problems posed by information technology. The use of biometric scanners at airports and other border crossings, which identify individuals by certain measurable characteristics (patterns on a fingertip or iris) or traits (walk or voice), and the connection of these scanners to databases also connected to hotel reception desks or railroad ticket counters, for example, pose serious dangers to anyone trying to operate in an assumed or stolen name or changing identity once in a country. If Dubai has biometrics on the members of the assassination team, they will not be able safely to enter the country again using different names. If Dubai has shared the information with other countries that have, as Dubai does, an interest in capturing the team members, then they will not be able to travel to those countries in a different name either. How will the intelligence agency know with whom Dubai might have shared that information? A penetration, human or cyber, of the Dubai security service would be useful, but not conclusive. Also, if the identities used in the Dubai operation had been previously used, then their discovery in that case will possibly connect the organization that carried out the Dubai operation to other operations previously well hidden.[17]

The consistency required for operating in a world of biometrics and the requirement for data to confirm or backstop identities online are two ways in which the Panopticon raises the costs of intelligence operations. These higher costs do not mean an end to clandestine or covert espionage operations, however. Consider the most extreme case. If there were a worldwide database of biometric data that was retrievable from any point on the earth, say with a handheld device or automatically when one arrived at any port of entry, checked into any hotel, or rented any car, operating under an assumed name would be quite difficult. But if such a biometric database and surveillance system existed, whether in one country, regionally (for example, in the European Union), or worldwide, it would itself become a prime target for espionage, both human and cyber. The point of penetrating its technical or human infrastructure, or the organizations that designed, built, and maintained it, would be to manipulate it to protect intelligence operations. This would be a good example of how offensive counterintelligence might need to evolve in the information age. If such a system were known to be vulnerable to penetration (how could those who ran it be certain that it was invulnerable? Its size and complexity would surely multiply the points of vulnerability), that would sow doubts about its effectiveness.

The hope for a system of ubiquitous biometric surveillance arises from the same impulse as the hope for world peace and world government that we examined in Chapter One. It is an expression of the liberal or modern desire to overcome uncertainty or insecurity. Such a system seems now as unlikely to develop as world government and, as in that case, not simply for technical reasons. A number of countries have traditionally strong attachment to civil liberties and notions of privacy that are likely to prevent such surveillance systems. As the true reach and power of information technology become apparent, a reaction against it will set in. This has already begun.[18] On the other hand, if the perceived threats that ubiquitous surveillance might reduce become severe enough (for example, nuclear weapons in the hands of small groups of fanatics), civil liberties may erode. But even if a worldwide biometric database existed, it would not put an end to espionage carried out in true name. Van Male did his espionage in England without the use of any aliases, although in correspondence he did use false names for his sources. In this sort of case, there is no cover identity to protect. Thus, even if we imagine the most imposing obstacles to espionage prevailing, it seems possible to imagine espionage continuing. But the possibilities for espionage in the future might be broader. In addition to other considerations we have mentioned (for example hostile penetration of the Panopticon), no one can predict the technical countermeasures to biometrics and scanners that intelligence services may be able to develop, or how successful they will be. Still, information technology will raise the cost of human involvement in clandestine and covert operations. As is often the case when the cost of something rises, the willingness to pay may decline. This is especially likely to happen if there is a lower-cost substitute available. Assuming that the ability to operate clandestinely and covertly remains important, the higher cost of human involvement in such operations imposed by information technology is likely to lead to the greater use of machinery and information technology in these operations, as it does in any situation in which there is a cost difference between human labor and machine power. While human intelligence operations will not cease, as a more expensive resource they may be husbanded and used more sparingly.

If this husbanding occurs, it will do so only in places where information technology is pervasive, and against opponents who use it. Some places in the world are lagging in the use of information technology. In these places, the cost of clandestine human operations will rise more slowly, and they may be more prevalent, therefore, than in other places. If al Qaeda remains low-tech or no-tech and other terrorist and insurgent groups adopt this operational regime, then human intelligence operations will remain more important against such organizations than in other cases.[19] Bin Laden was caught with the aid of human sources, and such sources have played a role in other counterterrorism cases. Taken together, regional variations in the use of information technology and nonstate actor avoidance of it may mean that in the future human intelligence will be most important in Africa, for example, and in countering terrorism and other kinds of irregular warfare. (We turn to this latter case in Chapter Five.)

As information technology improves defensive counterintelligence capabilities, and thus raises the cost and perhaps limits the scope of espionage, it will likely make offensive counterintelligence, at least with regard to its most comprehensive objective, less effective. Offensive counterintelligence, to repeat, is an attack on the operations of another intelligence service, with the ultimate objective of influencing or degrading the decision-making that the intelligence service supports. Insofar as offensive counterintelligence is a branch of espionage (running human agents), it will fare as well or ill as other aspects of espionage in the information age. Although it uses all the techniques of espionage, offensive counterintelligence differs from other kinds of espionage in that its ultimate aim is deception:[20] to create a false version of reality that, when accepted by the target, benefits the deceiver. The offensive purpose of running intelligence agents inside another intelligence service is to deceive or blind the service and remove it as a threat. Another purpose is to get deceptive information to the decision-makers informed by that service, so that they make decisions advantageous to the deceivers. Among counterintelligence professionals, deception of decision-makers is claimed to be the most important and most neglected use of counterintelligence, which they often call "strategic counterintelligence."[21]

It is strategic counterintelligence that is likely to be less effective in the information age, at least for the United States. To see this, consider perhaps the most famous example of strategic counterintelligence, the "double cross" system run by the British during World War II. Controlling not all German sources of information on Great Britain but all German agents in Britain, the British were able to defeat German espionage and, ultimately, help deceive the Germans about British and Allied plans, particularly the Normandy invasion. This deception was possible for specific reasons, including skilled operations, luck, and wartime conditions. The latter included the fact that access to Britain during the war was controlled and only permitted from Portugal or Sweden. By limiting the ports of entry, the British could more easily identify enemy agents. Wartime conditions and controls also limited the information on British activities available to the Germans, other than what the compromised agents were reporting. As for luck, the British faced a weak opponent. The Abwehr, the German intelligence service, was corrupt, filled with self-serving individuals who failed to pay attention to counterintelligence issues (signs their agents were under British control) when doing so conflicted with their self-interest. Skill entered into the success of the British deception in several ways. Of decisive importance was the "powerful centralized control" of their strategic deception activities that the British put in place.[22] This allowed the British to coordinate and control activities across their different military services and departments of government. First, they had to get agreement on what information their double agents could pass to the Germans to establish their credibility in German eyes. If the information was not important enough, the Germans might suspect the agents were being controlled. If it was too important, then turning it over to the Germans would do more harm to the British than to the Germans. Second, the British needed to be sure that they used the carefully established and costly credibility of their agents only for worthwhile or truly strategic objectives.

This brief review of the British success at strategic counterintelligence suggests that in the information age such success will be less likely. Publicly available information on a country, including that derived from aerial or satellite reconnaissance, is more plentiful now than when the British carried out their deception, and it is available in real time. A government can limit or control at least some of this information, but the more it does so, the more costly it is. Economies are so dependent now on information technology that limiting its operation is likely to be unsustainably damaging to the overall war effort. The availability of information is likely to make strategic deception harder, if not impossible. The more sources of information a government has, the harder it is to control that government's perception of reality. The more sources of information, therefore, the harder it is to deceive. For the United States, a more pressing problem in conducting strategic intelligence, perhaps, is the notorious inability of the federal government to centrally control and coordinate its activities. Because of this inability, it seems unlikely that the United States could succeed at strategic deception, although this might change in wartime.[23] Information technology is not the cause of this lack of coordination, but, since its causes are not principally technical, it is unlikely to be its cure either. The judgment that strategic counterintelligence is likely to become more difficult must be tentative, however, in large part because so many variables of perception and motivation affect deception. It may in fact take very little deceptive information to make a big deception succeed, depending on the disposition of the deception target.

In closing this discussion of counterintelligence, it may be worthwhile to consider how the ongoing development of information technology will affect what we might call the intelligence or information balance of power between states and their opponents. Information technology is unlikely to affect this balance of power between states, since all states over time will have more or less the same access to information technology. (Because it lowers the cost barriers to entry into the information gathering and analysis business, information technology will allow some states to have an intelligence capability that they could not previously afford.)[24] It will affect the balance of information power between states and nonstate actors, however, as the development and diffusion of information and destructive technologies increase the power of nonstate groups. The case of al Qaeda suggests that in the struggle between states and nonstate actors, the Panopticon will give more power and, hence, a net advantage to states. Al Qaeda, both its central organization and its far-flung affiliates, has found it difficult to realize its ambitions for weapons of mass destruction, while it found itself vulnerable to the intelligence operations of the United States and its allies. So far, it has been easier for states to use information technology to gather information on covert state-actors than it has been for those state actors to acquire and use destructive technologies.[25] Not only is a combination of human and technical intelligence likely to continue to locate nonstate actors (we return to this issue in Chapter Five), but any such actors who have political ambitions will find that increasing their operational security by isolating themselves or avoiding information technology will make it harder, if not impossible, for them to satisfy those ambitions. Hacktivist groups like Anonymous and Wikileaks may continue to strike at states but are unlikely to do more than annoy them, and in the latter case, as in the case of the more damaging revelations about NSA activities by a former contract employee, the damage to the state results not from nonstate actors but from state employees. It is true that information technology increases the power of these individuals to annoy or harm, but it also increases the power of the state even more. (The revelation of thousands of classified U.S. government documents by Wikileaks resulted from a policy decision rather than the power of the nonstate activists. Following 9/11, in an attempt to prevent another such attack by making sure that no one was prevented from "connecting the dots," the U.S. government moved from allowing access to information only to those with a need to know it to sharing it more widely. This created the opportunity for someone with new access to give the documents to Wikileaks.) An advantage to the defense and a net disadvantage to nonstate actors is the opposite of what some predicted would be the effect of modern information technology.[26] That outcome is in keeping, however, with the information dominance established by states throughout their history.

Covert Action

Covert action is any activity undertaken by a government in which it hides its responsibility for the action. When the Department of State issues statements and provides information to journalists, that is public diplomacy. When an agent working for the U.S. government publishes information in the newspaper he writes for or on the blog he runs without attributing it to the U.S. government, that is covert action. When the U.S. military blockades a country, that is a military operation and may be taken to be a casus belli, or act of war.

When agents working for the U.S. government plant mines in a harbor, without allowing that action to be attributed to the United States, that is a covert action and with no one to blame, not a cause of war. In language once classified but now public, covert action is

> all activities (except as noted herein) which are conducted or sponsored by [the U.S.] Government against hostile foreign states or groups or in support of friendly foreign states or groups but which are so planned and executed that any US Government responsibility for them is not evident to unauthorized persons and that if uncovered the US Government can plausibly disclaim any responsibility for them. . . . Such operations shall not include armed conflict by recognized military forces, espionage, counter-espionage, and cover and deception for military operations.[27]

Covert action is action undertaken by a government that it can plausibly deny it had anything to do with.

While covert action has acquired a bad reputation over the years and elicits supposedly high-minded calls for restraint and reform,[28] it serves a good purpose. It is in effect another example of the honor that vice pays to virtue or necessity pays to morality. In the world of warring states, governments will and should do what they must to defend themselves and their people. Doing so covertly helps lower the political costs of all such necessary action. It clearly lowers the costs to the nation carrying out the covert action because in hiding its authorship or allowing it to plausibly deny its authorship, it avoids the consequences of its action. But the benefits of covert action actually extend to the targeted nation and others. By hiding its authorship of covert deeds, a government reduces the challenge it poses to the targeted nation. If the perpetrator avows what it has done, it explicitly challenges the state it has attacked, compelling a response. Such overt actions challenge conventions of international life that help maintain the peace. Overtly harmful action announces with regard to the nation attacked, and implicitly every other nation, that the attacking nation will do what it will without regard to law. Doing what it will whenever possible is of course an implicit principle of every nation, but making it explicit makes it a challenge to which all nations must respond as they can. A nation that makes its challenge to law and convention explicit announces that it believes that its power makes it exempt from the rules that others obey. It announces itself a bully, if not a tyrant. It thus encourages every other nation to break the law and makes the world a more dangerous place. Covert action strengthens the rule of law and custom in international affairs, or at least minimizes erosion of support for the rule of law and thus benefits all. This is why it has long been part of international life. Spanish ambassadors conducted it in the sixteenth century.[29] Even in the information age, and age of openness, concealment has its uses.

Whatever one may think of this justification of covert action, the secrecy covert action requires differs from the secrecy required by the clandestine intelligence collection we call espionage. Covert action is less secret than espionage. We can see this difference and its consequence by considering the case of Mahmoud al-Mabhouh outlined above. Those who killed him had to know his travel plans, at least that he was going to Dubai and roughly when. Al-Mabhouh spoke on a cell phone about his travel to relatives.[30] Perhaps those targeting him were intercepting his calls. Perhaps they also had a human source who was privy to al-Mabhouh's plans. If those targeting the Hamas official had these sources of information, then they could have used them to collect information on Hamas's military plans and arms purchases. As long as these sources and their activities were unknown, as long as they remained clandestine, this collection could continue. Once al-Mabhouh was found dead, Hamas must have realized, if it had not before, that its enemies had sources inside its arms buying activity. Whereas stealing information from Hamas on its activities might have gone on undetected, the covert action that resulted in Mabhouh's death was sure to be noted. Covert action informs an enemy in a way that espionage tries not to and is therefore less secret.

Less secret than espionage, covert action is therefore more risky and more costly. Alerted by al-Mabhouh's assassination that their operations had been penetrated, Hamas would try to fix its security problems. The covert action, then, might well lead to the end of the clandestine collection that made it possible. This was a loss for the sponsor. Balancing the loss is the benefit, noted above, that as long as the author of the covert action was not known, organizing a concerted response would be more difficult. Countries objected to having their passports misused and complained to Israeli ambassadors, some expelled Israeli diplomats or enacted diplomatic sanctions of various sorts, but the lack of definitive proof of Israeli sponsorship prevented, or offered an excuse for not taking, further action. The different risks and costs and benefits of espionage and covert action explain the historical bureaucratic antagonism between those responsible for these two different kinds of intelligence activity.[31]

Although espionage and covert action differ in their secrecy requirements, they are alike in their reliance (until recently) on human agents. Espionage relies on human agents because it is the agent who has access to the desired secret information. Covert action relied on human agents because hiding the author of the action meant that no one connected to the author could be involved. If the U.S. government is trying to hide its hand, then one of its citizens should not be involved. For example, if the covert action is political and the political effect depends on its appearing to be the case that opposition to a government is entirely indigenous, the effect will be entirely spoiled if it is evident that the U.S. government is behind what is going on.[32] We may see the operation in Milan as an example of how having Americans involved erodes deniability, but this operation was apparently not conceived as a covert action. A better example comes from the U.S. government's efforts against the government of Nicaragua in the 1980s. When two Americans were killed and a third, Eugene Hasenfus, was captured as the result of the Nicaraguans shooting down a cargo plane carrying supplies to their opponents, the Contras, it was difficult for the U.S. government to deny plausibly a connection to the flight, especially when the plane's true identification number and its connection to the U.S. Air Force became known.[33]

Even though having your own nationals involved makes deniability implausible or less plausible, some operations meant to be covert still take this risk. They do so for two reasons. First, the operations are inexpertly run or inadequately financed and must fall back on inexpert or expedient methods. This appears at least part of the reason behind the poor tradecraft in the extralegal effort to support the Contras.[34] Second, and more important, actions apparently meant to be covert are done by the personnel of the country carrying them out because while operating through agents increases deniability, it decreases control and reliability. In response to the Clinton administration's decision to go after Osama bin Laden, the CIA recruited some Afghans and turned them into a team whose purpose was to kill or capture bin Laden. On at least one occasion, the case officers handling the team developed a plan to capture bin Laden when intelligence sources had located him. Ultimately, the director of the CIA and other senior leaders in the agency and the Clinton administration declined to approve the operation. A principal reason was that they simply did not trust the team of non-U.S. personnel to carry out the operation successfully. Women and children would be present, and there were fears that the team would not have enough fire discipline to spare them. The operation presented other tactical problems, and no one beyond those agency personnel directly in contact with the team was confident they could solve the problems as the operation unfolded.[35] While one may fault the decision-makers for their timidity, the story makes clear the problems of control and confidence that arise when using agents in covert operations. They are inherently less controllable and reliable than U.S. personnel. Although not a covert operation, another example of the difficulties of controlling and relying on non-U.S. personnel was Operation Anaconda in Afghanistan in 2002. After the operation, Afghan forces were criticized for allowing the escape into Pakistan of a significant number of Taliban and al Qaeda forces, including possibly Osama bin Laden. In addition to judging the potential tradeoff between the value of information and the effects of the covert operation, those deciding whether to engage in a covert action must also weigh the value of deniability against the benefit of greater control and reliability that comes from using their own personnel. To repeat, if they use their own personnel, the operation is not truly covert.

One reason control and reliability may be more difficult in covert operations as opposed to espionage is that in the latter case the politics of the agent may be less important.[36] In clandestine collection, one might use as an agent a committed Marxist, Islamist, or monarchist. The agent's political objectives are irrelevant, as long as he or she collects the necessary information. On the contrary, in Afghanistan, political objectives mattered. The objective of the Afghan forces the United States worked with was to control Afghanistan or share in its control, not to kill or capture bin Laden, which was the U.S. objective. Getting rid of the Taliban was necessary both for the Afghans to get control of Afghanistan and for us to get bin Laden, so directing the Afghans to that objective was not difficult. Once the Taliban was gone, the overall political objectives of the Afghans and the United States diverged. The Afghans wanted to focus on controlling Afghanistan, the United States wanted bin Laden. The ineffectiveness of the Afghans in Operation Anaconda was in part the result of this difference of objectives.

Covert action, then, often presents more serious issues of agent control than does espionage. All the more reason to have the most expert agent handlers in control. This is one reason why the National Security Council gave the CIA responsibility for covert action when the agency was established. Covert action required skilled use of human agents, and the CIA's clandestine service was supposed to have expertise in dealing with agents. Another reason the agency became the default covert action arm of the U.S. government was that carrying out covert action required the kind of clandestine operational expertise presumably resident in the agency. This is not just a question of operational expertise, however. Clandestine activity requires spending government money on activities and in circumstances not typical for government bureaucracies. For this reason, a law in 1949 made the CIA exempt from the reporting and accountability requirements under which other government agencies operate. While clandestine activity requires such exemptions, they should be kept to a minimum. Democratic control of government functions is a compelling reason not to give this exemption to two agencies, if one is sufficient. To these reasons for making the CIA the government's covert action organization, a retired formerly high ranking CIA officer, Henry Crumpton, has added two others. The agency collects intelligence that is necessary to run covert operations; and the agency does not have policy preferences and so can conduct covert action that serves the policy of the U.S. government.[37]

These additional reasons are not sound, especially the first. The agency's clandestine service collects intelligence necessary for all the policies and activities of the U.S. government but does not run them all. Interestingly, Crumpton seems to suggest at some points that it should. The agency achieved victory in Afghanistan (he is silent about the contribution of the U.S. military, especially U.S. Special Forces) because it devised the strategy, collected intelligence, analyzed it, and conducted operations "as the pointy end of statecraft and war." Who needs the Defense or State departments, Crumpton suggests, those unresponsive, dysfunctional organizations? But the problem in this argument is more than its origin in the preferences of a myopic intelligence officer. Collecting intelligence connected to covert actions that the agency itself is running risks injecting a bias into the intelligence gathering to justify the covert action either prospectively or retrospectively. A high-ranking DoD official reportedly made this argument.[38] Separating intelligence operations and analysis, as the agency historically did, mitigates this risk. Combining them in counterterrorism centers, as is now commonly done, increases it.[39] As for the agency's policy neutrality, Crumpton's other reason why the agency should be responsible for covert action, some may doubt that it exists; but assuming it does, the agency is not the only organization in the U.S. government that can claim such neutrality. Any operational organization, whether the military, the U.S. Marshall Service, or the agency, should subordinate itself to government policy. There is no evidence that the agency does this better than other operational organizations; in fact, one can cite evidence of the agency's policy preferences that at least in one case differed from those of the president and affected its operations.[40] In addition, Crumpton himself undercuts the importance of policy neutrality on the part of operational organizations by later claiming that there is no clear line between policy and operations, only "a broad common ground where ops and policy overlap and where the fuzzy boundary lines can shift [and sometimes] . . . evaporate."[41] If there is no clear line between policy and operations, then neutrality with regard to policy is not necessarily a virtue in operators.

Finding Crumpton's arguments unpersuasive, we are left with the argument that the agency's primacy in conducting covert action rests on its skill at dealing with agents and operating clandestinely. Developments in information and military technology undercut this claim to primacy. In general, information technology does not carry with it the same kind of identifying information that a human being does. We may believe that personnel with the skills and knowledge to write needed computer code only reside in certain nations, but that code in itself does not carry cultural or personal identifiers tying it to a particular nation. Information technology is inherently more covert than a human being, therefore. In addition, lethal or destructive technology is developing in such a way that it can be directed remotely, without putting humans at risk of being caught. These developments together can reduce the importance of using agents to carry out operations covertly. If so, then the National Security Agency or the military, both adept at the use of technology, could in some cases have a better claim to conduct covert operations than the agency. This argument also extends to covert political action conducted with social media. These media have been useful in organizing and directing political movements around the world. Such media and other forms of communication could be spoofed or manipulated covertly to support or undermine future political movements without the use of human agents. Again, if no agents or other covert mechanisms are involved, there is no reason why the CIA would have to be in charge.

It is true that any of these technological covert actions could be discovered or leaked. Indeed, as we have noted, the assumption should be that they will be discovered, since something noticeable is going to happen as a consequence of them. But the key thing for a covert action is not that it be undiscovered but that it be plausibly deniable. Technological operations will be deniable, even if they are discovered. Leaks pose a somewhat different problem, in that someone in the government carrying out the covert action, perhaps because they disapprove of it, reveals it to the press. This makes the action more difficult to deny, since someone in the government is claiming it. It may still be officially denied, and if there is nothing in the operation itself to tie it to the sponsor, this may maintain plausible deniability. Claims about covert action do get the attention of the media, but if, in the case of the United States, the proper procedures have been followed to initiate it, there may be no controversy between the administration and Congress and thus the story is less likely to remain news. In 2005, for example, news reports based on leaks raised questions about the role of the Defense Department in intelligence operations. An initial flurry of reports died away as it became clear that both Democrats and Republicans supported the military's new role and had in fact voted to authorize it.[42] This differs from what happened with the Contras during the Reagan administration. In that case, the action was hardly deniable (for example, a U.S. citizen flying a former U.S. Air Force plane), was undertaken without congressional authorization, and hence was a source of great controversy and thus news. In the U.S. context, plausible deniability now requires proper authorization, as well as competent conduct of the operation. But these requirements can be met when agencies other than the CIA carry out the operation, as well as when the agency does.

In the discussion to this point, we have focused on technical and operational issues, arguing that information technology is inherently covert and removes the presumption that the CIA alone is best suited to carry out covert action. But covert action involves important political considerations. By avoiding public insult, we have argued, covert action minimizes the need of the targeted government to respond. Would this be the case if military forces carried out the covert action? Of course, because the action is covert, this question should not arise. But the risk/benefit analysis before undertaking a covert action should consider the possibility of exposure and thus should consider whether, if the action became public, military involvement would raise the political risks. Is it less acceptable to a targeted government, does it increase its need to respond, if it is harmed by a military rather than a civilian action? Would Pakistan have felt better if the raid that killed Osama bin Laden had been carried out by non-U.S. citizen agents under the control of the CIA? In some cases it might lower the political costs of a covert action if the CIA rather than the military carried it out, but it does not seem to be the case that this is true universally, especially if the operators involved are Americans. Perceptions of legality may affect the perception of costs by both the sponsor and the target, but the legalities do not suggest that it matters which agency carries out the covert action.[43] In many cases, perhaps most, the political value of covert action will be preserved no matter which agency of the U.S. government carries it out, as long as the operation is truly covert. And again, if the operation is technological, deniability is enhanced no matter which agency is involved.[44]

A final reason that some might give for keeping the CIA the default covert action arm of the U.S. government is the greater operational flexibility of the agency compared with the military or other U.S. government organizations. Historically this difference may have existed, but since 9/11, under the relentless pressure of operations in Iraq and Afghanistan, certain elements of the military have increased their flexibility significantly. But in any case, flexibility must be weighed against military expertise. If the covert action is a military action, its success is likely to depend more on the military skill than the flexibility with which it is carried out. If military skill is important, this suggests that the organization with the most military skill should be in charge. That consideration would tip the decision in favor of the military as the covert action agent. Similarly, if the operation requires agent handling and the covert support of agents, then that consideration would tip the decision in favor of the CIA. This argument ignores the traditional military dislike of acting covertly as conduct incompatible with the ethos of an officer and a gentleman. This is an important issue and should be weighed in any consideration of whether to increase the role of the military in such activity.

It is hard to escape the conclusion that the CIA claims primacy in covert action now as a matter of habit and bureaucratic reflex. When we examine the reasons why the agency was given that primacy and then consider the possibilities created by information technology, we see that there is no reason why the agency should have primacy in all covert action. Its primacy should be restricted to those cases where it rests on its distinguishing expertise, the use of human agents. (If the cooperation of another foreign intelligence agency is necessary for the covert operation, then this might be another reason for the CIA to be in charge.) True expertise in handling human agents is so difficult to gain and maintain, we might argue, that no organization with that responsibility should be burdened with others. The law is no barrier to giving other organizations the responsibility for a covert action, since the law currently gives the president the authority to assign a covert action to the agency he deems best suited to carry it out. And, in any case, of course, laws may be changed.

In discussing who might carry out covert action, we have begged the question of whether it needs to be done at all. The argument we have made that covert action is a good thing because it helps preserve some respect for the rule of international law and for sovereignty (noninterference in the affairs of other nations) depends on this respect remaining a guiding principle of international life. To the extent this is no longer true, it becomes less necessary for nations to hide their interference in each other's affairs. Some have argued that such a change has occurred, that globalization has decreased unnecessary concern for sovereignty, allowing moral concerns and respect for human rights greater scope to guide the policies and actions of governments. Whereas we had to covertly support democracy right after World War II, we now openly support it with the National Endowment for Democracy.[45] Or, following through on the late liberal aspiration for world government, we appeal to the United Nations to approve our open interference. Political covert action, therefore, has become passe and unnecessary.

While there might be something to such arguments, they seem overblown and misleading. As a matter of fact, the "new openness" appears to justify open action only against the weak. Powerful nations such as Russia and China do not tolerate interference, and the United States pointedly refrains from it in dealing with them, except to express its concern over some of their practices.[46] With regard to the powerful, therefore, the situation does not appear to be fundamentally different now from what it was during the Cold War. The only difference is that for the time being the United States lacks a global peer competitor of the sort it had in the Soviet Union. Thus the "new openness" of the United States with regard to "covert" action is not so much the product of the information age or globalization as it is the consequence of the United States not having a serious competitor to constrain its power. The United States and those who act in alliance with it are now open and bullying when they were previously covert and accommodating, but only with regard to weaker, isolated nations. As power among nations equalizes in the future or as a peer competitor reappears, covert action may well again appear to be necessary for the United States as it pursues its interests in or near those competitors. Certainly the likelihood or fear of war with such a competitor would increase the rationale for covert action. What need not return is the primacy of the CIA in such operations.

Military covert action is likely to have a future as well, whether conducted by the military or an intelligence agency. First, man-hunting has become an important part of countering terrorism. Once terrorists are indicted, they can become the object of overt or clandestine manhunts. Not all terrorists can be indicted; not all those indicted, captured. Some may, therefore, be the object of covert action. The imperative for clandestine and covert action is also likely to increase as technology continues to put greater power in the hands of small groups and individuals. This will make covert action against labs, logistics and other infrastructure, as well as individuals appealing. Second, if the conditions return that make political covert action as attractive as it once was, they will also make military covert action as a coercive measure more appealing as well. Historically, this has been the most common use of military covert action. On numerous occasions during the Cold War, the United States undertook covert military action—insurgency, sabotage, subversion—against states whose policies it did not like but could not effectively oppose overtly. North Vietnam, the Sandinista government in Nicaragua, and the Soviet-supported regime in Afghanistan are prominent examples. The latter two, of course, became overt or known while they were occurring, and the last was perhaps the first so-called overt covert operation, since it had the support of the American people but was done covertly largely to satisfy the Pakistanis, through whose country weapons went to those fighting the Soviets in Afghanistan.

While military covert action may return, it is not clear that it should, in either of its forms. Questions have been raised about the long-term or strategic efficacy of man-hunting, whether overt, clandestine, or covert, although it can produce shorter-term benefits. (We discuss this issue in Chapter Five.) It is much less clear that covert coercive action can produce any benefit. Coercion is difficult, no matter how it is done. To coerce means to get the target to reverse itself. In reversing itself, the target declares its weakness and opens itself to further coercive pressures from the state that targeted it and from others that now see it as vulnerable. Coercion is more difficult when it is done covertly. To coerce successfully, the coercing state must demonstrate that it has the credibility to coerce and the capability to do so. Covert action undermines credibility and capability. If a state acts covertly, it signals that it sees political difficulties in carrying out its coercive measures, either with its own or international populations. Political difficulties suggest that over time the will to coerce, the credibility of the coercive threat, and, thus, eventually coercion itself will fail. The covert aspect of covert coercion undermines, therefore, the coercive aspect. Covert action also limits capability because in carrying out the action deniably, the coercing state does it with agents and thus presumably with those less capable than its own presumably better trained and equipped personnel. Information technology, by permitting a coercing state to act covertly but directly and not through agents, would not decrease the capability of covert coercion, but it will not enhance its credibility. In the case of technological covert coercion, preserved coercive capability will be offset by reduced credibility. While future circumstances suggest the continued relevance of military covert action, they do not suggest that covert coercive action will be any more likely to succeed than in the past.

Conclusion

The claim that transparency has finally overcome secrecy seems, at least at this point in our current information revolution, exaggerated. Through its effects on counterintelligence and covert action, information technology changes the cost/benefit analysis of clandestine and covert action and may make some traditional espionage activities obsolete or more difficult, but it does not put an end to espionage or covert action and leaves the core of espionage, the officer-agent relationship, untouched. Information technology actually appears to open up new covert action possibilities both with regard to what is done and which agencies of government do it. These possibilities are appearing as the need for espionage and covert action to counter newly empowered nonstate actors increases. Technology benefits these actors, of course; increased deniability is useful to them, as well as to governments. On balance, however, the greater resources of states will increase the benefit of technology more to them than to nonstate actors. The principal effect of information technology will be to reallocate increasing power among state agencies, rather than to shift it from them to nonstate actors.

The information revolution has effects on instruments of state power in addition to espionage and covert action. In the next two chapters we discuss intelligence and the military instrument, in the second returning to the issues raised by the struggle between state and nonstate actors.

4   Intelligence and Warfare

If information is essential to state power, and war is the ultimate decider of affairs between states, then one might think that information or intelligence would be decisive in war. No one, at least until very recently, ever entertained such a thought. Similarly, until recently, no one thought that information technology, upon which states have built power for centuries, could undermine that power, for example, by making secrecy impossible. Oddly, given the historical connections between information, military power, and the state, over the past several decades, analysts have come to see information as a revolutionary power in warfare, at the same time that they have come to see information as a threat to the power of the state. If the power of the state is in decline and information technology part of the cause, as it is a cause of the supposed revolution in warfare, then we are witnessing an important historical reversal. In the past, information was decisive for state power but not in warfare, although war was decisive for state power. Now, information technology undermines the state but is claimed to be decisive for war, as war itself for a variety of reasons is thought to be less important for state power.[1]

Is information weakening the state and revolutionizing warfare? In the previous chapter, using counterintelligence and covert action as tests, we argued that information technology did not undermine state power as is often supposed. In this chapter, we will examine information technology or intelligence in warfare. We will consider intelligence during battle, before war, and behind the lines or beyond the strict limits of the battlefield. In turning to warfare we leave the realm of secrecy and privacy, in the sense that we are no longer considering only the intentional withholding of information, whether compulsory or voluntary, but an inherent withholding of information. Theorists of war have seen war as a domain in a sense constituted by its resistance to illumination by information. War is thus a good test case in any discussion of the role of information as a transformative power, especially because war has been at the heart of state power. Beyond issues of the state, the role of intelligence in warfare may tell us something about the human condition itself. Whatever its regularities, war is thought to be dominated by chance. As we argued in Chapter One, the modern state and modern intelligence, the liberal tradition, were the offspring of the urge of humans to conquer fortune, the uncertain, the unpredictable, what appeared to be merely chance or God's will. By claiming to have lifted the fog of war, proponents of the information revolution in warfare are carrying on the work of Francis Bacon and the revolution in human affairs that he helped pioneer.

During Battle

Until recently, no one thought intelligence or information was decisive in war, even if one defined intelligence broadly as "every sort of information about the enemy and his country."[2] Chance and uncertainty, not reason and planning, dominate battle. Intelligence, human knowledge in general, is limited by the impenetrable fog of war. The classic expression of this view was given by Carl Von Clausewitz, whose long book on war makes short shrift of intelligence. According to Clausewitz, the intelligence reports that emerge from the fog "are contradictory; even more are false; and most are uncertain." This uncertainty is not the result only of human limitations. When we grasp fully the nature of war, we realize that there is something unpredictable and in that sense unknowable about it. Small things, such as a rain storm, a broken wheel, a wrong turn—what Clausewitz called the friction of war—themselves chance events, can have outsized effects, depending on a host of other chance circumstances, and there are almost innumerable small things at play in war. Most fundamentally, perhaps, all events in war, small or large, occur within the action and reaction of independent forces, which makes it inherently unpredictable and uncertain. For example, on each side, the contending army and its commanders continually interact with the passions of the people and the rational calculations of policy. The consequence is that "war is the realm of uncertainty; three quarters of the factors on which action in war is based are wrapped in a fog of greater or lesser uncertainty."[3] Numerical and material superiority is important in dealing successfully with this uncertainty. Taking the initiative is as well, because it decreases the attacker's uncertainty (he knows for example when and where he will attack) and increases the defender's. Overwhelming force or decisive action reduces uncertainty by shortening battle, thereby decreasing the opportunities for friction and chance to operate. Above all, however, what is essential in the face of uncertainty is not information or intelligence but the genius, the intuitive judgment, of the military commander, his ability to see some truth through the fog of war and his courage to act on his insight.[4] The genius of the commander serves the role in battle that prudence, as we noted in Chapter One, serves in politics more generally.

Of course, in Clausewitz's day even if intelligence—any sort of information about the enemy—was available, it would have been difficult to communicate it. Regardless of the nature of war, the limited ability to communicate during it restricted the utility of information or intelligence, especially espionage. (This is one reason why in what follows the focus is broader than just traditional espionage.) If one followed Sun Tzu's advice and had an agent in the enemy camp or capital who got access to the enemy's plans, how would the agent communicate them in a timely fashion? For those who today take their bearings from Clausewitz (we may call them neo-Clausewitzians), the development of modern communications, which allows for the timely exchange of information, has not increased the utility of intelligence in war. As technology improved the ability to communicate, it also allowed the power, size, and complexity of military forces to increase. However much industrial technology allowed for improved command and control and thus in theory increased the utility of intelligence, it simultaneously introduced even more uncertainty into warfare, according to the neo-Clausewitzians, leaving unchanged the dominance of uncertainty over information.[5] Ultimately, however, in the neo-Clausewitzian or traditional view, intelligence and command and control are not technological issues and are not in a race to overcome uncertainty. The nature of war itself creates uncertainty or is uncertainty. War is a clash of wills, which is to say that war, despite its mechanization and its brutal technological slaughter, is a world where human freedom predominates, bringing forth the unexpected and previously unknown to a degree that dwarfs human capacities, no matter how enhanced by technology. If we understand war this way, we can see why it is such a problem for the liberal tradition with which Kent identified himself. That tradition seeks to conquer uncertainty in human life; it must then put an end to war, which is uncertainty. Whatever may be the prospects for vanquishing uncertainty in other realms of human endeavor, the neo-Clausewitzians doubt it is possible in war, since they agree with the financial management expert cited in Chapter One: "[T]he true source of uncertainty lies in the intentions of others."[6]

While neo-Clausewitzians see war and thus to some extent human life as dominated by uncertainty, they accord some importance to information or intelligence. For example, they agree with the intelligence officer Henry Crumpton that self-knowledge is critically important. A natural inclination to overestimate one's strengths can lead to disaster. (The traditionalists are quick to point out that self-knowledge may be even more difficult to come by than knowledge of the enemy, a point we examine in detail in Chapter Six.)[7] Also, a commander does need to know where the enemy is and, to increase the chance that his attack will succeed, where the enemy's weak points are. In certain kinds of battle, for example submarines versus surface shipping in World War II, intelligence (in this case interception and decryption of radio messages) was especially important, at least according to one neo-Clausewitzian. Yet the traditional view is that at most intelligence is of secondary importance in war, at best a force multiplier, never sufficient for victory, often not even necessary.[8] No matter how good one's intelligence is, the battle must still be fought. It will be fought with weapons and skill and numbers employed by good or bad commanders. Intelligence can help achieve victory, but it can only help—and may not always do that. The irremediable dominance of uncertainty in battle explains, perhaps, why soldiers are reputed to rely more than others on prayer, one of the traditional means of dealing with uncertainty.

For the traditionalists, war remains a realm of chance and uncertainty in which material factors and the genius of the commander remain the most likely routes to victory. Even stealing the enemy's plans might not help, because the fog of war guarantees, as the old saying has it, that plans will not survive first contact with the enemy. Once the fighting starts the contest of wills takes over, and one has entered the realm where, because of uncertainty, not plans but the genius of the commander dominates. If plans do not survive contact with the enemy, then the corollary for intelligence must be that there is little reason to steal them. But certainly there must be at least some advantage in knowing when and where an enemy will strike? There is, but it is not necessarily a decisive advantage, according to the neo-Clausewitzians. The British knew the timing of the German attack on Crete as well as the plan of attack but still lost. It is true that if one has poor intelligence, one is more likely to be surprised. Yet those who carry out surprise attacks seldom win, at least in the long run, which indicates that a lack of intelligence (by those who are surprised) does not necessarily lead to defeat, nor does an information advantage (for those who surprise) necessarily lead to victory. The reason those who achieve surprise do not necessarily win is that they are often the weaker side in the conflict. That is why they resort to surprise attack. This is true of terrorists, who have almost nothing going for them except their ability to surprise. Despite this information advantage, which we will examine in more detail in the next chapter, terrorists seldom achieve their political objectives.[9]

What we have dubbed the traditional view of the relationship between intelligence and war may be called traditional because it purports to describe the historical, if not eternal, relationship between intelligence and war and because it is the view that dominated discussion of the topic until recently. It is not the only view, however. An older view and a newer one contest the traditional understanding of information in warfare. As noted in Chapter One, Sun Tzu claimed that intelligence was a significant determinant of military outcomes. "Know the enemy and know yourself; in a thousand battles you will never be in peril." Sun Tzu asserted that one must know the condition in neighboring states and the terrain on which one will fight. He emphasized the use of secret agents. Since one can only learn the enemy's plans by penetrating his camp with human agents, Sun Tsu devoted a chapter to the description and management of these agents, calling their secret operations "essential in war."[10]

If Sun Tzu thus seems to suggest that the fog of war is penetrable, this may be so only because of the fog or mist that envelopes his own oracular utterances. Undoubtedly there are compelling *apercus* in the work attributed to Sun Tzu that readers have felt revealed the nature of war. Presumably his pronouncement that "operations of war require one thousand fast four-horse chariots, one thousand four-horse wagons covered in leather, and one hundred thousand mailed troops" is not one of them.[11] Those utterances we find still insightful are confirmed by the experience of war we have gained independently of Sun Tzu. His writing thus neither explains nor justifies a view alternative to the traditional understanding of war and intelligence, but merely inspires those dissatisfied with the traditional understanding. Sun Tzu's aphorisms have become a sort of herborium from which one may pluck ingredients for a potion to ward off the dangers of mass and attrition warfare.

Nevertheless, it is not clear that Sun Tzu disagrees with the traditional view. Plucking from the herborium for our own purposes, we note that one of his aphorisms states that "in battle there are only the normal and the extraordinary forces, but their combinations are limitless; none can comprehend them all."

This seems very similar to the view of Clausewitz. Furthermore, Sun Tzu is famous for his emphasis on deception.[12] But if deception is effective in war, it must mean that intelligence is not able to uncover it. This again suggests that intelligence is limited in warfare. In this view, Sun Tzu would not so much disagree with the traditional view of warfare as suggest different ways to deal with it. Instead of struggling to overcome it with firepower, numbers, and decisive action, he appears to counsel working with it through deception and guile.

Apart from such considerations, we should also note that in emphasizing the importance of intelligence, Sun Tzu may have a broader perspective than Clausewitz. Sun Tzu argues that subduing "the enemy without fighting is the acme of skill," that "those skilled in war subdue the enemy's army without battle," and "thus what is of supreme importance in war is to attack the enemy's strategy."[13] Writing in the warring states period, Sun Tzu was concerned not only with battle or with war as consisting of a string of battles, but also with conflict as a persistent underlying condition. He was concerned, therefore, with what we might call grand strategy as well as with war. Intelligence may be more important or more useful for grand strategy than for battle or campaigns, a point to which we will return. This may explain why Sun Tzu did not dwell on the difficulty of timely communication with one's agents in the enemy camp, as Clausewitz did. In the long-term perspective of grand strategy, "timeliness" has a different meaning than it does in the heat of battle. This would also explain why Sun Tzu did not worry about stolen plans becoming irrelevant once the battle began. His purpose was to win without the battle. Knowing the enemy's plans would allow for a disposition of forces or the creation of an alliance that would show the enemy that battle was futile.

The newer objection to the traditional view that information is of limited utility in warfare is associated with the recent improvements in communication and information technology. As early as 1975, officials associated with the development of defense technology were speaking of a transformation in the technology of conventional warfare brought about by the conjunction of precision strike weapons, increasingly powerful surveillance and reconnaissance capabilities, and improved command and control. These developments were creating revolutionary effects and bringing the world to "the threshold of a new era."[14] Fifteen years later, the American military seemed to have stepped across that threshold in the first Gulf War. With its new technology, it had an unprecedented vision of enemy dispositions and an equally unprecedented ability to strike precisely what it saw. Reflecting on the Gulf War and on the history of change in military affairs, a number of defense analysts came to the view that a revolution in military affairs (RMA) was occurring. As gunpowder and railroads had at different times in the past revolutionized warfare, so was it now being revolutionized by advances in information technology. This was not a matter of technological determinism. New technology created new opportunities. Exploiting them to the fullest required revolutionary changes in organization and doctrine. Not all militaries seized these opportunities. Any that did acquired decisive advantages over those that did not.[15]

As the argument for an information technology RMA developed, it led some to believe that the U.S. military could develop dominant battlespace knowledge. Our intelligence, reconnaissance, and surveillance capabilities would be so good that decisions would "be made with something approaching perfect knowledge." While this was perhaps a more optimistic view than most held, the information technology RMA did promise to lift the fog of war, as a book by one proponent explained.[16] That it had done so with the promised revolutionary effect appeared to be the case in American operations in Afghanistan after 9/11. There, a small number of U.S. Special Operations Forces (SOF), assisted by less skilled indigenous forces and airpower, routed the numerically superior forces of the Taliban and its al Qaeda supporters. SOF spotted targets, indicated them with lasers, communicated with pilots above, and directed devastating attacks on their opponents. No one had expected the small deployment of SOF—a few hundred personnel—working with the Northern Alliance to win the war with the Taliban, but to everyone's surprise it did. "The unexpected outcome did not occur because of a particular technology or tactic." In keeping with the now received wisdom about RMAs, success, it was held, came from "the synergy of a series of new capabilities [that] transformed the nature of the campaign into something revolutionary."[17] Numerically inferior forces on the offensive are not supposed to win, but they did. Not only were the Taliban forces numerically superior, they were often better trained and had more firepower than SOF's indigenous partners. Yet the Taliban lost. An important part of the victory was the degree to which information dominance (achieved through command and control, surveillance, and reconnaissance technology) had revolutionized the dynamics of war. Contrary to the traditional view, information and by extension intelligence appeared to be, if not decisive for victory, more important for success than ever before. And Afghanistan was not an isolated event. The revolutionary developments manifest there worked in northern Iraq as well, and could work in a wide range of other conflict environments.[18] Proponents of the RMA agree with the traditionalists that however good one's intelligence, the battle must still be fought, but contend that the information revolution has changed the *way* battle is fought.

Advocates of an RMA had always met with skepticism, and events in Afghanistan and Iraq did not change this. Some skepticism was probably simply dogmatic. But some arose from hard-won experience on the battlefield.[19] Other doubts about the revolutionary power of information arose from more general reflection about battle. For example, just as the first Gulf War was about to ignite the debate about the information RMA, a scholar noted that an enemy subject to the new technologies could use cover, concealment, and deception to defeat them, while those deploying them were themselves subject to the friction of war.[20] The experience of the first Gulf War and the growing power of information technology in society generally overwhelmed such doubts, however, and built a good deal of enthusiasm for the idea of an information RMA. Yet not all analysis of the first Gulf War supported the view that information was becoming decisive in warfare. One anomaly in the war was that U.S. casualties were much lower than predicted by models of warfare. Research into this unexpected outcome, using sophisticated social science methodology that would have made Sherman Kent proud, led eventually to the view that the new information technology had not, in fact, revolutionized warfare.[21] Acknowledging that a number of factors including information and communications entered into battlefield outcomes, this view held that force employment or the skill of those engaged in combat was more important than informational, technological, or numerical advantage. The ability to capture and use increasing amounts of information would not change this, for three reasons. First, as the earlier skeptics noted, cover and concealment can defeat information technology, and deception can inject false information into a collection system, which creates uncertainty. Second, the information revolution will not remove the organizational and personal causes of misperception. Most victims of surprise, for example, had ample information to avoid being surprised but fell victim to it because of self-deception. Third, the initiative that belongs to the attacker imposes constraints on defenders that prevent them from using to full advantage whatever information they have on the attacker's location and intentions. The information technology RMA is limited, then, by the deception of others; our unwitting deception of ourselves; and the inherent dynamics of offense and defense.[22]

Since these claimed limitations on the latest RMA are important in assessing the role of information and intelligence in warfare, we should consider them in more detail, beginning with deception. During the first Gulf War, Iraq aimed to tear apart the coalition opposing it by striking Israel with mobile SCUD missiles launched from Iraqi territory. If Israel retaliated against Iraq for the attacks, the fear was that the Arab members of the coalition would leave it in protest. Destroying the SCUDs before they could be fired thus became an important objective for the coalition. It failed in this mission. The ability of the Iraqis to set up decoy missiles and use other deception techniques was an important part of the failure. Thus at the same time that the coalition's operations seemed to herald the arrival of an information technology RMA, the Iraqis' ability to fool the coalition's information collection and processing capability indicated a limit to that revolution. About a decade later, in the Kosovo campaign, U.S. and other NATO forces were "unable to discriminate between real ground vehicles (tanks, armored vehicles, etc.) and mock vehicles (plywood, dead hulks, etc.)."[23] Deception has proven an effective counter against the enhanced intelligence, surveillance, and reconnaissance capabilities made possible by the communications and information revolution. To the degree that the United States emphasizes the information-enabled RMA, its adversaries have an incentive to develop their deception capabilities. The reported ability of the Russians to move into Crimea in 2014 largely undetected may be an example of this dynamic.[24] The ability of plywood tanks to defeat advanced sensor-driven aircraft suggests that the cost/benefit ratio will favor the deceiver.[25] This may be particularly true if we take into account the lower cost and increased ability to deceive that our enemies will have in the digital domain, a critical domain for the information RMA. In the previous chapter we considered the effect that digital operations have on secrecy. While secrecy may not have come to an end, we should have no doubt that our enemies will be inside at least some of our digital domains, giving them additional opportunities to deceive us. The Israelis were able to get their aircraft safely to a Syrian nuclear facility they wanted to destroy reportedly by deceiving the sensors in the Syrian antiaircraft system. Deception also reportedly played a part in the successful employment of the so-called Stuxnet virus that attacked Iran's nuclear program.[26] Knowing that such digital deception is a possibility will itself introduce uncertainty into our military operations, whatever our opponents actually do. Uncertainty and the fog of war will remain even in a digitally enabled military force.

The deception activities of others mean that whether we are considering the immediate tactical sensor-shooter loop or the more strategic, mediated intelligence cycle,[27] we will not operate in an environment free of "noise," allowing us to have perfect information and knowledge of what is going on around us. Furthermore, whatever information or "signal" reaches us is subject to further distortion because the individuals and the organizations in which they work inevitably interpret the information they receive based on what they already know and what they expect and hope will be the case. In Korea, Douglas MacArthur refused to accept intelligence reports that contradicted his belief about what the Chinese would do. The American Navy did not accept reports about Japanese naval technology before World War II because it "knew" that Japanese technology was inferior to its own. Intelligence analysts concluded that Saddam Hussein was pursuing weapons of mass destruction programs even though there was little evidence of this, because they "knew" the Iraqis were good at deception. Thus, in their interpretation, the absence of evidence became evidence of presence, to paraphrase then Secretary of Defense Rumsfeld.[28] These are just a few examples illustrating the many ways that we misperceive and misunderstand our surroundings, even if we have plentiful information about them. For the information revolution to change this, it would have to change the human proclivity to discount the inconvenient.

In addition to deception and self-deception, the power of information is limited by the dynamics of combat operations. On the offense, precision strikes enabled by information technology are not effective enough to destroy targets and accomplish what a ground offensive aims to do: remove opposition on contested ground. Offensive forces must still mass to try to exploit weak points in the defense. Cover, concealment, deception, suppressive fire—in short, tactical skill allows an offensive force to mass and move in the face of enemy fire. To counter these attempted offensive breakthroughs, the defense must defend in depth. Only a defense in depth gives the defense the flexibility to counter an offensive that manages a breakthrough. But a defense in depth must be prepared well in advance of the offensive, while the offensive can be feigned at one point then launched at another at the last minute. Concealment and deception allow the offense to mass at one point, while appearing to mass at another, or the offensive force may have superior numbers at more than one point. Intelligence is not able to confidently predict where the point of attack will come.

> Even if the defender reads the attacker's true intentions perfectly up to the very minute the defender must commit, the defender thus still risks being drawn into overcommitment if they [*sic*] try to meet the attack in advance: if the attackers themselves do not know that they will delay until the last minute, the defender cannot possibly know any sooner, yet defenders have to commit long before

the attacker moves if they are to be ready to fight in time on the key sector, and once committed they can be held there by pinning attacks using a fraction of the attacker's strength.[29]

Held in place by the feints and deception of the attacker, the defenders are no longer able to respond at the key sector. Once it is clear where the key sector is, by using cover, concealment, dispersion, and other measures, skillful defenders will be able to move even in the face of information technology–enhanced attacks, even if less efficiently. The need for such attacks on defensive forces as they move to counter a breakthrough assumes in the first place that the attacking force is skilled enough to cause the breakthrough in the face of modern technology-enabled precision firepower.[30] On both the offense and the defense, this analysis claimed, skill is more critical to the outcome in modern battle than is information.

In addition to these three general considerations, empirical evidence from Afghanistan and Iraq supports the view that information technology has not revolutionized warfare as its advocates claim. SOF and its allies did not always succeed, even though they always used their high-tech information systems. When SOF and its allies fought less skilled forces, they won. However, when they fought more skilled enemies, they did not always. The new information technology did not trump skill. For example, in one Afghanistan engagement, skilled and unskilled indigenous forces fought together with SOF and U.S. air support. Thus both groups of indigenous forces had the benefit of America's information enabled precision strike capabilities. First the unskilled and then the skilled forces attempted to take the same objective. Only the skilled force succeeded. This is a good test of the claims about the relative importance of skill and information technology because important variables (for example, terrain, force strength, information technology) were constant. One of the few things that varied was skill, and in this case not information but skill was decisive. Again, in initial engagements in Afghanistan, Taliban and al Qaeda forces were slaughtered by American and allied forces, which used their information technology advantage to devastating effect. But the Taliban and al Qaeda learned how to use natural and constructed cover and concealment to defeat American sensors. They also improved their ability to move and fight in the face of American information and precision fire technology. In short, they became more skilled combatants. As they did, the tactical advantages of American and allied forces declined, even though America's technological and informational advantages remained.[31]

To this evidence about the role of information and skill in warfare, we may add what occurs in a particular form of combat, special operations. A special operation is an operation carried out against a specific, fortified, critical target by specially trained, equipped, and supported forces.[32] (Not all operations carried out by SOF are special operations; the operations that SOF carried out early on in Afghanistan were unconventional in that SOF worked with foreign forces but were otherwise typical military operations: infantry forces supported by airpower seized and held defended positions. Moreover, not all special operations are combat operations of the sort we discuss in the following examples.)[33] The target in a special operation is critical either for military or political reasons. The more critical the target, the more intelligence resources will be brought to bear in support of the operation. Such an operation may in fact be so important that it will have priority for all national intelligence resources. It would appear this intelligence support is critical, since the mystery of a special operation, at least from the viewpoint of traditional military theory, is how one ever succeeds. Special operations are conducted typically by forces that are smaller and have less firepower than those they attack. Thus they should not succeed. Nor are they always more skilled than those they attack, yet they may still prevail.

Regular and special operations have much in common. They both require information derived from reconnaissance, careful planning, rehearsal, speed, secrecy, and skill in execution. They both succeed, when they do, because they manage to create relative superiority over those they attack.[34] A regular combat operation aims to manufacture relative numerical superiority at a particular point to create and then exploit a breakthrough.[35] The ultimate purpose is to take and hold ground. This is the principal difference with a special operation. A special operation is not designed to take and hold ground. Its purpose is to destroy a target or, in the case of a hostage, effect a rescue. Thus it aims to create not relative numerical superiority at a given place but relative temporal superiority. The special operations force is typically smaller than the defending force. It creates through its attack a limited period of time in which it is superior to the numerically superior force only because it acts before the defenders can react. It will not suffer from its numerical inferiority in the long term because it will withdraw, having destroyed or rescued the target, before the defenders have a chance to respond and bring their superior firepower to bear.[36]

Given its characteristics, we might think that intelligence or information would be of decisive importance in a special operation. A smaller unit can succeed against a larger one if it acts before the larger unit can respond. This means it must surprise the larger unit. Surprise is an information advantage: the attackers act before the defenders know what is happening. It is not possible, however, to say definitively that an information advantage is necessary for the success of a special operation. In theory it may be. But as we all know, there is theory and there is practice, and in practice the role of information superiority is less clear than in theory. The case studies used to illustrate the theory of special operations contain examples in which the attackers achieve surprise but the operation fails, and others in which surprise is lost but the operation succeeds. In the raid on Saint-Nazaire, the British did surprise the Germans but the complexity of the operation led to its failure. In the rescue of Mussolini surprise was compromised at the beginning but Otto Skorzeny, who led the raid, acted so boldly that the raid worked anyway. Skorzeny did use some deception (he took an Italian officer with him on the assault, which apparently confused some of those guarding Mussolini), and deception creates information superiority. On the other hand, it is not clear that the deception was the difference between success and failure. In the raid on the Son Tay prisoner of war camp in North Vietnam, "complete surprise . . . was probably not essential to mission success." All in all, as the theorist of special operations has written, "[T]he importance of the principle of surprise [hence of information advantage] should be neither understated nor overestimated. Surprise generally provides only a momentary advantage, and although it is usually necessary for success, it alone is not sufficient for success."[37] In theory, "surprise is essential, but it should not be viewed in isolation. It is only valuable as part of the complete [set] of principles."[38] In practice, the key to success in special operations appears to be not one principle or all of them but the relation of the principles to each other and to the specific characteristics of the operational environment, including the will, alertness, and competence of the enemy. It appears that, to some degree, more of one principle may compensate for less of another.[39] It is not possible to state precisely, therefore, what the importance of information is in special operations. It is preferable to have an information advantage, of course. Success is more likely with it, but this may be said of any of the principles. In particular in the context of the current argument, would anyone versed in special operations say that an information advantage is always more important for success than the skill of SOF?

If special combat operations are like regular combat operations, may we reason by analogy from them to regular combat operations? It appears so. By the time the debate took place over the role of information in SOF's operations in Afghanistan and Iraq, no one was defending either of the extreme positions— that information technology had dissipated none of the fog of battle or that it had done so completely. The issue was, as it is in special operations, how to weigh the relative importance of all the elements of warfare, including numbers, skill, intelligence, firepower, and leadership. The conclusion is that the relationship of these elements is multiplicative rather than additive. If all the values for the elements are high, the result will be even higher; if any is zero, the result will be zero. Higher values for some elements can compensate for lower values of others.[40] In this view, all of the elements are important; none, including information or intelligence, is decisive. Putting the elements together in the proper balance to maximize the chances for success is an example of the kind of intuitive expert judgment that we considered in the case of espionage in Chapter Two.

This irenic interpretation of the debate may not satisfy those who argued for the revolutionary effects of information technology in warfare.[41] On balance, however, it seems an accurate outcome and one that settles more on the side of the neo-Clausewitzians than their revolution in warfare opponents. Yet, in fact, the neo-Clausewitzians always accorded a more important role to intelligence in warfare than Clausewitz did, which tempers the revolutionaries' loss. For example, in a seventy-page essay, one of the prominent exponents of the neo-Clausewitzian view of intelligence explained its role in the following ways: "[I]ntelligence is [only] a force multiplier"; "intelligence remains essential in some measure"; "it is natural that intelligence, like logistics, should always play a supportive role; yet the word supportive as used here is not synonymous with secondary or unimportant"; "the Battle of the Atlantic was decisively influenced by the successes and failures of intelligence on both sides"; "intelligence is of the utmost importance in war but is not a prerequisite for military conflict or even victory."[42] Or consider the various claims of another stringent proponent of the view that intelligence and information are of only secondary importance in war: intelligence was not decisive in the Battle of the Atlantic, was critical to Stonewall Jackson's success in the valley campaign, but insufficient, even when good, to guarantee favorable outcomes in Crete and against the Germans' V-1 and V-2 weapons in World War II.[43] Perhaps we should expect the traditionalists' judgments to vary so. Their account sees uncertainty and fog as defining war. If uncertainty is essential to war, then it may well be the case that intelligence, while generally not critical for success, is critical in some circumstances, in specific battles, or at some times. It would suit the traditional view of war as paradoxical, if war's uncertainty, the enemy of intelligence, made intelligence essential on occasion.

If our analysis gives credit to the traditional view of the limited role of information in warfare, then it will be worthwhile to consider what else this view might tell us about this relationship. From the uncertainty of war, the traditional view has distilled three principles about intelligence: intelligence may be more important in sea and air warfare than in land warfare; when forces are on the defensive; and at the operational level or in the formulation of strategy. In discussing these principles we should remember that "general principles distil only with reluctance from the mass of particulars" in any battle or campaign.[44] So resistant to distillation are general principles about warfare that we might more accurately refer to them in this instance as suggestions.

Intelligence may be more important at sea or in the air than on land because the sea and air are vast, and even two enemies who seek engagement may not be able to find each other. On the other hand, targets are harder to hide in these environments, since the earth affords greater opportunities for cover and concealment than the sea or air do. Thus, for these two reasons, intelligence may play a greater role in sea and air battles than in land battles. In the battle of Midway, for example, each side sought contact with the other. Intelligence helped bring the battle fleets into proximity; a chance sighting led to the decisive engagement and poor decisions by the Japanese commander to the ultimate U.S. victory. Whether one argues that intelligence, particularly the intelligence advantage of the United States (reading Japanese coded messages), or chance, or mistakes by the Japanese were most important in determining the outcome of the battle depends on how one weights these various factors. This weighting in turn requires immersion in the details of the battle, attention to its timeline, and knowledge of each side's capabilities. If one concludes that intelligence was more important at Midway and other sea battles, such as the Battle of the Atlantic, than in land warfare, then one might consider whether, as one analyst has claimed, the apparently greater importance of intelligence in sea warfare is only an artifact of the easier time we have in isolating the importance of intelligence in the simpler combat environments of the air and the sea.[45]

The traditional view also accords more importance to intelligence for those on the defensive. We have seen that going on the offensive, taking the initiative, creates uncertainty for the defense. Intelligence is one way to reduce this uncertainty. As noted, the dynamics or action/reaction of offense and defense means that even with foreknowledge, the defense could not with full confidence pre-position its reserves to counter an anticipated attack. Nevertheless, intelligence can reduce uncertainty and allow for more effective defensive action. Although significantly outnumbered and on the defensive, Stonewall Jackson succeeded in the valley campaign because he used superior intelligence to great advantage, consistently outmaneuvering and outfighting Union forces, achieving what one historian, a traditionalist, has called the "model of an active intelligence victory."[46] Caesar reported that an outnumbered Roman cavalry force faced the Gauls resolutely because they knew the enemy's plan of attack and how the Romans would counter it.[47] These isolated examples, of course, do not prove anything definitive about the relative importance of intelligence to the offense or defense. After testing this claim more systematically, toting up data points from "battles of worldwide importance" to "tactical actions," one analyst has concluded that intelligence was essential for the defensive but not for the offensive.[48]

While we conduct our own empirical investigations to decide where we stand on the issue, we might consider the use of intelligence at the higher levels of command. At the operational or strategic level, if a commander takes intelligence seriously, as Eisenhower most often did, it may have a greater effect than at the tactical level or in the midst of battle. This is the third principle cautiously advanced in the traditional view to explain the role of intelligence in warfare. Intelligence may have a greater effect in strategy because strategy and planning are "war on paper" rather than "real war," to borrow a phrase from Clausewitz.[49] Although strategy and planning need to take the fog of war into account, they will not be defeated by uncertainty or friction, if they are, until they are put into practice. Since uncertainty does not operate in strategy and planning as it does in war, intelligence may have more scope in these activities. For example, as noted in Chapter One, train watchers behind German lines in World War I were able to inform British intelligence about the movement of military trains. Since the tracks the trains were on went to known destinations, the British were able to anticipate where the next German offensive was going to occur. Similar operations were effective in World War II, among them those carried out by the coast watchers in the Pacific.[50] In the same war, information from Ultra (signals intercepts) that targeting its supplies was affecting the Afrika Corps's ability to fight helped the Allies direct their scarce resources in the most effective way, while informing Montgomery that he could go on the offensive and outslug the Germans as his own resources increased. Ultra again had a strategic effect by confirming that the Germans were expending more resources and suffering more casualties in Italy than the Allies, supporting the strategy of fighting the Germans there to create vulnerabilities for them elsewhere in Europe.[51] In all these cases, of course, the fighting still had to occur. At that level intelligence was subordinate to or at least not more important than or a substitute for other factors, such as numbers, skill, leadership, and determination. And, of course, even the most accurate intelligence cannot help decision-making if material conditions constrain decisions. The British did not have the resources to take advantage of the complete and accurate intelligence they had on the German attack on Crete. Rommel could not take advantage of his intelligence and tactical superiority because of constrained fuel supplies, constrained because Ultra intelligence was guiding Allied attacks on those supplies. Because of Ultra, Eisenhower knew in detail and in advance the German plans for landing at Tunis but did not have the resources to respond.[52]

That intelligence generally may have more effect at higher decision-making levels suggests that espionage may as well, as the train- and coast-watching examples just mentioned suggest. Perhaps the most famous example is the one discussed in the previous chapter, the British control of German espionage in Britain during World War II and the use of it and of German agents in other parts of Europe to deceive the Germans. Yet, if intelligence has greater effect in strategy and planning, it may also be less necessary. What is needed to make strategy can often be known without intelligence. Strategic decisions may be more determined by domestic political requirements, one's own resources and capabilities, or the needs of allies than what one knows of the enemy. If in principle intelligence may have more effect in strategy than in fighting, in practice it is not so much greater as to be always decisive or even necessary. As one descends in war from strategy to engagement, uncertainty and friction increase, which is to say that intelligence becomes, perhaps paradoxically, more necessary but less effective.

The greater importance or effectiveness that intelligence may assume on the sea and in the air, on the defensive, and at the strategic level does not alter the traditional view that intelligence or information, no matter how good or abundant, will not revolutionize warfare. As one proponent of this view has put it:

> [B]efore the development of communications and intelligence, militaries relied on material superiority, refinement of the art of war, and the cultivation of military genius to cope with uncertainty . . . . [E]ven though intelligence finally came into

its own in the mid-twentieth century, these traditional remedies for uncertainty continue to hold sway.[53]

It is certainly the case, as we have seen, that the precise relationship of intelligence to warfare is difficult to specify in the traditional view. If the traditional account is sure of anything, however, it is that intelligence or information, no matter how technologically enabled, will not change the nature of war. War is not a realm of thought and thus not a realm in which intelligence or information is decisive. It is a realm of action.[54] Whatever intelligence one has, the war must still be fought, and it is the fighting that ultimately determines the outcome. Intelligence may enable one to fight more cost effectively, but war is not an enterprise in which calculations of cost necessarily determine action or the results of action.

The traditional or neo-Clausewitzian account remains convinced that advances in intelligence collection cannot overcome uncertainties in warfare and remains unimpressed with the claim that information has produced a revolution in military affairs, perhaps because it has already taken into account an information revolution. The advent of electronic communications technology and the ability to capture and decrypt the messages it carried constituted a mid-twentieth century intelligence and information revolution. Consequently, "between the beginning of this century and 1945, the role of intelligence in war increased, until from 1942 onwards [as the full effect of this new signals intelligence came to bear on the war] intelligence exercised an influence it had never known before."[55] That unprecedented influence now appears less than decisive for yet more than inconsequential to the Allied victory.[56] It was perhaps most important in the submarine versus convoy engagements of the Battle of the Atlantic and naval campaigns in the Pacific but much less so in the Russian defeat of German forces in the East, the decisive ground engagement of the war. For the rest, the significance of intelligence to the outcome varied, but in no case did it mean the fighting did not have to take place and thus in no case, according to the traditionalists, did it mean that intelligence overcame the chance and uncertainty that are war. That the earlier revolution did not change the nature of war encourages the traditionalists to believe that the recent information and communications revolution will not do so either. Neither revolution overcame uncertainty.

In noting that during battle or in a campaign, intelligence might be more effective at the operational or strategic level, we open up the possibility that the true importance of intelligence in warfare may be before the war begins.

Before the fog of war settles in, it may be possible to see more clearly what is happening. In addition, to extend a point made above about the strategic level of war, before war begins (if not in the crises that may immediately precede it) there may be time to sift through what one can see, make better sense of it, and learn important things. Analysis takes time and if allowed time, may improve on what is collected. For example, detecting deception is time consuming and so may be more likely to occur at the often slower pace at which things unfold outside of war. More time may also increase the relevance of espionage and other forms of human intelligence, which as we have explained, also take time. In addition, during war, counterespionage efforts are heightened and citizens are warned to beware of spies, suggesting that espionage may be more effective before war. For these reasons, we may hope that intelligence will be more useful before war begins when time is more plentiful. As we will see, however, this hope is not fully realized.

Before War

Following World War I, Poland was in a difficult position, caught between Germany and Russia. As the Nazis gained power in the former and the Bolshevik revolution stabilized in the latter, the Polish position became worse. Recognizing Germany as a principal threat, Polish intelligence began working to intercept and decipher German radio transmissions in the late 1920s, almost as soon as the Germans began to use the Enigma machine, which encrypted their messages. Work on the German codes began in earnest in 1932. With the aid of a commercial version of the Enigma machine purchased by the Poles and documents supplied through liaison with French intelligence, which acquired them from a human agent "walk-in" who worked in the German cryptology office, the Poles were able to decipher the encrypted German messages. By 1938, in a test, the Poles deciphered about 75 percent of the messages they worked on.[57] In addition to its intercept operations, Poland also had agents of various sorts operating in Germany. Polish attachés in Berlin and other cities, as well as reconnaissance flights over the Baltic, provided additional information. Thus the Poles were well informed on German intentions and capabilities right up to September 1, 1939, when Germany invaded. Although not a negligible military force, without the vigorous support of allies Poland was unable to resist the power of Germany and eventually Russia. Its brilliant signals intelligence success allowed it only a good understanding of its approaching demise.

The Polish case is not a fair test of any claim about how important intelligence is for national security. Given Poland's position, intelligence would never have saved it, especially given the weakness of France and Great Britain. The Polish case is worth considering, however, because it does illustrate several things about intelligence before war begins. First, it illustrates the fact that weaker nations are inclined to focus on intelligence. The Poles understood the threat they faced and saw intelligence as critical for trying to handle it. Their position was essentially defensive; they needed intelligence to use what force and strength they had to best advantage. The Polish case also highlights the difference in time horizon between peace and war. The Poles had time to work; their signals intelligence effort against Germany proceeded for about a decade before the war occurred. Espionage and other kinds of intelligence gathered from humans was an important part of Polish intelligence activities as well. Again, they had the time to piece together the puzzle of German signals encryption. Through liaison, espionage played a critical role in their success, reminding us that human intelligence has played such a role in technical collection since such collection began, not just since the appearance of the Internet. The Polish success in signals intelligence also reminds us of the value of liaison, official sharing of information between intelligence agencies of different countries. Open information sources were also important. In addition to attaché reporting, diplomatic reporting provided information, as did newspaper reports.

Among the points illustrated by the Polish case, it is worth considering a bit more the importance of open sources in intelligence prior to World War II, since one supposed effect of the information revolution is the increased availability and importance of such sources. Insofar as war or the approach of war is concerned, open sources have always been important. An American naval attaché in Tokyo before the war estimated that he got 95 percent of his information from open sources, including debates in the Japanese Diet about naval construction, newspaper articles, conversations with businessmen, ship visits, and tours of aircraft manufacturing facilities. Open sources were also important in the European theater. A practitioner of French intelligence has claimed that "at least 80% of French military intelligence" came from open sources. (Interestingly, an al Qaeda document from the 1990s claimed that "openly and without resorting to illegal means, it is possible to gather at least 80% of information about the enemy.")[58] British newspapers and military journals contained valuable information about British Army tank maneuvers from which the British had barred attachés. At the request of the American attaché in Germany, Charles Lindbergh visited various Luftwaffe facilities and aircraft manufacturing plants, "providing a treasure trove of information on the German air force." Other Americans involved in aircraft manufacturing also visited German plants and talked to American attachés in Berlin.[59]

Open sources were also important in the years preceding World War I. In 1910, German analysts read French parliamentary budget debates and deduced correctly, for example, that the French no longer considered the Italians to be potential enemies. British publication in 1912 of detailed studies of Belgian roads, rivers, bridges, and locks indicated to the Germans that the British thought they would be fighting in Belgium, important information for the Germans given their plan of attack on France. When in 1912 a French staff officer was reported by the press to be hospitalized in Namur, Belgium, the Germans concluded, again correctly, that the French and Belgian staffs were cooperating. Nor was it difficult for the Germans to understand the meaning of the French loaning money to the Russians to build railroads, the Russians nationalizing some rail lines in Russian Poland, or the Russians in 1913 replacing German gauge track in Poland with Russian gauge.[60]

The historical record, then, suggests that with regard to the coming of war and preparations for war, most of what needs to be known has always been openly available. Preparations for industrialized warfare are hard to hide. "The Lion's share of all intelligence, it appears, comes from the public domain, from the national and regional press, from recent books and book reviews, from journals specializing in everything from transportation systems to agriculture and from military affairs to medicine."[61] Intentions are implicit in preparations, even as those preparations are revealed indirectly in parliamentary debates. Geography provides the basis for other deductions about enemies and their plans, indicating where attacks might originate or counteroffensives have most chance of success. Railroad tracks point where troops will go, as does the length of a recently built train platform in a small Polish town, longer than necessary for any civilian train but just right for long mobilization trains.[62] Warfare in the information age is no different. If there is a confrontation between the United States and China in the future, it should not be a surprise if information technology or cyberweapons play a role, given extensive Chinese and American activities in these areas reported in the press. Even the broader outlines of American capabilities and hence plans are apparent in published reports, congressional debates, and official budgets.

The availability of open sources on preparation for war suggests that clandestine sources might be less important. The fact that open sources did not supply everything suggests that clandestine sources are still necessary. Accordingly, before World War II, as before World War I, a number of countries, although they had officially proscribed the use of clandestine human sources, engaged in espionage, often using their attachés to run agents. In many cases, the espionage does not appear to have produced much of importance. In some cases, as in the previously mentioned French success against German cryptology, it did. Less significantly, human sources gave the American attaché in Tokyo "important technical information" concerning a new torpedo and other naval armaments that the attaché could not have procured otherwise.[63] During the Cold War, both the Soviet Union and the United States, at different times and to different degrees, collected through espionage information that was vital to understanding the intentions and capabilities of their principal adversary. Officials on each side have claimed sufficient knowledge of the other side to have crippled it, if war had come.[64]

Such benefits of espionage did not come without costs. Early in the twentieth century, some governments hesitated to engage in espionage because, for example, they felt that the benefits would not exceed the costs to the attachés who carried out the operations. And, inevitably, attachés were expelled because of their involvement in espionage. As the century wore on, this problem was dealt with by separating the espionage function from the legitimate work of attachés and diplomats, as we noted in Chapter Two. Another problem, less easily overcome, was deception perpetrated through human agents. Prior to World War I, both the French and Germans paid a Hungarian count for information he provided, most of which he appears to have made up. In the 1920s, Russian emigres desperate for money and with declining access to information in Russia fabricated information that they gave to British intelligence, which at the time had little way to corroborate the information. In self-defense, the Czechs tried to deceive their British and French allies in order to draw them into a confrontation with Germany. Before the invasion of Iraq in 2003, an Iraqi defector fabricated information that he provided to German intelligence, which passed it to the United States. Lack of other sources to assess this information, particularly human sources with access to Iraq's weapons programs, was one reason it was believed.[65] The greater availability before war of the time to assess and consider before acting does not necessarily lead to better detection of deception.

The problem of deception leads us to the greatest problem with intelligence before war: not that enemies may deceive us but that we may deceive ourselves, as we do in numerous ways. Military staffs misconceive what future warfare will be like and thus fail to understand the significance of what their enemies are doing. Racist or nationalist prejudice devalues the reported efforts of one's supposed inferior enemies. Commitment to carefully contrived plans made in accordance with doctrine survives the arrival of intelligence showing these plans will almost surely fail. The preoccupations of civilian and military leaders convince them that their enemies must have the same concerns. A desperate situation encourages "best-case" analysis and wishful thinking. Intelligence agencies strive to make the actions of others rational, as those agencies conceive rational action. Faced with ambiguous situations, analysts look for evidence to confirm what is already supposed. Assessment of technological developments or material conditions is easier than accurate assessment of enemy intentions, and therefore guides decisions, but assessment of enemy intentions is more important. Mission justification prompts military analysts to make worse case assessments of enemy intentions and capabilities, while domestic concerns competing for scarce dollars prompt civilian leaders to make best case assessments. The admonition to keep an open mind, the well-intentioned remedy for our prejudice, is undercut by the recognition that an open mind is an empty mind and that an empty mind would be defenseless in the face of experience. Not only does self-deception blind decision-makers to what their enemies are doing, it also blinds them to the capabilities of their own forces. So powerful and pervasive are the causes of self-deception in this matter, that Ernest May concluded that objective net assessment (comparative analysis of our own and the enemy's forces) was "nearly unobtainable."[66] For these and other reasons, self-deception may be more powerful before war than during it, when enemy success may finally break through the delusions that easily go unchallenged in peace. During war, uncertainty limits the effectiveness of intelligence; this uncertainty derives principally from enemy freedom of action. Before war, we are our own worst enemy, generating a self-enveloping "fog of peace," as one author has put it, that no less than the fog of war limits the effectiveness of intelligence.[67]

It is hard to see how the greater and more detailed information made available by the information revolution would solve all of these problems, or even any of them. For example, the intelligence available to the U.S. government and MacArthur's staff indicated that the Chinese were already operating in large units in North Korea and had massed more troops to intervene. Presumably today we could read the shoulder patches on the Chinese troops and listen to

them breathe in real time, but this would not make the intelligence more effective than it was when MacArthur ignored it and bullied others into doing
likewise.

Behind the Lines

So far, in discussing intelligence in warfare we have been considering what
information we need to collect before or during war to wage war more successfully. But the term "intelligence" also refers to clandestine or covert activities
beyond the collection of this information. These activities are done secretly, in
peacetime sometimes deniably, as we saw in the previous chapter, and until recently through human beings. (They can now be done through software, as in
cyber-espionage and cyber-sabotage.) In wartime they are done secretly but do
not need to be done deniably and occur behind the lines, as guerrilla warfare
or escape and evasion nets for downed pilots, or in the enemy's home country
as sabotage. As we noted in the previous chapter, in peacetime, collecting information clandestinely and doing things covertly may conflict, and they may in
wartime as well, as the history of the British Special Operations Executive and
MI6 illustrates.[68] In war, the activities of intelligence may be favored in their
conflicts with collection because these activities are more warlike than collecting information and thus may appear more relevant to the immediate need.
The history of such activities suggests caution in accepting such an appearance,
however.

A number of senior leaders in World War II, both civilian and military, were
fascinated with the secret world of intelligence. Stephen Ambrose recounts an
episode in which Winston Churchill became almost giddy at the thought of being involved in a clandestine operation to meet French officials in North Africa
prior to the Allied landings there.[69] This fascination is in part what had earlier
prompted Churchill to order that secret intelligence work on the Continent
set Nazi-occupied Europe ablaze with sabotage and resistance. This fascination and a lack of alternative means to attack Germany led to an overestimate
of what such intelligence activities could accomplish. In retrospect, it is hard
to find evidence that all of the secret operations (sabotage, partisan warfare,
and the occasional assassination) carried out behind enemy lines accomplished
much at all. Even at the time it was being carried out, the lack of effectiveness
was evident in some cases. Riding out of Norway as the war ended on a railroad
line he had recently blown up, William Colby, later a Director of Central In-

telligence, was "chastened" to discover how quickly the Germans had repaired it.[70] In retrospect, it has become even clearer that despite their great courage, sacrifice, and ingenuity, those conducting operations behind enemy lines accomplished little, if anything. They helped the war effort only when acting in proximity to conventional military operations, as in the area surrounding the Normandy invasion, or as part of a larger strategy. For example, partisan destruction of a key bridge in the Balkans helped crimp the flow of supplies to Rommel's Afrika Corps. Yet even in these cases the effect was small, the contribution to victory negligible. Breaking the German codes was much more important in limiting Rommel's supplies than partisan activity, since it directed Allied aircraft to vulnerable German shipping in the Mediterranean. Supporters of the effectiveness of operations behind enemy lines often mention partisan operations in southern France against the Das Reich Division as it made its way to Normandy following the invasion. But the most detailed examination of this case shows that the partisan operations had an effect largely because the Germans decided to respond to the partisans instead of ignoring them and pressing on to Normandy.[71]

A number of reasons explain the lack of success of these various intelligence operations. In World War II, the forces engaged were vast. Compared with them, the efforts of small groups armed with light weapons and explosives amounted to little. Given the redundancy and strength of the German economy and the economies conquered by German arms, sabotage was incapable of producing much effect, even if it was more cost effective than so-called strategic bombing, as one analyst has claimed.[72] Partisan bands conducting guerrilla warfare were hampered by the fact that, in Europe, "few places existed where one could safely build up large guerrilla forces," and those places where such forces could establish themselves were peripheral to the war.[73] In addition, the Nazis used an array of means both traditional (for example, torture) and modern (such as radio finding technology) to suppress hostile clandestine activity in territory they controlled. John Keegan has claimed that reprisals against the populations of countries the Germans occupied increased the number of those willing to act as informants for the Nazis and persuaded the British in some cases to encourage less partisan activity. How the former effect can be known to have occurred is not clear. We do have some evidence, however, that German reprisals limited partisan activity.[74] We have some evidence of the opposite effect, as well. As a lieutenant in the German Army, Kurt Waldheim, later secretary general of the United Nations, pointed out to his superiors that ruthless reprisals embittered the population and made them more supportive of the partisans. Perhaps reprisals achieved both effects, or perhaps, like the partisan activity and sabotage they were meant to stop, they accomplished little, other than killing people.[75] Another reason for failure, at least in those operations sponsored by the American Office of Strategic Services (OSS), was that the OSS was often amateurish and incompetent.[76]

If the OSS contributed little, if anything, to victory in World War II, it did succeed in creating a template for the later use of operations behind enemy lines or in enemy-controlled territory. As James Q. Wilson argued, when an organization is first established, a powerful leader can stamp it in his image, giving the organization a set of operating norms that govern it thereafter. William Donovan, the founder of the OSS and to many in its ranks an inspiring leader, did this with the OSS, not to the advantage of the organization and its successor, the Central Intelligence Agency (CIA), certainly when it came to operations behind enemy lines. As the Allies approached Germany, Donovan believed that the OSS should parachute agents into Germany, as it had into France, to carry out sabotage, encourage dissent, and collect intelligence. Several of his subordinates argued that such operations were pointless. Unlike France, in Germany there was no already existing opposition to the government, the population was hostile to Allied personnel, and virtually every German was connected to the state police. Donovan was not dissuaded. Operations went ahead, and, as even a sympathetic biographer reports, accomplished nothing. Undeterred by this failure and others, or unable to acknowledge them, Donovan did not lose faith in the power of intelligence operations behind enemy lines. While ambassador to Thailand, he argued after the French defeat at Dien Bien Phu (1954) that the United States should undertake such operations in Vietnam, where conditions for them were as unfavorable as they had been in Germany.[77]

Donovan's unwavering belief in the effectiveness of covert action despite all evidence to the contrary set a pattern that the CIA would follow. After World War II, it persisted in parachuting agents into communist-controlled countries. All of these operations were failures. In the Korean and Vietnam wars, it sent agents into the enemy homeland, again without any success. It continued the missions, getting its agents killed or captured, even when those running the operations acknowledged that they were not working. In Vietnam, it continued to claim that agents or agent teams were operating in the north even when on two occasions, although under North Vietnamese control, the team radio operators managed to send messages reporting that they had been arrested.[78]

Despite a lack of any success, the agency persisted in its effort to operate behind enemy lines for a number of reasons, including a desire to do something, the freedom it felt to waste non-American lives, and a lack of effective oversight.[79] The causes of failure in these operations are likely to pertain in the future. In wartime, operations behind enemy lines will suffer from heightened enemy counterintelligence efforts and the coercive power available to states at war to discourage cooperation with the enemy. Those operations that avoid counter-intelligence may produce an effect, if closely tied to conventional military operations. Even if they do, given the scale of forces at play in war, the historical record suggests that the effect will be negligible.

Some have argued that if not sabotage or guerrilla operations, then deception operations behind enemy lines can be effective. For example, they cite an operation aimed at convincing the North Vietnamese that they faced an indigenous opposition movement. Evidence for the effectiveness of this operation is that the North Vietnamese made the cessation of it one of their demands during negotiations to end the war.[80] Tradecraft in the deception operation was so bad, however, that it is clear the North Vietnamese knew that they did not face indigenous opposition. Their demand was in effect, then, a demand to cease efforts to affect North Vietnamese opinion through the radio broadcasts and leaflet drops that were part of the supposed resistance movement. The breach in their complete control that the broadcasts and drops indicated did irritate the North Vietnamese, but it was no more than an irritant, hardly something critical to the decision to begin negotiations or to their outcome.[81]

Better evidence for the effectiveness of operations behind enemy lines is the assistance given to downed pilots and escaped prisoners in World War II, which allowed many to reach safety. Behind-the-lines operations and work with resistance forces also provided a good deal of valuable intelligence. This was in fact probably the most important contribution that the operations behind enemy lines made to the war.[82] In acknowledging this, we return to the question of the role of intelligence in warfare, a question we have answered by saying that intelligence or information, no matter where or when gathered, is not decisive in war.

Conclusion

We opened this chapter by noting that whereas in the past both war and information were critical in building state power, information was not thought to be decisive in war. We noted as well the recent reversal of this claim: information technology undermines state power, yet is critical for success in war. In other words, the claim is now that neither the state nor war can keep their secrets any longer. In Chapter Three we argued that this was not true of the state, and in this chapter we have argued that it is not true of war. We should add that state power developed and thrived even though its information capacities failed to conquer the secrecy of war because it has always been more important for the state to know about itself and its occupants than to know about its enemies. For the British, for example, it was more important to know how many heads of cheese there were in Cheltenham than how many casks of gunpowder Napoleon had in Gonesse. Counting cheeses was essential to increasing the revenue of the state. That revenue was essential to waging war. The information that states require for their power is above all information about their own people, their activities, and resources. Therefore, if it is true as we argued in Chapter Three that the current information age threatens privacy (the voluntary withholding of information) more than secrecy (the compulsory withholding of information), then our age promises in principle an increase in state power rather than a decline. In any case, with regard to what they need to know, the state and its military have something critical in common. Given the opacity of war, it remains the case that the most important thing a military commander needs is information about his own forces, rather than information about his enemy's. Self-knowledge remains the most important knowledge of all. The difficulty of acquiring such knowledge in organizations, especially espionage organizations, is the theme of Chapter Six. Before turning to it, we will consider the role of information in irregular warfare.

5   Intelligence and Irregular Warfare

Toward the end of his book on intelligence in warfare, the eminent military historian John Keegan defended the traditional view of intelligence in warfare by arguing that if enemies seek battle, they will find each other. Thus intelligence is not critical for success in war. When enemies meet, not intelligence, but will and force decide the outcome.[1] As we saw in the previous chapter, this is true, although in some cases (war at sea or in the air), finding each other can be difficult, even with modern technology. But what if an enemy does not want to be found? What if the enemy does not have uniformed organized forces that seek battle? What if it hides by mixing with the people at large? This kind of hiding and fighting, of course, is a distinguishing feature of what is known as irregular warfare, the most important examples of which are terrorism and insurgency. The German forces massing for the attack on France in 1940 were visible. Those who carried out the attacks on 9/11 were indistinguishable from the other passengers on the planes until they began their attack. If the hiddenness of the 9/11 attackers is illustrative of irregular warfare, it would seem that intelligence is more important in this warfare than in regular warfare. Keegan suggests as much, mentioning in an introductory discussion that in the eighteenth century American wilderness intelligence was at a premium, "and usually provided the basis of victory or defeat."[2] The explanation for the importance of intelligence in this case is not far to seek. For the most part, the Indians fought what was referred to as a "skulking" kind of warfare, refusing to stand and fight, merely skirmishing and running away, setting ambushes and raiding.[3] If the Indians could be found and engaged, most often they could be defeated. So the Indians hid and fought only when they chose to. Finding them, and therefore getting intelligence about them, was decisive, although how it was acquired differed from the classic espionage described in Chapter Two.

In one sense, intelligence was less important in fighting native Americans than it is now in fighting terrorists and insurgents. Having no easy way to find the Indians, the colonists eventually settled on the expedient of attacking what the Indians could not hide—their villages and crops or sometimes their women and children. Against these attacks, the warriors had to stand and fight, or lose what they most valued. Against nomads such as the plains Indians, the U.S. military used its resource advantage to keep after them, especially in winter, and burned villages and supplies when they found them, exhausting the natives, at which point they had to fight or surrender. (Slaughter of the buffalo by civilians for commercial purposes was a perhaps decisive element in the wars against the plains tribes.) Historically, village burning and other such tactics have been common in campaigns against tribal societies. When a tribe used the forests to hide, Caesar burned their villages and farms and took hostages. This forced the enemy to deal with him, although in this case they decided to treat, rather than fight. The British used these tactics in their "small wars," substituting bombing villages for burning them once they had the aircraft to do it.[4] (As we have seen in the previous chapter, the Germans also used them in World War II to deal with resistance forces. The idea in this case was to make resistance actions too costly to continue.) It is much easier to find a village than to locate warriors, who possess intimate knowledge of the land and a way of life adapted to its every contour. As long as village burning was acceptable, intelligence was less important for irregular warfare in practice than in principle: village burning could take the place of finding the warriors. The weaker side in an irregular war can adopt guerrilla or hit-and-run tactics only if it has nothing of value that is easy to find, or if its stronger opponent operates within moral and political limits that prevent it from attacking these valuable things (principally noncombatants—that is, women and children). If neither of these conditions applies, then guerrilla tactics are unlikely to work. By the early twentieth century, the moral climate in the imperial countries had changed enough so that village burning was becoming a questionable tactic. Before long, it could no longer be done, at least not openly.[5] Morality thus made intelligence decisive in irregular warfare. In regular warfare, intelligence is a force multiplier. In irregular warfare, we might say it is a morality multiplier or, at least, that good intelligence in irregular war makes it more likely that combatants will observe moral principles.

The Dynamics of Intelligence in Irregular Warfare

Although the superior power in an irregular war is likely to need superior intelligence, it is unlikely to get it, at least at first. Having a preponderance of force and accustomed to the dynamics of regular warfare where the enemy can be more or less forced to engage, for example to protect its capital or its citizens, the superior force will tend to rely on that superiority in all its conflicts rather than on superior intelligence. The Romans, for example, did not have a highly developed intelligence system as they expanded their empire, because they had confidence in their military superiority. Only as they became relatively weaker did they take their intelligence needs more seriously.[6] The United States, for most of its history holding a preponderance of power over its local enemies and protected by ocean barriers, has not been notably adept at intelligence. It lagged other powers in institutionalizing this capability, for example. The superior power is likely to carry its disregard for intelligence into its irregular conflicts. Even if a superior power has a tradition of paying attention to intelligence, a claim made about the British,[7] history suggests that it will need to learn over and over again the value of intelligence and the means of acquiring it when it confronts enemies who hide. For example, despite its experience dealing with irregular warfare throughout its imperial history, the British effort in the early years of the most recent troubles in Northern Ireland was not distinguished for the adept use of intelligence.

The hidden insurgents, on the other hand, are likely to do better with intelligence from the start because it is easier for them to collect and analyze. An intelligence officer for the Irish Republican Army (IRA) could learn almost everything he needed to know simply by walking or driving around his operational area. Targets—policemen, soldiers, police stations, barracks, other government buildings—were all plainly visible. Furthermore, the terrorist's analytical task is rather simple. Observation of normal daily activity allows him to identify the routines of his target, if the target has a routine. Doing so is important because, like all intelligence, this knowledge reduces uncertainty in operations. For example, a target always goes to his pub on Friday evening at six o'clock. The ambush, including safe movement to it and especially away from it, can be meticulously planned, therefore. Because the routine is predictable—that is what makes it a routine—the terrorists can better anticipate various contingencies or chance events that might occur. In planning for them, they reduce the risk to themselves.[8] In searching for a target's routine, terrorists seek a pattern in all the confusing rush of daily activities. In trying to find the terrorists, the counterterrorist does the opposite. He looks for an anomaly in the established routines and patterns of daily life: an unfamiliar car left in a neighborhood or an unexpected package with oil-like stains that comes in the mail. The potential target protects himself by varying his routine, by injecting as much apparent chance into his activities as possible, and thus uncertainty into the planning of the terrorists, while the terrorist protects himself by making his activities appear as routine and normal as possible. Both are engaged in versions of the regularity/anomaly recognition noted in Chapter Two as part of the process by which humans sense danger and opportunity.

The hiders (the terrorists or insurgents) and the finders proceed typically in two different ways, then. Generally speaking, the finders (looking for anomalies) proceed deductively and the hiders (looking for routines) proceed inductively. The finders must get to the hiders based on what they know about the operational environment they share with the hiders. Based on that knowledge and some more or less common-sense notions, they formulate hypotheses about where the hiders might be and then test them. For example, an insurgent group with an ethnic agenda is likely to have a base of support in its ethnic group. The members of that ethnic group, say in a village, would be of interest, therefore. The question would then be which individuals in the village—perhaps by reason of their work—might be in the best position to aid the insurgents by acting as couriers or in other support roles. Once those individuals are identified, a pretext might be found to question them, but in a way that does not single them out. They might be included in a larger group selected for questioning because of minor legal infractions, for example. Based on these interviews and information available from other sources or perhaps given up by one of the other villagers selected for questioning, one or two of the individuals identified as most likely to be assisting the insurgents might appear to be the best candidates for surveillance and further investigation in hopes that they would lead to the insurgents. Frank Kitson, a British military officer with experience in counterinsurgency campaigns, whose example we have been paraphrasing, described this deductive process as one of moving by a progressive series of hypotheses from the general to the particular, from background information to contact information, to information that allows the counterinsurgents to find the insurgents.[9] Sherman Kent would certainly point out that Kitson's method is a prime example of how even the most particular operational tasks rely on the scientific method—and we would add intuitive judgment—so scorned by Alexander Orlov.

The example of the hypothetical-deductive finding method just given assumes a rural operating environment, but it could work as well in an urban setting. For example, if the threat comes from an ethnic or religious group, the neighborhoods or communities in the city dominated by those groups become priorities. Since it is a common experience that recruits to terrorist or insurgent organizations come from social contacts, places where people congregate (such as places of worship, athletic or social clubs, or schools) would become priorities within the targeted communities or neighborhoods. Perhaps some of these could be singled out because of the rhetoric their leaders use. Or some might engage in a lot of fund raising in the absence of signs that the organization was particularly well off or engaged in local charitable work, suggesting that the money raised might be going somewhere else. The authorities might select such organizations for closer scrutiny. Again, this is a process of moving by progressive hypotheses from general background information to particular targets.

Kitson offered his own example of deduction in an urban environment. Urban terrorists, he argued, like all insurgents, act for a political purpose. They thus must have some connection to the political movement that their violent actions are meant to support. Usually this means some connection to the political wing of the terrorist organization. Often this political wing will itself be hidden in a larger, completely legal political movement or party. Not knowing who the terrorists are, the counterterrorist must work from this larger political movement down to the individuals carrying out the acts of violence. To shorten Kitson's analysis of this problem, we may say that discussions or negotiations with political elements, from block committees to national directorates, allow the authorities to collect background information that, along with information from other sources, permits them to formulate hypotheses about who in the overt political organization might have connections to those in the covert political organization, who in turn have connections to the terrorists.[10] The authorities then test their hypotheses by conducting surveillance on the individuals they suspect are the links between the outer, overt political elements of the organization and its inner, secret military elements. Negotiations are only one context in which such an approach works. More generally, the inevitable cooperation between the overt supporters or sympathizers of a violent political movement and those carrying out attacks is one reason why traditional approaches to espionage (although not necessarily going to cocktail parties) can work against terrorist organizations.

If we take deduction to mean moving from general or background information to specific or contact information, then we can take as another example of an urban deductive method an ingenious technique deployed by the British in Northern Ireland. Recognizing that support for the IRA was stronger in some areas or neighborhoods than others, the British targeted those communities. In one case, the British ran a laundry service in selected areas that, in addition to collecting, cleaning, and returning clothes to customers, also submitted the clothing to forensic examination. If anomalies appeared, clothing that did not fit the demographics of the house or stains or residue that might indicate work with electronics, guns, or explosives, one might hypothesize that the inhabitants of the house were involved in IRA activity and deserved further investigation.[11]

As this example makes clear, the hypothetical-deductive method requires both recognizing a pattern and what deviates from the pattern. The background information that the authorities collect establishes a pattern of life for a community. This term, used by Kitson and now in vogue again,[12] refers to the habitual or regular patterns of activity that one observes in a community or neighborhood. Once one understands this pattern, anomalies will stand out. The anomaly might be an unusual number of visitors to a particular house, or a house that sent to the cleaners what appeared to be an unusually large number of adult-size men's shirts, given who was supposed to live in the house. A parked car not registered to someone in the neighborhood might indicate a car bomb or, if occupied, surveillance. Any anomaly may, and most often does, have an innocent explanation—but it alerts the authorities and any citizens who support them that something might need further investigation.

As noted, the deductive approach is necessary if the finders have little or no information about the hiders. It is a time-consuming and expensive approach, since hypotheses often turn out to be wrong or anomalies innocent events, wasting the resources spent investigating them. But it would be even more expensive and time consuming if the finders did not use this method. Not operating on the assumption that some locations are more likely to hold targets than others would mean investigating everywhere and wasting most of one's efforts. Soldiers who are absent without leave could be anywhere but most often they are back home. The process of deduction relies on such probabilities as a way of focusing the search and saving resources.

Finding hiders would be much easier, of course, if targets carried signs identifying themselves. From the perspective of the terrorists, this is exactly what happens. Military personnel and police wear uniforms, government buildings fly flags, the dates of elections and location of polling places are announced in advance. In this abundance of information, deduction is not necessary. An inductive approach or one that starts with individuals is possible. This is the approach taken by terrorists. For example, observing a police station or an embassy, they can identify the officers or diplomats. They can then follow individuals to find out where they live and the routines they follow to figure out how to ambush them. They might also receive tips from sympathizers identifying the location of police or other officials. In any event, the insurgents can usually begin with individuals or facilities and through surveillance develop their operational plans.

The terrorists who attacked the U.S.S. *Cole* in 2000 provide an interesting illustration of the difference between the deductive and inductive approach to intelligence in irregular warfare, while reminding us that the usefulness of each approach derives not just from one's strategic position in the conflict but more from one's operational task. Sometimes the terrorists also face the task of finding one fish in the sea, so to speak. In one of their operations after attacking the *Cole* the terrorists set out in a small boat hoping to find and destroy a U.S. warship in the Gulf of Aden. Even in this relatively small body of water, however, that turned out to be an impossible task, not unlike trying to find an individual insurgent in a sea of people by wandering around until one bumps into him. They ended up attacking a tanker, the *Limbourg*, which they happened upon. They thus experienced the intelligence problem, finding the enemy on vast seas, that Keegan shows bedeviled all naval operations until more recent technological advances (which have not entirely overcome the difficulty). The terrorists could have mitigated their problem deductively, by hypothesizing where U.S. ships were likely to be found. This is in essence what they did in preparing for the attack that eventually targeted the *Cole*. They knew, as everyone did, that U.S. ships refueled in the port of Aden. They simply had to rent a house near the harbor, prepare a small boat for the attack, and wait. They moved from a general principle (where U.S. ships docked) to a particular target.

The contrast between the deductive and inductive approaches we have presented, which is a measure of the varying difficulties of the intelligence tasks faced by hiders and finders, best describes the situation at the beginning or in the early stages of an insurgency. It is one way to highlight the fundamental difference between the starting positions of the two sides in irregular warfare. The hiders are rich in information (virtually everything they need to know is openly available) but poor in resources; the finders are poor in information (their enemies are hidden and hard to find) but rich in resources, at least relative to their enemies. As time goes on, this situation can and usually does change. If the insurgents gain resources, including public support, and do not lose their information advantage, then they will win or at least not lose. If the counterinsurgents gain information about the hiders and do not lose their resource advantage, including public support, then they will win or at least not lose.[13] This formulation of the strategic struggle in irregular warfare highlights the key role of information or intelligence in such conflicts.

Even if helpful in understanding the role of intelligence in irregular warfare and the different approaches to intelligence taken by insurgents and the authorities, we should not take the distinction between deduction and induction as absolute. For example, even in the early stages of its counterinsurgent campaign, the government might get a tip about an individual or uncover his activities. For example, an alert customs inspector in 1999 noticed anomalies in the behavior of someone entering the United States from a ferry in Washington and decided to investigate further. This led to the arrest of Ahmed Ressam, who was trying to smuggle explosives into the United States as part of a plot to bomb the Los Angeles International Airport. Interrogation of an arrested suspect can provide information that will lead to other conspirators. If the suspect cannot or does not need to be arrested, then surveillance might lead the authorities to other plotters. This would be an example of operating inductively. In addition, the deductive method will ultimately lead to individuals, and then the authorities will proceed inductively, as surveillance of the individual or information he provides following his arrest leads the authorities to other insurgents and supporters. Also, governments, at least some of them, can now use advanced data collection and analysis tools to identify a needle in a hay barn full of communications and Internet postings by tracing particular connections. The man who blew himself up inside Camp Chapman in 2009, killing CIA officers and others, came to the notice of the Jordanians who recruited him reportedly because of his postings online, from which apparently the authorities were able to figure out which house he lived in. Intelligence analysts now also use social media to locate people, a potentially powerful technique.[14] More generally, as the counterinsurgent or counterterrorist campaign progresses, the government will probably be able to use induction more frequently, as it comes to know more about the insurgents and their operations, and information from one captured terrorist leads them to others. U.S. forces in Iraq, exploiting information technology, developed and refined this approach into a powerful weapon against insurgents. In its essence, however, it was not a new approach but one that was used in Vietnam against the Viet Cong infrastructure, for example, and in other conflicts.[15]

For their part, the insurgents may need to use deduction, since their targets may start to hide themselves once the threat from the terrorists manifests itself. In addition, as the authorities gain knowledge about the terrorists and find them, they may be able to "turn" some, getting them to remain apparently loyal members of the organization as they report on it to the government. As terrorist operations begin to fail, the terrorists will come to think that traitors may be at work. In trying to find them, the terrorists will operate deductively, formulating hypotheses about who the traitor might be and testing them. This is counterintelligence, which often proceeds deductively.[16] Generally speaking, the relative importance of deduction and induction to both sides will depend on how the campaign progresses. If the insurgents gain or maintain public support, for example, they will always tend to proceed inductively, since tips from the community will identify targets, even if they try to hide. A chance observation by a bartender of an identity card in a wallet, for example, is enough to expose an auxiliary or reserve police officer or soldier, even though he does not normally wear a uniform or have daily contact with official installations.[17] Similarly, if the population provides information to the authorities, they will be more able to proceed inductively.

Techniques

Whether proceeding inductively or deductively, both the authorities and the insurgents will use in varying degrees the same basic array of intelligence collection techniques, with the better resourced authorities relying more on technical means, and the insurgents more on informal human sources or informants. Both sides are likely to receive tips, many of which may be useless, while others could be falsehoods invented to set up persons who, apart from having gotten on the wrong side of the tipsters, are innocent. The side seen as winning or as most friendly is likely to receive the most tips. If money is offered for information, the quantity of information provided is likely to increase, although not necessarily its quality. Interrogation of captured opponents will be another source of information. The evidence suggests that if interrogation techniques are enhanced, people will talk.[18] The problem with this is not that they will make things up if subjected to coercion. What they say can be checked while they are held and if found not to be true, they can be interrogated again. The problem with enhanced interrogation is twofold. First, as noted in Chapter Two, forced cooperation might not get from a subject all that he knows, particularly the most important things he knows, which are likely to be least known to the interrogators. Second, to abuse detainees, who might after all be innocent, is to invite long-term adverse political consequences, which should be a compelling argument against it, if humans did not tend to discount the future. The authorities are likely to have more people to interrogate, since they are the hunters. This will be especially true if they offer an amnesty for those who surrender and talk. Captured documents or electronic devices will be helpful. Both sides will also try to exploit social connections (and hence social media) for information. This is likely to play most against the insurgents, since social connections will act as bread crumbs leading counterinsurgents inside the clandestine organization of the insurgents.[19] In Nicaragua, in the 1920s, Marines who invested time in understanding the dynamics of local patron-client networks and making friends with the patrons reaped significant returns of information. The patron's client network, spread across the countryside, became a collection network.[20] Finally, both sides may recruit agents, in the sense discussed in Chapter Two, but this is likely to be a technique used most often by the authorities, who have the resources, organizations, experience, and above all the incentive to make it work. Agents are likely to be useful to the government throughout the campaign, because their enemy is hidden, but only to the insurgents later in the campaign or as it draws to a negotiated close, when it will be advantageous to know the hidden negotiating positions and priorities of the government, as well as its factions and disagreements. We should recall here the remark from an al Qaeda publication, mentioned in the previous chapter, that 80 percent of what al Qaeda needs to know is available in the open. This is probably an underestimate, and it certainly indicates that clandestine collection is not likely to be very important to terrorists or insurgents for most of their campaign. Generally speaking, the insurgents are likely to be more focused on and therefore be more adept at counterintelligence than intelligence, because they are under a constant threat, whereas the government will tend to focus on intelligence and be better at it, because it needs to find its hidden enemies, but less adept at counterintelligence, because through most of the campaign, its enemies have a limited incentive to try to penetrate it, since again most of what they need to know is in the open.[21]

As for human intelligence in irregular warfare, when used by the authorities it will be most akin to the police work of man-hunting and different from the traditional practice of human intelligence as described in Chapter Two. To repeat the formulation we used there, intelligence in irregular warfare will be an issue of getting information to get the man, rather than, as in traditional espionage, getting the man to get the information. Espionage tends to be less important in man-hunting than in other activities because in man-hunting there are other sources of information. The information critical in man-hunting is, first, often overt background information, not the secrets that traditional espionage deals with, and second, contact information, which may be secret or guarded but is tactical in nature—again unlike the information that traditional espionage usually seeks. It is not military plans or the intentions of leaders but the location of individuals and information on impending attacks those individuals might carry out that is most important. Those working with the authorities may be agents but not always, probably less often than in the traditional practice of intelligence. (MI-5, the British domestic intelligence agency, ran agents in the IRA.) In irregular warfare, as in regular warfare, information may come from the captured who are turned or the neighborhood or village informant. Insofar as human intelligence in irregular warfare is aimed at killing or capturing an individual, it is like covert action in that it will produce a change in the world. Hence, the security requirements involved may differ from those in traditional espionage. The human source, for example, may be thought of as a short-term asset, in that his or her information may well be unnecessary after the killing or capture of the targeted individual. If the insurgency or terrorism campaign becomes a long-term effort, both sides will have the time to develop and run agents. The insurgents may see the need to do this, as they feel the effect of the government's human intelligence operations. The evidence seems to suggest that few insurgent or terrorist organizations have done this.[22] The government may prove vulnerable to penetration, since it is likely to underestimate the intelligence capabilities of the insurgents. As we have already noted, if the counterinsurgent campaign enters a phase of negotiation, then the work of traditional espionage and its agents is likely to become more relevant for both sides. Tradecraft skill will be particularly important for the government whenever the point of finding an individual is not to kill or capture him but to use him against his organization, a strategy we examine shortly.

How good are the authorities likely to be at man-hunting? Will they, like the Royal Canadian Mounties reputedly, always get their man? In asking this question, we are looking from the other side at the question of the end of secrecy discussed in Chapter Three. If the state may keep its secrets, may those outside the state keep their privacy? Does the evidence from the past ten years, when man-hunting passed from a law enforcement issue to a national security priority, indicate that hiding has come to an end? This question is in reality a question about the power of intelligence or information gathering more generally and, since it is states that are most often the ones doing the finding, about the power of the state.

The most obvious answer to this question is no—hiding has not come to an end. Terrorists and insurgents continue to hide. Indeed, the more effective finders are, the more incentive hiders have to hide. But this obvious answer is also a trivial answer. What we want to know is not just whether hiders can hide but whether they can succeed in not being found. Is hiding effective? Can an individual prevent the state from finding him? In Chapter Three, we examined aspects of this question by considering the case of bin Laden, who managed to hide for ten years. Here, we want to address the question more broadly before returning to bin Laden to make a few additional points. To address the effectiveness of hiding, we should consider two factors: the environment in which a person hides, which may afford the person some protection; and the power of the state doing the finding and the priority it attaches to finding the person hiding. For example, if a terrorist has the protection of a state power, he or she is more likely to be able to hide without being caught. In this case, the protecting state is not going to use its power to find the hider and, more important, will try to prevent another state from using its finding power. Similarly, if a terrorist has the protection of a population, he or she is more likely to be able to hide without being found, although the protection provided by a population is likely to be less effective in many cases than the protection provided by a state, since most populations are subject to the control of some state and, for that reason, lack coercive or defensive power. Still, as we have seen in certain areas of Pakistan and Afghanistan, a population with coercive power and a state not sufficiently motivated to challenge it will provide a good environment in which terrorists may hide. If a terrorist has ceased to operate, neither moving internationally nor communicating with other terrorists, or perhaps not using electronic means to communicate with anyone, he or she is more likely to be able to hide without being caught. Turning to the second factor—the power of a state and the priority it places on finding someone—we should note that if only one state is looking for a terrorist, if that state is a weak state, or if the terrorist is a low-priority target, then he or she is likely to be able to hide effectively. Conversely, if a terrorist participates in operations, communicates frequently, uses electronic means to do so, lacks the protection of a state or population, and is a high-priority target of a powerful state or a coalition of states, he faces a high probability of being found.

The cases of Mir Aimal Kasi and Imad Mughniyeh exemplify some of these considerations. After he killed two and wounded three CIA employees outside the agency's headquarters in 1993, Kasi hid in his Pashtun tribal homeland in Afghanistan and Pakistan. The FBI and the CIA were highly motivated to find him; the Pakistani government had no reason to protect him; a reward was offered to anyone providing information about him that led to his capture. Kasi was betrayed, captured (four and a half years after the shootings), brought back to the United States, tried and executed. Mughniyeh was perhaps responsible for the deaths of more Americans than any other terrorist before September 11, 2001, including those killed in suicide bombings in Lebanon in the early 1980s. He also organized the killing of Israelis. He was known to be very careful about his security, avoided publicity, reportedly had plastic surgery to alter his appearance, and had the protection of the Iranian government. He survived and operated for 25 years. Still, he was found. He was killed by an explosive device in his car in Damascus in 2008.[23]

What is the probability of being found? It is not possible to say in the case of terrorists or insurgents, since much of the information remains classified. A terrorist the state has found may not be exposed because he is still being followed in hopes that he will lead to colleagues. More may have been found, therefore, than we are aware of. In addition, there is no reason to assume that all kill-or-capture operations are publicized or that all those killed or captured are actually terrorists who are trying to hide. Terrorists and insurgents do surrender, and some that are killed or captured are not terrorists or insurgents. Data in these matters have not been highly reliable. Again, the circumstances in which someone hides and how much effort is put into finding him or her varies from case to case, and we have no way of knowing how these variations affect the probability of being found in different cases. In nonterrorist criminal cases, the probability of being found, at least by states with competent law enforcement, seems rather high. The U.S. Marshals Service, which began its Most Wanted Fugitive list in 1983, reports that it has found 211 of the 226 people it has put on the list, a 93.4 percent success rate. The Federal Bureau of Investigation, which began its 10 Most Wanted list in 1950, reported in 2010 that it had located 463 of the 494 individuals on the list, for a success rate of 93.7 percent, almost identical to but of course a little better than the rate reported by the Marshals Service.[24] Although some of the cases on the FBI and Marshals lists include fugitives found overseas, for the most part the cases were domestic and involved people with little protection other than what they could provide themselves. They were also priority cases. We should assume that when dealing with terrorists overseas, protected by a government or population, the success rate will be lower. The more protection available to a terrorist, the lower the finders' success rate will be.

It is not just the probability of being caught that is important, however. How long it takes to catch someone is also important, especially perhaps for terrorists and insurgents. Mughniyeh operated for a couple of decades. Abu Musab al-Zarqawi did not operate for long in Iraq but long enough to foment a civil war in the country through his attacks on Shia Iraqis. As we might expect, there is no one answer to how long someone may hide. A variety of circumstances, everything from personal appearance to the competence of one's pursuers and the quantity of publicity about the hider, affects the answer to this question. One safe generalization is that the longer one hides, the more likely one is to be found, assuming that the motivation and resources of the finders remain constant. Although likely to be caught eventually (according to the Marshals Service and the FBI), a domestic fugitive in the United States runs only a very small risk of being caught in his first month of flight.[25] But hiding for a long time does not necessarily indicate success for the hider, since long success at hiding is likely to come at the expense of operational effectiveness and political achievement. Osama bin Laden was able to hide for much longer than Abu Musab al-Zarqawi, who remained operationally active until he was found and killed, but only by following stringent security measures,[26] in effect isolating himself from his movement and losing control over it. He did continue to communicate, offering advice, and he did have some influence, but nothing like what he had before hiding became his priority.

Bin Laden's case allows us to consider some issues related to the finding power of states and the effect that power has on those who are trying to hide from it. Bin Laden claimed in a letter to colleagues that it was possible to hide even inside what he called "the circle of espionage," if one followed security precautions:

> It is proven the American technology and its modern systems cannot arrest
> a Mujahid if he does not commit a security error that leads them to him, so
> adherence to security precautions makes their technological advance a loss and a
> disappointment to them. In addition to that, adhering to security precautions is
> not an issue that a person will commit a human error in, if he really understands

the importance of his mission and is capable of staying in hiding until the situation opens up.[27]

Bin laden wrote these words a few days before U.S. forces found and killed him. In one sense, his death does not prove him wrong. The error that led to it was not made by him but by his courier, who responded to the (presumably) innocent question of a friend (not a member of al Qaeda) in a cell phone call. The caller asked what the courier was doing these days, and the courier replied that he was working with the people he used to work with. Given what the United States had learned about the courier through interrogations and possibly other human and technical sources, and the high priority that the United States placed on finding bin Laden, this minor slip was enough to bring to bear on the courier the full surveillance power of the United States. Eventually but not inevitably, the courier led U.S. forces to bin Laden.

In a larger sense, however, bin Laden was wrong about how successful one could be at hiding. It is impossible to function without having contact with others, particularly if one wants not merely to survive but also to have some political influence. It is not possible, then, as bin Laden claimed it was, for anyone to ensure their security by adhering to security precautions, no matter how well they understand the necessity of such precautions. One must also ensure that one's contacts adhere to such precautions, and that is much more difficult, if not impossible. For one thing, it is not possible to know with any certainty what those looking for us know. If we do not know this, then we cannot know what additional piece of information, no matter how trivial it may seem, such as the remark by the courier, will reveal our hiding place. If we have contact with others, which we cannot avoid, we will reveal some information. We are all necessarily embedded in social or human networks of one sort or another, and it is not possible to separate completely a clandestine network we may be part of from our open networks. Before anyone becomes a terrorist or insurgent, he is a son or brother, friend or schoolmate. These connections, and many other kinds, do not cease to exist when one joins a clandestine organization, even if the person joining ignores them. Most do not or cannot ignore all of them. Bin Laden's courier took the call from his friend. We are all parts of networks, and networks are inherently bad at security.[28] Just as so-called air gaps (physical separation) between classified and unclassified physical communication networks do not provide security, they do not provide security—they do not exist—between open and clandestine social networks.

In addition to showing the inherent difficulties of securely hiding from motivated and powerful finders, the bin Laden episode is clear evidence that the surveillance and coercive power of the United States extends thousands of miles beyond its borders. Although Ayman al Zawahiri, bin Laden's colleague and the current leader of al Qaeda, has not been found, most of the original leadership and those involved in the 9/11 attacks have been. Particularly vulnerable have been the so-called number threes in the organization, who run operations, since their job requires them to move and communicate. In Iraq as well, the United States and its allies eventually proved adept at finding members of the clandestine insurgent networks carrying out attacks. In Afghanistan and Pakistan, bin Laden's letter suggests, American surveillance and coercive power is effective enough that its targets feel they are faced with a choice between death and imprisonment. Other sources report that those hiding from the United States in the remote tribal areas of Pakistan live in fear, with reason, of being found and killed.[29]

This recent success at finding suggests that if irregular warfare is an intelligence contest between nonstate hiders and state finders, it has become a one-sided contest, as long as the finders are competent, sufficiently resourced, and motivated. In truth, this has always been the case. In Vietnam, once the United States focused on the problem of the Viet Cong infrastructure (VCI) and provided resources to fight it, that infrastructure proved vulnerable, and for the same reason that more recent terrorists and insurgents have proven vulnerable. Political activity, even as a violent clandestine conspiracy, requires contact and communication between clandestine and overt networks of people. Various security measures can make the finders' job more difficult, but the basic circumstances of political work that hiders are involved in, which requires contact and communication bridging the "gap" between overt and clandestine networks, even incidental but unavoidable bridging, favors the work of finding. Once the finders get inside the network of hiders, they can move from node to node or person to person. Recently, electronic means of communication and interception and analysis have enhanced this ability, as it did in the case of bin Laden despite his rigorous security measures, but it was effective long before the existence of such means of communication and ways of exploiting them. In Vietnam, operations in the Phoenix program against the VCI unfolded much as they did years later against terrorists and insurgents in Iraq.[30] The only difference was that moving from contact to contact in Vietnam might take days, while in Iraq, because of the electronic communication involved, it might take only hours. Without the advantage of electronic communications, the operations of finders would be slower, but, of course, so would the operations of hiders. And the evidence suggests, again because of the inherent political character of the hiders' work, that even at a slower pace, the finders would have an advantage. Of course, the hiders can give up their political work. As bin Laden said, they can stay "in hiding until the situation opens up." Over time this approach might cause the finders to scale back their hunt because they believe that the hiders have given up. In fact, this would effectively be true. This is essentially what the notion of leaderless resistance amounts to: give up political mobilization and any hope of controlling a movement, to commit a few random acts of violence, which, because they are severed from any political purpose or mobilization, are likely to appear senseless and undermine the cause. A group of hiders reduced to this condition has lost, even if it occasionally manages to kill some people. Such killing would be a protest, but only a protest, against the overwhelming power of the state.

To note the tactical advantages of finders in the contest of hiders and finders that is irregular warfare and to speak of the strategic defeat of the hiders does not imply that the tactical advantages lead automatically to the strategic defeat. To imply such a result would be to leap at a single bound the gap, so to speak, between tactics and strategy. As the case of Vietnam reminds us, tactical and operational advantages or excellence do not automatically translate into strategic success or victory. If irregular warfare is now and has always been a contest in which finders have advantages, it has never been a contest in which success at finding automatically leads to definitive success. Thus, once the hiders have been found, the important question arises: what should be done with them? How can success at finding be turned into strategic success? In asking this question, we are asking about the strategic value of intelligence in irregular warfare.

Intelligence and Strategy in Irregular Warfare

Generally speaking, there are four ways of dealing with hiders once they are found, which in effect amount to four different strategies for dealing with terrorism or insurgency, four different ways to turn tactical information superiority into strategic victory. First, all of those found may be targeted for killing or capturing. Second, those found may be targeted selectively, in hopes that killing or capturing the skilled will collapse or render ineffective the network they are part of. Third, those found may be targeted selectively, in hopes that taking out key network functions will lead the network to collapse or become ineffective.

Fourth, those found may be used in such a way as to encourage the collapse of the terrorist or insurgent organization. (The third and fourth approaches differ because the networks in an organization are not necessarily synonymous with the organization.) We may consider these strategies in order. As we will see, they imply different roles for intelligence, especially human intelligence, and in doing so, also imply different command and control arrangements and organizational structures.

Killing Insurgents. There is a kind of forthright, even elegant simplicity in the notion that one may counter a terrorist or insurgent campaign by killing or capturing the terrorists and the insurgents: no insurgents, no insurgency; no terrorists, no terrorism. This approach is really a strategy of attrition, an effort to beat the enemy into submission by the unrelenting application of force. It was the apparent strategy behind the Phoenix program, a kind of mirror image of the overall strategy in South Vietnam through much of the war. The objective was simply to kill or capture so many members of the VCI that the VCI would cease to be effective, if it did not simply cease to exist. At some points and in some accounts, this seems to have been the strategy against al Qaeda in Iraq as well, although the leading commander of the effort argues otherwise.[31] In this strategy, the role of intelligence is to locate targets. Depending on circumstances, including the degree that the insurgents use communications technology, human intelligence may be more or less important. Analysis is simple. It is limited to putting together information from captured documents, intercepted signals, and interrogation reports to locate targets or support further interrogation. Organizationally, intelligence is in a subordinate position to operations and driven by operational dynamics. It must speed up its processes to keep operations going at a tempo sufficient to produce the collapse of the enemy.

Despite its elegant or merely brutal simplicity, attrition is unlikely to be a successful strategy in irregular warfare. The conditions that allow attrition to work do not always apply even in regular warfare, and probably apply less often in its irregular version. For attrition to work, the opponent must be following or be forced into a strategy based on resource superiority; his resources must be limited or vulnerable; his morale must be weaker than his attacker's; and moral or political constraints must not impede killing the opponent.[32] Few if any of these four conditions apply in irregular warfare. Certainly, the first rarely does. Terrorists do not pursue strategies based on resource superiority, since they have few resources. While they may be able to count on the support of a sympathetic population, they cannot count on an endless supply of recruits or money. Thus, the first two conditions for a successful attrition strategy do not exist when dealing with terrorists. The third—inferior morale in the target of attrition—may apply but often does not. For the insurgents and many of their supporters, the cause is often more self-evidently one of life and death than it is for the counterinsurgents. Finally, seldom if ever does the last condition for success at attrition prevail in irregular warfare. Counterinsurgents no longer operate without moral or political constraints on their ability to kill, as we noted in the opening of this chapter. Imperial counterinsurgents lost this advantage decades ago and now criticize other counterinsurgents who wish to hold on to it.[33] Drones are a technological fix to the problems of moral limits on attrition warfare as a counterterrorism strategy, because their precision allows those using them to kill terrorists without harming others. This at least is the claim of the U.S. government, a claim disputed by those who believe that U.S. drone attacks have, in fact, killed significant numbers of noncombatants.[34] Even if improved intelligence collection allows counterinsurgents to operate within the moral constraint on attrition warfare (an example of the morality multiplier effect mentioned at the beginning of this chapter), it is clear that the other conditions that allow attrition to work are not present in irregular warfare.

We might qualify this conclusion by noting, as mention of the changing sentiments of imperial populations indicates, that the moral and political restrictions on the counterinsurgents' use of force are not written in stone. To some degree, they depend on the level of outrage that terrorist or insurgent attacks generate. In 1981, 82 percent of Americans said they could never support political assassinations as a way of dealing with terrorism. By contrast, two months after the September 11 attacks, a poll found that a majority of Americans (60 percent) supported assassinations in the war on terrorism. One-third approved of the use of torture, and 27 percent the use of nuclear weapons.[35] As subsequent events have shown, however, not even the 9/11 attacks suspended or altered the moral constraints on counterinsurgents. These moral issues are important, perhaps decisive, given the close connection, even etymologically, between "morale" and "moral." The morale of the people counted on to support the counterinsurgency back home depends on their assessment of its morality. The moral constraints remain, therefore, even if technology allows counterinsurgents to operate more lethally within them.

The restraint on the use of force in irregular warfare arises not just from the sentiments of the imperial population and its allies. It also arises, of course, from the reaction of the population against which it is used. The very webs of human relationships that allow counterinsurgents to find insurgents also restrain their ability to deal with them once found. Because insurgents are part of a web of human relationships, killing them produces collateral damage to the government's cause, even if noncombatants are not killed when the insurgents are. The more legitimate the insurgents' cause appears, the more outrage their family and friends are likely to feel when they are killed. If noncombatants are killed, the cost to the government may of course be even higher. The more the state has reserves of affection and loyalty from its citizens, and the more that the insurgents are seen as merely self-interested, as indistinguishable from organized criminals, the less the state will suffer from tearing up the human web. But in tribal states or states where ethnicity is more powerful than nationalism or loyalty to the state, any attack on insurgents is likely to damage the standing of the counterinsurgents. Often counterinsurgents assume that their use of force will not have negative effects because the innocent are not harmed; but this view assumes the universal validity of the counterinsurgent understanding of who is innocent. (It is important to note that arguing that an attrition strategy is likely to fail in irregular warfare is not to argue that killing or capturing terrorists and insurgents is a bad tactic. We return to this point shortly.)

Selective Targeting: the skilled. The requirement to limit collateral damage suggests that selective targeting is a better strategy to deal with insurgents and terrorists than attrition. One principle of selection would be to target leaders or otherwise critically skilled personnel in hopes that removing them would cause the organization to collapse or lose effectiveness. In this strategy, the role of intelligence is still to locate targets. Human intelligence might be more important in this case, since insurgent leaders are likely to be well protected and may even limit or avoid using electronic means of communication. Human sources, even agents, as that term is traditionally understood, might be critical sources of information. Analysis will be more important than in a simple attrition approach, if only because it is necessary to find specific well-protected individuals in the insurgent organization, rather than just anybody. Organizationally, intelligence remains subordinate to operations because killing or capturing is still the principal task in the strategy. But operations would no longer simply dictate the pace. Operations should proceed at a pace no faster than intelligence could identify and locate targets, because the intent of this strategy is to make targeting more discriminating. Analysis is more important in this strategy, therefore, and analysis takes time.

Leadership targeting has succeeded in some instances. For example, the more that an insurgency depends on a charismatic leader, the more vulnerable it may be to this approach. When U.S. Marines occupied Haiti in the 1920s, they were able to snuff out an insurgency or rebellion by killing its leader, Charlemagne Perrault, who had a mystical standing among his followers. Even without charismatic leadership, an organization may be vulnerable to counterleadership targeting, especially in the uncommon circumstance that most of the leadership can be killed or captured almost simultaneously. A tip from a captured member of the Hukbalahap rebellion in the Philippines provided information that led to the capture of most of the rebellion's top leadership in 1950, along with numerous documents. This was a crippling blow, although lower levels of the leadership struggled on until other measures finally brought the rebellion to an end. The near total and simultaneous arrest of the Sendero Luminoso leadership in 1992 almost destroyed that organization. What survived and regrouped has never been as effective as the organization was under its first leaders. In other instances, targeting leaders has failed to end an insurgency or to make its organization less effective. The Baader-Meinhof organization survived the death of its leaders and lived on for years through succeeding and operationally effective generations of leaders and followers. Killing Baitullah Mehsud, the leader of a Taliban faction in Pakistan, did disrupt the faction and lead to infighting; but rather quickly Baitullah's cousin, Hakimullah Mehsud, gained control. He led the faction into "a dangerous new course." The *Economist* reports that since Abubakar Shekau replaced the former leader of Boko Haram, "who was killed in police custody, . . . he has radicalized the movement and overseen more deadly and co-ordinated attacks."[36] Technical skill may be more susceptible to selective targeting than political skill, but insurgents do not necessarily need an impressive level of technical skill to stay in the fight or even win. And others can learn these skills sufficiently for the fight to go on.[37]

Selective Targeting: Networks. Another approach to selective targeting is not to target individuals as such but rather their function or position in a network, a network in this case understood to be some combination of people and the connections between them. The key to targeting in this case is not function in an organization but function in the network that is the social structure of the organization. For example, someone identified as a leader on an organization chart may not be as critical to the functioning of the organization as someone, perhaps even in a relatively inconspicuous position on the chart, who informally conveys information among many people in the organization. If these critical people are identified and killed or captured, according to this strategy, the network will collapse or function less effectively. In this approach, the role of intelligence is again to locate targets. The relative importance of human and technical intelligence will again depend on circumstances. Analysis will be more important than in the previous two strategies, however. Success depends on understanding the network and identifying the critical nodes. ("Critical" may mean with regard to the strategy being used against the insurgents or the metrics used to analyze networks; these are not necessarily the same and may conflict.)[38] Organizationally, intelligence remains subordinate to operations in this strategy because killing or capturing is still the principal task, but as in the previous case of selective targeting, operations would not alone dictate the pace. Operations should not proceed at a pace faster than intelligence analysis can identify and locate the critical targets.

As indicated, the success of the counternetwork approach depends on identifying the right nodes to target. Indeed, if this is not done, counternetwork targeting amounts to no more than attrition. If we cannot remove the right or critical nodes because we cannot identify them, then we are simply removing nodes in hopes that we can do so faster than they can be replaced, leading the network to collapse or become ineffective. But which are the right nodes? Elaborate mathematical models purport to answer this question; but it is not clear that they have been adequately tested. No effort was made in the heat of battle in Iraq or Afghanistan to use or test them systematically, although some were applied here and there and became the anecdotes upon which strategy or the presumption of strategy rested. Moreover, the models exist outside any strategic framework, as if the networks themselves and the logic of the models were the entire world. Proceeding to target networks on the basis of these models would be similar to turning over strategic planning to individuals who were good at manipulating the artificial rules of chess. Chess masters make good intuitive judgments and powerful computers are good chess players, but that is because chess has a high-degree of regularity.[39] This seems unlikely to be true of the social networks encountered in irregular warfare. Absent an ability to identify the key nodes to remove, in practice counternetwork warfare is merely attrition warfare.

The problem with the counternetwork strategy is not just that we do not know which nodes we need to neutralize. It is the whole way in which the network is conceived. When discussing their work, counternetwork warriors and their admirers speak of the network they are targeting, by which they mean the set of nodes and links on their powerpoint presentation. But this diagram represents not the network but only the limit of their knowledge of it. Every node in a network, even a clandestine network, links to some nodes outside what we think of or know as the network.[40] These "outside nodes" may not be critical to the organization. They may not be financiers, foot soldiers, religious sanctioners, tactical leaders, or strategic masterminds. They may only be family, friends, or former schoolmates. They may not have critical roles in the network, as network analysis defines "critical." But as those "inside nodes" are killed or captured, the outsiders could move in to take over for them. Networks, in other words, typically have a latent capacity to restore themselves because what we identify as the network is only a snapshot of a limited set of a much larger dynamic set of human relationships that extend well beyond the area illuminated by our knowledge. The speed at which latent becomes actual operational capability in a network depends, of course, on how quickly the new "nodes" can learn the skills they need. This may not slow the replacement process much, since most skills that terrorists need are simple and can be effective in the production of violence, even if simple. If we recognized that "the network" was much larger than the briefing slides indicate, we might be less sanguine about destroying it. The latency or redundancy of opposition networks is likely to make them "faster" in the long run than our operational tempo.[41] This is an instance in which in the long run not everyone is dead.

The latency of social networks, like the redundancy of infrastructure networks, is a strength. It takes time for that strength to work, however, and for the government to counter it. The government has the long term it needs for this effort only if it survives the short term. Targeting insurgents, whether leaders, the skilled, or the network nodes, particularly to prevent them from carrying out attacks, helps get the government through the short term. Part of this may be the positive effect on its population's morale if a government carries out a targeted killing campaign. Targeting killing may also cause some insurgents to reconsider the cost/benefit calculation of being a terrorist and make other counterterrorist measures more effective. Those favoring targeting insurgents would be right to say, then, that although their approach may not work in the long term as a strategy, it can work in the short term as a tactic. This is true, but of little use if the tactic causes the strategy to fail. In the late 1950s and early 1960s, the government of South Vietnam carried out a ruthless campaign aimed at the communist underground organization.[42] Indiscriminate targeting and brutal methods, including the use of torture during interrogations, led to the near destruction of the communist infrastructure, at least in some parts of South Vietnam. Information was critical to the success of this campaign, but the South's information dominance was not ultimately decisive. Short-term success came at the long-term cost of alienating the population, and as we know did not definitively deal with the problem of communist subversion and insurgency.

The differences and trade-offs between the short term and the long, as well as variations in the quality of the data used and questions about measures of effectiveness, may explain in part why rigorous examination of targeted killing, whether as part of an attrition, leadership, or network targeting strategy, has produced such varying results. One study that looked at 298 cases of leadership targeting found that targeting leaders did not make an organization more likely to collapse and, in fact, with some kinds of organizations, made it less likely. Other studies have found that targeted killing does shorten the life of a terrorist organization or lessen its effectiveness (defined as its lethality—but is lethality a good measure of effectiveness?), while others have found that in the long run it increases the number of terrorists or is less effective than other methods of countering terrorism.[43]

Attacking the Organization. Targeting members, those with critical skills, or the networks that bind organizations together have much in common as strategies. In one way or another they focus on the individuals in the organization. They all use intelligence in a similar way, to locate individual targets, and make intelligence subordinate to operations. The final strategy for dealing with hiders differs in all these respects. Attacking the organization through which hiders carry on their work does not aim at individuals or their functions in an organization or network. It aims instead to attack what makes clandestine organization possible. This approach is based on the understanding that clandestine organizations, organizations of hiders, rely more than other organizations on the trust that exists between members. Hiders are at risk. Therefore, to survive and function, they must trust that those they deal with will not betray them to those looking for them. If this trust can be undermined, the clandestine organization will cease to function or at least lose its effectiveness. If hiders cannot trust other hiders or people outside the clandestine organization, they will not communicate with them or will impose ever tighter security measures to shield themselves from those they are unsure of. But, as we saw in the case of bin Laden, such security measures isolate individuals and make it harder to carry on the work of the clandestine organization. In the strategy of attacking the trust essential to clandestine organizations, the role of intelligence is to gather information on individuals in the organization in order to manipulate them. Technology can help with the gathering and the manipulating, but in the intensely human business of destroying trust, human intelligence is most effective. In this strategy, everything else done against the hiders is subordinate to the task of penetrating their organization through human agents. Analysis will be important in this strategy only insofar as it supports the work of penetrating the clandestine organization. Organizationally, military and police operations should be subordinate to intelligence operations because killing and capturing are subordinate to penetrating the organization and running agents in place. Trust among members of the organization is the target, not the individuals themselves.

A RAND study published in 1964 argues that in Malaya the British used a counterorganization strategy based on human intelligence.[44] Written a few years after the conflict ended and based on documentary evidence and interviews with a variety of people involved, the report traces the development of the British counterinsurgency effort but argues that at its most effective it was guided by the idea that penetrating the communist apparatus was the highest priority for all counterinsurgent operations. Every effort was made to capture, not kill, insurgents, and to turn them and send them back into the organization in the hope not only that they would gather and report information that would allow the security forces to capture and turn others but also, and most important, that they would persuade others to defect or surrender. According to the report, the British believed that as their penetration of the organization progressed, it would become increasingly difficult for the insurgents to operate. Ultimately, if it progressed far enough, the organization itself would collapse like a house whose timbers had been hollowed out by termites.

The highest purpose of the Malayan counterinsurgency, then, was to make the insurgent change sides. The report describes this as the "covert aim" of the British effort.[45] It was covert, of course, at the beginning because if the British had publicly announced the purpose of their efforts, they would have forewarned the insurgents about the double agents operating among them. This raises the possibility that more recent kill or capture efforts may have the covert aim of penetrating and hollowing out the insurgent organization. If so, this has been an unusually well kept secret. But in fact, the ever-increasing speed at which these kill and capture operations were conducted (at least in Iraq) indicates that their purpose was to remove individuals from the organization, rather than to return them to it so they could help destroy it. As the general who perfected this attritional approach put it, "[E]very operation is a fight for intelligence," so that another operation can be mounted as quickly as possible before the next target is aware that he is in danger.[46] As the operations in Iraq and Afghanistan developed, their targets had less and less time to consider defection. Indeed, the aim of the operations was to proceed faster than the insurgents could think and respond. Any operation to turn people must allow time for them to calculate what they would lose by continuing in the insurgency and what they would gain by defecting.

In Malaya, according to the study we are considering, so intent were the British on penetrating and destroying the organization that they subordinated even military operations to achieving this objective. For example, the British would run military operations in an area not primarily to make contact with the insurgents so that they could be killed but to drive the insurgents into other areas where the British had informants and agents in place who could make contact with the insurgents in preparation for trying to turn some. This caused some friction between the intelligence apparatus and the military. Unaware of the overall purpose of the British effort—or perhaps unconvinced by the plan and thus unconcerned with how a particular operation fit into that purpose— commanding officers felt they were being given futile missions. They may have appeared so from the military viewpoint, in which engaging and destroying enemy forces is paramount, but they were hardly futile in the counterinsurgent effort. Similarly, the principal purpose of interrogations was not to extract information that could be fed into the targeting machine but to win the cooperation of the subject, in hopes that he would agree to return to the insurgent organization under the control of counterinsurgent intelligence officials.[47] The difference between extracting information in order to target, even if this is done by winning willing cooperation, and interrogating to recruit agents to penetrate an organization is the difference between a military or law enforcement approach and an intelligence approach.

It is important to understand the mechanism by which the British aimed to destroy the insurgent organization in Malaya. The aim was not primarily to affect what the insurgents did or were capable of doing but to affect what they thought and felt. The purpose was to convince them that they could not win because the government was inside their organization. Their operations would fail and they could not trust their colleagues. At the same time, the British promised independence for Malaya, isolated the population from the insurgents, and conducted civil-military programs to win and maintain the support of the people. This led to people offering information about the insurgents but also created the sense that the insurgents could achieve their nationalist aspirations peacefully, as part of a process already in motion, that would leave them behind if they stayed in the fight. Another important component of the counterorganization campaign was the ability of the British to interdict food and other supplies to the insurgents. This was possible because of the control (through resettlement and in other ways, such as curfews) that the British had over the population. Hunger as well as despair, the report notes, were the principal means by which the British turned insurgents and ultimately hollowed out the insurgent organization. The British approach in Malaya, in short, aimed to defeat the insurgents by targeting principally their minds, not their bodies. This is an important qualification to John Keegan's argument that bodies are more important in warfare than minds.[48] In irregular warfare, minds may be at least as important as bodies.

The approach followed by the British in Malaya differs from the targeting approaches we have previously considered. All of those are in one way or another either intentionally or in fact attritional approaches to counterinsurgency, in which human intelligence provides support. The approach in Malaya was what we might call a maneuver approach to counterinsurgency, in which human intelligence was the principal fighting arm. The British sought not simply to increase the number of battles or engagements with the insurgents so as to remove them from the fight but to put the insurgents in a position in which they came to see that any engagement was futile. The British did kill insurgents in the course of their campaign—their increasing competence at this was an important tactical support to the overall strategy—and did seek to increase contact with them for this purpose, but the principal target was ultimately, again, not the bodies of insurgents but their minds and their will to fight, which the British sought to affect by undermining the trust their organization depended on. The underlying principle of the campaign in Malaya was that turning an insurgent and directing him back at the organization was, compared with simply killing or capturing him, a way to multiply the force or the effectiveness of the time and effort spent in finding those who were hiding. Insurgents who end up in prison may return to the fight when they leave. Those who turn or surrender, on the other hand, have given up the fight and in giving it up discourage others from continuing or joining in the first place. This is a more comprehensive approach to counterinsurgency.

It is certainly possible to overpraise or misinterpret the British success in Malaya. To some degree, the British were forced into the measures they took. Since Malaya was part of the British Empire, the counterinsurgency was considered a police action. This ultimately came to mean a police intelligence operation, since the police were not institutionally inclined to think that slugging it out with an enemy was the key to success. In addition, the British effort was resource-poor. Not only did this encourage the use of less costly but arguably more effective approaches; admission of limited resources led to the general imperial retrenchment that made it possible, indeed necessary, for the British to offer Malaya independence. To a degree, therefore, British policy coincided with Malay and insurgent wishes, so the argument was really only about the means to achieve that end. Resolving a conflict over means is easier than resolving one over ends. Put another way, in the face of impending independence, the insurgents had a hard time finding ideas that could legitimate continuing the struggle. Circumstances also assisted the British in persuading the insurgents to adopt peaceful means: the insurgents were based in an ethnic minority; they could be cut off from their supporters and resources, such as food; they had no external sanctuary. The insurgents could not increase their resources sufficiently to carry on the struggle, even if they could have legitimated such an effort. In addition, the British were in charge in Malaya and did not have to operate through and with the permission of a local government, whose vested interests made it difficult to pursue effective policies. This set of circumstances is rare, perhaps unique to Malaya, and limits the applicability of the Malayan model and perhaps the praise the British deserve.

One might suppose that the British approach in Malaya worked there but would not work against al Qaeda, its affiliated organizations, and its associated movement, because our current enemies are more fanatically devoted to their cause than were the communists whom the British fought. This may be true, but we should remember that some of the communists stayed in the field and fought on in an increasingly hopeless cause and some members of al Qaeda have turned. Although it is not clear, it may be the case that tribal and religiously based insurgencies are harder to break than those with an ideological base. Kin and religion may touch something deeper in humans than do the words of Lenin or Mao. There is enough variation in humanity, however, that generalizations of this sort are not likely to be of much use. Counterinsurgents, unlike Caesar heading into Britain, should know the character of their opponents before they begin to operate.

However particular the circumstances the British found in Malaya, it remains the case that the kind of counterorganization effort they ran, with intelligence operations as the principal weapon, has appeared in other counterinsurgency or counterterrorism efforts. For example, the Central Intelligence Agency ran such a campaign, on a smaller scale, against the Abu Nidal Organization (ANO). The ANO was the al Qaeda of the 1980s, running operations on several continents, carrying out simultaneous attacks and killing a lot of people. Little was known about the true scope of its operations until a defector revealed details of a commercial network that supported the ANO's operations. The information the defector supplied allowed an analyst to draw together bits and pieces of information and develop a more comprehensive understanding of how the ANO worked. This included identifying or confirming the identity and location of members of the ANO, as well as identifying the location of its commercial enterprises. The State Department provided versions of this information to countries that were wittingly or unwittingly hosting ANO commercial entities and asked that they be shut down. Except for those in East Germany, they were. At the same time, based on information the analyst had put together, the CIA approached a number of ANO cadre and cold-pitched them. The idea was not so much that those pitched would agree to work for the CIA (cold pitches do not have a high success rate, as we noted in Chapter Two), although perhaps some did. The hope was that the pitches could be done in such a way as to suggest that the CIA already had agents inside the organization or that certain individuals in the ANO—their identities suggested by the way the pitch was made—were cooperating with the CIA. The British reportedly used similar techniques against the PIRA.[49]

Another example of a counterorganizational operation about which a good deal is now known is the work of the FBI in the United States against the Ku Klux Klan, the Black Panthers, various communist parties, and other groups. The program, referred to by the FBI as COINTELPRO (an abbreviation of counterintelligence program), used an array of techniques, many of them illegal or extralegal, to disrupt the targeted organizations. For example, the FBI broke into the offices of the organizations or the homes of their members and planted information or forged documents that discredited other members. It pursued the same end through forged letters or anonymous phone calls to members or their friends and associates. It leaked derogatory or fabricated information about the organizations and their members to the press. It published leaflets with false information to disrupt mobilization efforts and recruitment meetings. The bureau also set up fake competing organizations to dilute the efforts of the original organizations. It put pressure on employers and others so that organization members lost jobs and other kinds of support or feared they might. The FBI also used the legal system to harass COINTELPRO's targets, by trumping up charges, conducting heavy-handed surveillance, and using other means. Again, the evidence suggests that these measures were effective.[50]

Finally, it is possible, according to published reports, that the United States and some of its allies are using some of the techniques we have just mentioned, adapted to electronic communications, against al Qaeda and its movement and associated organizations.[51] Deception is a part of these techniques. In that connection, and since deception is traditionally part of human intelligence, particularly counterintelligence, as we saw in Chapter Three, it is interesting to note that the British in Malaya used deception sparingly and only tactically. They did not use it to attack the organization at large, although destroying the organization was their overall objective. For example, as their knowledge of the insurgents increased and as they gained the cooperation of some high-ranking insurgents, the British could have simulated a guerrilla headquarters, at least for a while, and tried to sow dissension or confusion among the insurgents by issuing orders and communiques from this fake headquarters. They judged such efforts too expensive and uncertain, however, and did not undertake them. On the other hand, they did stage engagements between "guerrilla" and government forces using turned guerrillas, who then remained in the area of the engagement seeking help, in hopes of having members of the insurgents' support structure contact them. Those who did then became targets for arrest and recruitment by the counterinsurgent intelligence organization. Also, the British did aim to sow suspicion in the insurgent organization in Malaya, but not through deception. We have noted that the effort to penetrate the insurgent organization was a covert aim, but over time it must have become apparent to the insurgents that the British had agents inside their organization. Indeed, it was to the advantage of the British at some point for the insurgents to know this, since it would have increased pressure on the insurgents by decreasing the trust in their clandestine organization. The report written in 1964 indicates that the British knew this and exploited it.[52] This was not deception, however, since the British did actually have agents inside the insurgent organization, and they did not apparently make an organized or sustained effort to exaggerate their penetration.

It is not clear that it is possible to extract any general lessons about the use of deception in intelligence operations in irregular warfare from the small sample we have considered. In general, however, the claim that deception is complicated and expensive, while yielding unpredictable results, is true. Maintaining an alternative reality requires a lot of energy and attention. Security must be tight, so that the truth does not become known and deflate the deception. Coordination across perhaps multiple government agencies will be necessary as well, for the same reason, as we noted when discussing counterintelligence and the British deception of the Germans in World War II. The high costs to maintain deception explain why intelligence organizations will tend not to engage in it unless they need to. The higher the level at which deception is tried (at the strategic level, for example), the more security and coordination it requires, and the more expensive it becomes. Since deception operations are always unpredictable, especially as they increase in scope and complexity, this increases the chance that there will be little or no return on the investment of time and energy they take. At the strategic level, coordination becomes a particular problem. Such coordination is difficult to attain, especially in a presidential system of government like that of the United States, in which independent departments and agencies carry out government policy. In addition, if the military is in charge of the counterinsurgency campaign, closing with and destroying the enemy will appear, for institutional reasons, to make more sense than trying to fool him. Finally, deception requires a thorough understanding of the opponent. If one possesses such an understanding, uses for it other than deception will suggest themselves, especially since the success of a deception campaign is hard to assess, given that, even if successful in the short term, deception may later have unintended adverse consequences. The ANO tore itself apart in response to the agency's deception, but other more competent organizations have responded by improving their security, making operations against them more difficult. In the long run, then, deception may cause more pain than gain. All in all, deception may be useful in some tactical situations, especially if the enemy does not have the time to assess adequately what is happening, but it might be best to use it only when other means are not available, as was arguably the case in the campaign against the ANO.

However they intend to use intelligence, analysts of irregular warfare typically claim that in order to get it, those engaged in this kind of conflict must at least initially get it from the people. One reason Stonewall Jackson succeeded in the valley campaign, although it was not insurgency as typically conceived, was that he had the support of the locals, who supplied him with valuable intelligence.[53] In order to get it from the people, the people must be disposed to give it. While coercion may pry information out of the people, it is more efficient to have them give it willingly. Besides, neither the United States nor any of its allies will tolerate the kind of coercion once routinely used against the people to force their cooperation. Therefore, the argument goes, the key to success in irregular warfare is not killing insurgents or terrorists but winning the favor of the people. The insurgents operate among the people or by, with, and through them, so the people know about the insurgents. If the government wants to find them, it will need in effect to make the people transparent, so looking through them it can see the insurgents. It will need to win the people to its side and away from the insurgents, thus removing the insurgents' cover and exposing them to the coercive power of the government. To use Michael Mann's terms, the government wins the people through its infrastructure power, so that it may apply its coercive power discriminately and effectively. In this view, the government wins the support of the people by addressing their grievances and responding to their needs. Intelligence helps create the conditions for finding those hiding by first and foremost identifying the people's needs and grievances.[54]

While generally sensible, this approach to irregular warfare overstates the importance of addressing grievances and, especially in a recent influential example, mistakes the role of intelligence and how it should be organized.[55] With regard to grievances, it is important to remember that the more the insurgents make themselves repugnant to the people through excessive violence or unacceptable objectives, the less the government will need to do to win over the people. If the insurgents or terrorists make basic errors in security, which they are likely to do when they are starting out, the government may be able to get inside their organization early on and proceed inductively, from member to member, relying not on information provided by the people but on information from those in the insurgent organization. This will be especially the case for a government with effective surveillance and coercive powers; governments are more likely than insurgents to have such effective powers. In addition, whatever may be the attitudes of the people at large, individuals will have a variety of attitudes and motivations that the traditional practices of human intelligence and law enforcement can work on, without physical coercion, to win their cooperation, without addressing the society's grievances.

Various other conditions may affect the degree to which grievances and needs must be addressed in an irregular warfare campaign, but, generally speaking, we need to remember that the connection between grievances and insurgency or terrorism is not simple. Grievances are common; insurgencies are not. Serious grievances are widespread; enduring insurgencies are not. At most, therefore, grievances are necessary but not sufficient for insurgency. A government may find it easier and less expensive to attack the other conditions (for example, leadership, legitimating ideas) that must be present if grievances are to lead to insurgency than to redress any grievances that exist. A government may be able to get the information it needs, even if it ignores grievances.

Whatever we may conclude about the need to address grievances to succeed against insurgency or terrorism, it seems doubtful that anything like an intelligence effort will be necessary to identify them. A military or political officer who travels around his district and talks to people will learn what is bothering them. If the hostility to the government is too great for such reconnaissance, then grievances (for example, brutal law enforcement, rank exploitation based on racial or ethnic differences, and so forth) are likely to be so evident to anyone who cares to know about them that such reconnaissance would be unnecessary. Generally speaking, learning about grievances will occur, as long as those in command understand it to be a critical task of command, which it is in irregular warfare. In regular warfare, a commander would be derelict if he failed to understand the physical terrain he was operating on. Similarly, in irregular warfare, it should be an inherent task of command, not the function of a separate intelligence staff, to understand the human terrain in which operations take place. Such understanding is inherent in command in irregular warfare not only because it is necessary to direct effective operations but also because of the nature of this warfare. Irregular warfare is ultimately about minds more than bodies. For this reason, in this warfare, the task of collecting information is inseparable from the task of building influence over those from whom one collects the information. In this regard, command in irregular warfare resembles the traditional business of espionage.

Conclusion

In regular warfare, intelligence was never considered decisive because the fog or uncertainty of war dominated. We argued in Chapter Four that developments in information technology have not changed this assessment. In irregular warfare, intelligence has typically been considered more important, perhaps even decisive. There is warrant for this claim, but the strategic value of intelligence in this kind of warfare depends on the degree of moral and political constraint under which irregular warfare campaigns unfold. The higher the moral constraints, the more important is intelligence. The value of intelligence also varies, we argued, depending on the strategy used against insurgents or terrorists. Moreover, in irregular warfare developments in information technology appear to favor the state more than the insurgents because the principal task of the state in this kind of warfare is to increase its intelligence on the insurgents, and information technology aids the state in this regard more than it aids the insurgents in their principal task, which is to increase their resources.[56] Bin Laden's fate is indicative of this result. The U.S. government's information advantage forced him to hide, and his use of information technology was not sufficient to overcome the disadvantages of hiding. The information advantage of the state does not necessarily determine the outcome of an irregular war, of course, because the state must still figure out the best way to use its advantage.

So far, by examining counterintelligence, covert action, and regular and irregular warfare, we have concluded that our current information revolution, although producing a number of changes, has not undermined the power of the state, at least relative to the privacy of individuals or the power of nonstate actors.[57] On balance, the information revolution helps more than it harms the state. Privacy seems more threatened than secrecy and nonstate actors more vulnerable than the state as a consequence of this revolution. In one area, however, to which we now turn, the revolution has not helped the state. The revolution has not overcome the state's inability to know itself.

6   Principals and Agents

In a memoir, a former high ranking Central Intelligence Agency (CIA) operations officer, Milt Bearden, recounts the following incident, which took place in 1991. He had just taken charge of Russian operations, when the head of counterintelligence came to see him. A CIA officer in Europe had reported to his boss that a KGB (Russian intelligence) officer he was meeting and developing had told him that the KGB had an agent inside the CIA. Any report of a penetration of the agency's espionage operations would have been a cause for concern, of course, but this report was especially troubling. First, the Cold War had just ended, but the KGB was still considered by many to be the principal antagonist of the CIA. Second, the agency had lost a number of its agents inside the Soviet Union in the mid to late 1980s. Many had been executed. The cause of those losses was not yet known (they would later be attributed to Aldrich Ames, arrested in 1994, and Robert Hanssen, arrested in 2001), so the report of a KGB penetration might explain perhaps the greatest disaster in the short history of American espionage.

Bearden recounts in his memoir that as he listened to the details of the report about the KGB penetration, he became uneasy. "I knew the case officer who had turned in the report," he wrote. "And I knew he couldn't be trusted. He had a track record that convinced me he played fast and loose with his intelligence reports."[1] The counterintelligence officer who had brought the report to Bearden checked on it by meeting with the case officer who was its source. During the meeting, the counterintelligence officer asked the officer to write down what the KGB officer had told him about the penetration. He then compared this written account with the original one. The second report had many more details than the first one, and they seemed to have been added to answer specific questions that the counterintelligence officer had asked in the meeting. This simple counterintelligence technique had raised further doubts about the officer's report.

Although the report seemed doubtful, it was so important that the agency had to try to resolve the doubts. Bearden tried to do this by meeting with the officer during a trip to overseas posts that he had already planned. When he met the officer, Bearden asked him to tell his story. As he did, Bearden's memoir recounts, he did not maintain eye contact with Bearden. When he finished, Bearden said nothing but looked at the officer "with what [he] hoped was a friendly if expectant look on [his] face." The officer broke "the painful silence" by elaborating on his story, adding details that he had not included in any of his previous reports or retellings.[2] It seemed clear to Bearden that the officer was making it all up.

Still, the agency was not sure whether the report was true or not. Bearden and others determined that they had to talk to the KGB officer who was the ultimate source of the report about the penetration. The agency was able to meet the KGB officer, using one of its own officers who spoke Russian, had served in Moscow, and was considered an exceptionally good human intelligence officer. He arranged the meeting with the KGB officer, who denied telling the CIA officer anything about a penetration of the agency. (Why the agency would trust a KGB officer to tell it whether the KGB had penetrated the agency, when, as Bearden relates, the KGB had already sent its officers to the CIA to report fake penetrations, Bearden does not explain.) By the time the meeting with the KGB officer took place, Bearden reports, the CIA officer who had reported the penetration had been brought back to headquarters and submitted to a hostile questioning. Under this pressure, his story unraveled, although he never admitted to fabricating it in the first place. He subsequently resigned from the agency. Bearden comments that "it was another chapter closed in the search for the truth [about the compromised agents], and it had itself involved nothing but lies."[3]

This episode is remarkable. In a case critical to the integrity of the agency's espionage, it was not able to determine whether its own officer was lying to it. Charged with discovering the truth in far-away places, it was unable to uncover it at the heart of its own business. Bearden tells us during his recounting of this incident that the officer who reported the penetration had a record that raised questions about his truthfulness. Apparently, the report of the penetration was not the first time this officer had made up information. "The CIA," however, "had never been able to catch him in an outright fabrication." On a previous occasion, concerned about his truthfulness, the agency had tried to get another officer to meet with the agent who was reporting to the suspect officer. Something always seemed to prevent this, however. The agent was never met with and the suspect officer continued on his career, presumably fabricating as he went.[4]

In discussing the role of intelligence in warfare, we encountered the traditional view of the limited importance of intelligence. The sunlight of knowledge cannot dissipate the fog of war. Uncertainty dominates. To operate effectively within this uncertainty, some argue, not knowledge of the enemy but self-knowledge is most important. As we have noted, a retired CIA officer has made the same claim for the importance of self-knowledge in the espionage business. The assumption in this view is that it is easier to know oneself than to know the enemy. Modern information technology has caused some to question this assessment. We can now know a good deal more about the enemy than we did before, although it may be that advocates of an information-driven revolution in warfare, regular or irregular, have mistaken locating an enemy for knowing him. In any case, whatever the capacity for knowledge of self and enemy that exists in military affairs, the episode Bearden relates suggests that in espionage, knowledge of self for an institution is particularly hard to come by. As we will argue, this is the case. But as in other matters, the problems of self-knowledge in espionage are only a more difficult case of a general problem in the relationship of knowledge to power. The limits of self-knowledge in intelligence organizations, which one might argue are quintessential organizations of the information age, point to limitations inherent in any use of information.

Principals and Agents

One way to understand the limits of self-knowledge in an organization, and thus the limited power of information, is to use a framework or set of ideas known as principal-agent theory. A principal-agent relationship "is one in which a 'principal' delegates authority to an 'agent' to perform some service for the principal." The "key feature" of an agency relationship "is that once the principal delegates authority" to an agent, the principal has trouble controlling the agent.[5] This problem arises because the principal and the agent have different levels of knowledge and different interests. The person actually doing the work, the agent, is likely to know more about how and whether the work is done than the person, the principal, who hired him to do it. This difference in knowledge or the knowledge asymmetry between the principal and the agent becomes a problem because the principal and the agent have different interests.

The agent has an interest in receiving the most reward for the least work; the principal has an interest in getting the most work, while giving the least reward. These basic conditions—knowledge asymmetry and different interests—apply in all principal-agent relationships. The principal-agent framework explains why problems arise between principals and agents and how principals try to mitigate the problems created by knowledge asymmetry and different interests.

The central problem in the principal-agent relationship is that differences in knowledge and interest between the principal and the agent create the possibility that the agent might shirk rather than work. The agent *works* when he does what the principal wants him to do in a way that is acceptable to the principal. A working agent—say, a roofing contractor—roofs a house with shingles of an agreed upon durability; or a human source collects intelligence on an adversary's weapons programs without violating human rights. The agent *shirks* when he could do what the principal wants him to do but does less than this, because he has an interest in doing as little work as possible, while maximizing his benefit. The agent is able to shirk because the principal has difficulty learning exactly what the agent is doing. A shirking agent uses inferior shingles but charges for the superior ones, while his (the roofer's) workers, paid on an hourly basis, take more breaks than the principal (the roofer) has specified, while he is away from the job meeting with potential clients—that is, his own future principals. Likewise, a shirking intelligence officer makes up a story about a penetration of his organization, rather than doing the harder work of recruiting a reliable source of information.

"Working" and not shirking does not mean blindly following the orders of the principal. The agent can argue with the principal or suggest better ways to do things, but once the principal decides what needs to be done and the agent agrees to do it, "working" becomes doing what the principal has decided should be done. The agent is shirking if she does something else, something less important, or puts an incomplete effort into doing what the principal has decided should be done. One discussion of principal-agent issues, in the context of civil-military relations, gives this summary description of working and shirking.

> The agent is said to work perfectly when it does what it has contracted with the principal to do, how the principal has asked it to, with due diligence and skill, and in such a way as to reinforce the principal's superior role in making the decisions and drawing lines of any delegation. The . . . agent is said to shirk when, whether through laziness, insolence, or preventable incompetence, it deviates from its

agreement with the [principal] in order to pursue different preferences, for instance by not doing what the [principal has] requested, or not in the way the [principal] wanted, or in such a way as to undermine the ability of the [principal] to make future decisions.[6]

In this description, the principal is clothed in legal and even moral authority beyond what would apply in other contractual relationships. The military is supposed to work in such a way as to "reinforce the principal's superior role," for example. This is appropriate for civil-military relations, given the commander-in-chief's constitutional status and the strong presumption in a liberal democracy that military power should be subordinate to civil authority. This sentiment is not entirely lacking in the relationship between the president and America's human intelligence collectors, perhaps because of the service's origins in the quasi-military Office of Strategic Services in World War II.[7] The fundamental point, however, is that "working" is doing what the principal wants done in a way that he wants it done, while "shirking" is not doing what the principal wants done.

Shirking and working may occur not just with individuals but also with organizations. In this case, we need to think of an entire bureaucracy as the agent and the president or Congress and ultimately the American people as the principal.[8] With bureaucracies, the principal-agent problem takes the form of bureaucratic drift, the "tendency for the actions of bureaucratic agencies to 'drift away' from the goals of the politicians trying to control them."[9] Bureaucratic drift occurs for the same reasons as other principal-agent problems: knowledge asymmetry and differences of interest between the principal and the agent. Interests that differ from the principal's move the bureaucracy in a direction different from that preferred by the principal, and the principal's lack of knowledge makes it hard for the principal to get the agency back on her preferred course. At least one former intelligence official has acknowledged drift among America's intelligence agencies.[10] Other examples of this phenomenon include the difficulty of getting the U.S. military to pay attention to irregular warfare and getting the Federal Bureau of Investigation to pay more attention to intelligence and counterterrorism than to normal criminal activity, its major focus in the past.[11]

Why are principal-agent relationships so problematic? Asymmetry of knowledge and different interests may create the possibility that shirking will occur, but is it really so hard to prevent? Often it is not, but in some cases it is. To explain this variation, we can use a schema developed by James Q. Wilson. After examining a large number of bureaucracies, Wilson argued that they could be understood as one of four kinds of organizations based on whether their outputs (their work) and their outcomes (the effect of their work on the world) were observable or not. The less outputs and outcomes are observable, the harder it is to prevent shirking. The less reliable information mangers have about the work their organization does and the outcomes it produces, the less power will they have to prevent shirking.

Wilson called the four organizational types he identified the production agency, the procedural agency, the craft agency, and the coping agency.[12] In a production agency, managers can more or less easily observe both what their employees do and the effect it has. In the Social Security Administration, for example, managers can see the work necessary to get checks to people (output) and they can determine if the checks get there (outcome). In this kind of organization, direct supervision limits shirking, even though those taking applications for social security have an interest in doing as little work as possible and may know more about their work than their supervisors might. In a procedural organization, mangers can more or less easily see what their employees are doing, but they cannot tell very well what effect their work might produce. The peacetime military, according to Wilson, is a good example of a procedural organization. Commanding officers can see training, review doctrine, and develop new equipment (output), but they have no very clear idea if all of this will allow them to win the next war (outcome). Because they can directly oversee output, they can mitigate shirking now, but they cannot be sure that working now will produce success later on. In a craft agency, managers cannot directly supervise the work their subordinates do, but at some point they will know whether it produced the desired outcome. As an example of a craft organization, Wilson offers the wartime military. The fog of battle often prevents commanders from knowing what their subordinates are doing (output), but commanders eventually will know if they took the objective (outcome). How will they know, however, what part of the work they did during peacetime led to that outcome? Finally, in a coping organization, managers have a hard time observing both the work their subordinates do and the effect it has. Wilson offers the police as an example of a coping organization. Police lieutenants have little direct supervision of their patrol officers (output) and cannot say with assurance that what they do produces the effects that the public wants (outcome). Lieutenants, therefore, cannot easily prevent shirking and cannot easily use the outcomes they see (decreasing or increasing crime rates, for ex-

TABLE 1. *Wilson's Four Forms of Organization*

Production	Observable	Observable
SSA	Issuing checks	Received checks
Procedural	Observable	Nonobservable
Military (peace)	Training	Victory or defeat
Craft	Nonobservable	Observable
Military (war)	Tactical action	Victory or defeat
Coping	Nonobservable	Nonobservable
Police	Patrolling	Public order

ample) to assess the work of their subordinates. Is the decreasing frequency of crime in New York City over the past couple of decades the result of what the police are doing (and which part of what they are doing?) or demographics, increased incarceration, or changing economic circumstances? Table 1 summarizes Wilson's schema. It suggests that coping organizations will find it hardest to prevent shirking, because the managers of these organizations have the least information about what is going on inside them and how that affects what occurs outside them. In the case of the military conceived as a procedural organization, the outcome (victory or defeat) is not observable because it has not yet happened and may not happen for years. In the case of the police, conceived as a coping organization, the outcome is not observable because the connection between the work the police do, no matter how much information they collect about what they do, and its outcome (public order) is hard to establish.

Wilson warned his readers to use his schema with caution. He noted it was not a theory and that many organizations did not fit its categories. One might argue, for example, that the highly developed training, simulation, and assessment techniques of the U.S. military, the result largely of applying information technology to military matters, now give the peacetime military a better sense of what to expect in the future than Wilson allowed for.[13] The argument would then be about the degree of certainty with which outcomes could be known, say, in distributing social security payments and thinking about future war. In this light, the distinction would still seem to hold. There is a great deal more uncertainty about who will win the next battle and why than whether a social security check will get to the right recipient. Still, it is important to acknowledge that information technology has made the state more legible to itself and undermined somewhat the distinctions Wilson made. For example, statistically driven policing and better information technology allows police commanders to have a better sense of what their patrol officers are doing. Various sorts of surveillance devices now give military commanders better insight into what both their troops and the enemy are doing during a battle. Yet, judging from accounts of battles in Iraq and Afghanistan, it seems that the fog of battle still prevails to a large degree, especially in larger battles. Furthermore, we might say that surveillance of one's own forces allows a military or police commander to see the outcome in process, as it were, but still leaves in doubt exactly how and why the outcome is coming about and, in the case of the military, how training, doctrine, leadership, and equipment developed in peacetime contributed to it. Even detailed and careful analyses designed to illuminate such questions after the fact remain controversial, as we saw in Chapter Four. As for espionage, perhaps one would argue that in man-hunting there is an observable outcome. Either the man is there or not. But if he is not, was the intelligence necessarily wrong? Without claiming perfection for it, then, it seems we may still use Wilson's schema to help us understand why shirking is harder to prevent in some organizations than in others.

How should we classify espionage organizations? They seem most like coping organizations. For the most part, those conducting espionage operate without direct supervision. One reason it was so hard to prove that the officer Bearden suspected was actually making things up was that no one observed the meetings in which he claimed to get the intelligence that he was reporting. The officer had a much easier time shirking than would a clerk in the Social Security Administration. Not only is the work of espionage a "low-observable," so is the outcome of this work. Even if the officer were accurately reporting what a KGB officer told him about a penetration, how should the intelligence organization evaluate that information? Obviously it must take it seriously, but how will it determine if it is true? After surveying the issues involved in assessing this kind of situation, a seasoned analyst of the intelligence world remarked, "[It] is very hard to know what is sensible," and concluded that it is not possible to know if it is true.[14] This kind of uncertainty also characterizes intelligence reports other than those about penetrations. Bearden indicated in his account that he suspected the officer's report about the penetration because he had come to suspect his previous intelligence reporting. Was it not possible to determine if the officer's reports were accurate? In some cases the report might be corroborated by other intelligence, although this could be planted as part of a deception operation. What a report predicts might come to pass, although that could be coincidence. In many cases, perhaps most, it might not be possible to verify with indisputable facts or events what is reported. If a report turns out not to correspond with what later happens, it does not mean that the report was wrong at the time it was made. If it is difficult to verify the output of intelligence work, it may be even more difficult to evaluate the outcome of the reporting. Even if reporting is accurate, it may not produce any outcome, since policy-makers may always ignore it or act on other information, as we saw in the case of Ryszard Kukliński, the Polish officer who reported on plans to suppress Solidarity. Even if policy-makers pay attention to intelligence, how do we measure its effect on something as complex and even vague as national security? For all of these reasons, managers in espionage agencies are likely to have a hard time both detecting shirking and using outcomes to asses the work of their subordinates. Espionage organizations are coping agencies and have a hard time coping, because all of the uncertainty and complexity they deal with "creates an atmosphere that is hard to cope with."[15]

If it is difficult to supervise and assess what intelligence officers do, we should expect to find shirking in intelligence organizations. Do we? Evidently, since Bearden provided an example. Others have reported finding such problems.[16] How extensive is it? Is it worse than in other coping organizations? Based on the public record it is impossible to say. It is likely to be worse for two reasons. First, as a public entity, an espionage organization is not subject to the discipline of the market, as are some other coping organizations. A private coping organization (Wilson offered a private school as an example) may find it hard to directly supervise the work of its employees (teachers) and may not be able to prove the connection between that work and a desired outcome (a happy life, admission to the best schools), but if its customers stop paying for its products and services, it will know it has problems it needs to fix. (The analogy for an intelligence organization might be when policy-makers stop making time to read its reports.) Second, no public coping organization has the protection that its necessary secrecy affords an espionage organization. For example, secrecy protects espionage agencies from scrutiny by the press or at least the same level of scrutiny that other government agencies receive. An espionage organization and those who work in it, therefore, are likely to find ample opportunity for knowledge asymmetry and different interests to have their full effect. Of course, this cannot be the whole story. If it were, then no espionage agency would perform well, and, as noted in the introduction, this is not the case. American espionage, for example, has had successes as well as failures, and many of its practitioners, not just by their own account, have worked extraordinarily hard in very difficult circumstances. Furthermore, the issue here is not whether there is skill involved in espionage. In Chapter Two we argued there was. Whatever the role of luck in espionage, it is not all a matter of luck. We can see that skill at work in Bearden's account. In the language of Chapter Two, the officer reporting the penetration was suspect in Bearden's view because Bearden's accumulated experience gave him an intuitive sense of the regularities of the espionage business and the officer violated those. He did not present the right cues (such as looking Bearden in the eyes). Skill or competence is not the issue then but, rather, whether the conditions in espionage or coping organizations allow it to flourish or instead encourage shirking. Ultimately, for our purposes, the most important point is the possibility of organizational self-knowledge in intelligence organizations, possibly the paradigmatic organizations of the information age. To address that issue, we need to consider the standard ways of managing principal-agent problems to see how well they might work in espionage. After that, we will consider an alternative approach to principal-agent problems. The point of this analysis is not to suggest ways to reform human intelligence operations but to understand the role of information in an institutional setting as another way of assessing the power of information.

Mitigating Principal-Agent Problems

Principal-agent problems are inevitable in all organizations because efficiency requires that principals delegate responsibility to agents. In intelligence organizations, security also requires delegation. Agents not only have access to information that no officer has, but getting an agent to do something is often more secure than having an intelligence officer do it. In covert action, delegation enhances deniability, for example. Whenever a principal delegates responsibility, however, he must worry about accountability.[17] How does he know that the agent is doing what he is supposed to do? Over time, principals have devised a number of ways to try to make agents accountable. Perhaps the most important way that principals do this is through structuring monetary incentives in the contracts they make with them.[18] To revert to the example used above, the homeowner (principal) might pay the roofer only part of the cost of the work at first, with the rest to be paid when the new roof is on the house and the homeowner has had a chance to inspect it. This contractual arrangement gives the roofer an incentive to finish the work and to do work of the specified quality. While pecuniary incentives may be easier to establish and use in the private rather than in the public sector, where espionage occurs, they still exist. As the Commission on the Intelligence Capabilities of the United States Regarding Weapons of Mass Destruction discovered, American espionage organizations promote (that is, under the current system, increase the pay of) officers in large part based on the number of agents they recruit.[19] Organizations also substitute other goods (such as better assignments) for pecuniary rewards when these rewards are restricted. Financial incentives may apply to organizations as a whole as well. A number of schemes, none a panacea, have been devised to use public sector budgeting to prevent bureaucratic drift.[20] The suggestion of one former espionage officer that "consistent funding" should be a reward for espionage "right practice" is an apparently unintended example of this.[21] For monetary rewards to be effective, however, the principal must know whom to reward. The principal must know which agents are doing what they are supposed to be doing and in the manner they are supposed to be doing it. This brings us back to the issue of knowledge asymmetry and the need to understand in detail why standard methods to mitigate this asymmetry do not work well in espionage.

One of the ways a principal can try to overcome knowledge asymmetry with an agent is to select trustworthy agents. If the agent were completely trustworthy, then the principal would not have to worry about the fact that he does not know exactly what the agent is doing. Vetting agents before contracting with or recruiting them is an important part of the espionage business, and is the point of the recruitment cycle. Lie detectors are also used to vet recruits or agents, but the polygraph is an interrogation aid rather than a good test of trustworthiness. The interrogations may be useful, but—insofar as they are interrogations and not tests of lying—are likely to be inconclusive. Aldrich Ames passed at least one polygraph exam while he worked for the Russians as a spy. At least some of the other agents who were supposed to be working for the CIA but were actually working for the Cuban, East German, and Soviet governments presumably passed such exams as well.[22] At least one American espionage officer expressed dislike for the polygraph, and it is not clear how widely it is used by intelligence services.[23]

It may also be the case that rigorous screening of recruits produces a version of what the literature on principal-agent problems refers to as an adverse selection problem.[24] People who want to cooperate with an intelligence agency for the good of the world or their country or out of some other sense of duty may be discouraged from doing so by what they view as the suspicious and untrusting attitudes of the intelligence agency. This is probably why the former head of MI6 wrote that trust and therefore the human touch were so important in espionage. On the other hand, some scam artists will see suspicion or a hostile reception as the price of business and be both motivated and prepared to deal with it. Therefore, the rigorous screening of possible agents may discourage the good ones but fail to catch the frauds. This suggests again why the traditional business of espionage stressed the need to take the time to assess a potential agent carefully. This would allow a blending of trust and scrutiny. Even over a period of time, this is likely to be a process that cannot guarantee that only the trustworthy will become agents.

Just as problems with espionage sources might be reduced by hiring trustworthy agents, so too principal-agent problems with officers might be reduced by hiring trustworthy, competent people for these positions. A former espionage official has noted, however, that despite its best efforts the CIA has not been able to come up with a profile of a successful recruiter that it can use in selecting its future case officers. More recent comments by former officers do not suggest the agency has solved this problem.[25] The background checks the agency uses will reveal if anyone has a history of illegal or duplicitous behavior and thus, presumably exclude them from the hiring pool. Yet, once someone is hired and comes to understand the knowledge asymmetry and incentives in espionage work, what is to prevent her from shirking? It is also true that once the individual is hired, and comes to understand the opportunities for shirking, he may well also become "one of us" and cease to fall under any suspicion. Something like this seems to have helped Ames accomplish his treachery.[26] In sum, then, while general tests or assessments of trustworthiness are prudent prior to contracting with an agent, they will not do away with knowledge asymmetry and differences of interest and, hence, principal-agent problems.

Once a principal has entered into a relationship with an agent, the principal can try to increase his information about the agent's activities (overcome his knowledge asymmetry with the agent) by monitoring the agent. Monitoring, however, is self-defeating. If the principal follows the agent around, constantly advising him and reviewing what he does, then the principal loses the benefit of the agency relationship. He might as well do the work himself. In the case of espionage, the constraint on monitoring is obviously not just a loss of efficiency. Security considerations prevent direct monitoring. ("Why is that American sitting in our war council?") Electronic or technical monitoring is possible, and may be better now than in the past thanks to the information revolution, but the only reason to have human agents is to get information that cannot be obtained in other ways.[27] If an intelligence agency can get the information it wants electronically to verify what an agent is reporting, why would it need the agent in the first place? It may happen that such monitoring is available in some cases, but often it is likely to be only indirect (observing or measuring an effect that does or does not directly corroborate human reporting) or not available. The reporting of another human agent may be another indirect monitoring device. "Cross-checking" in this fashion has been in use for some time.[28] Of course, the other agent is also subject to agency problems. If both agents are fabricating, then the odds are that the fabrications will not coincide (truth is one; error is many). This will not tell the intelligence organization which report is true, but if the reports contradict, it should alert it to the possibility that one or both are false.

An indirect way to monitor or increase supervisor information over both the espionage officer and the agent would be to review the reporting they produce. This is done by intelligence organizations, but it presents two problems. One we have mentioned before: what is the standard to be applied to judge the reporting? If what the report claimed was going to happen did not happen, was that because the report was false? Also, many intelligence reports do not make claims about what will happen and so cannot be checked against subsequent events in such a straightforward fashion. The second problem with such review systems is that over time they are themselves subject to principal-agent problems or shirking. At one time, MI6, the British intelligence service, had such a review process. Its official historian reports that

> as is so often the case with performance-indicator schemes, there is the risk that measures of performance themselves become targets. So it was with the crit scheme [the name for the service's report grading process]. It was found that stations sometimes pursued "A" crits on easy targets to the detriment of devoting effort to more difficult and more important requirements. . . . Thus a system introduced for the best of intentions did not always produce the desired result.[29]

Intelligence organizations, like all organizations the attainment of whose paramount objectives is hard to assess or measure, are likely to substitute more measurable objectives for more important ones. This substitution, however, simply encourages the organization to produce more of what is less important. Instead of measuring work, such schemes end up encouraging shirking. This is the "numbers game," quantity over quality, referred to in the Report of the

Commission on the Intelligence Capabilities of the United States Regarding Weapons of Mass Destruction.[30]

Another possible way to monitor in espionage would be to have two officers meet with one agent. The theory is that it is more difficult for two people to shirk than for one. In this case, a manager might hope to increase his information on what his subordinates were doing by, in effect, playing one employee against another. Sometimes, it seems, two or more intelligence officers might meet with an agent. Sometimes meetings are recorded. In the case that Bearden reported, the CIA tried to introduce the second officer post facto. For the most part, however, it seems that one officer meets with one agent, especially during the process of recruitment.[31] Efficiency would seem to suggest this arrangement, but security might also be an issue. Two officers meeting with one agent suggests twice the likelihood that a hostile security service would discover the meeting, but that would depend on the operational environment. Even if it were possible to have two officers always meet with one agent, this would not necessarily reduce shirking. In his discussion of police departments, which resemble espionage agencies in certain ways, Wilson reminded his readers that shirking and corruption can spread through an entire department. And police officers work in tandem more than intelligence officers.

A variation on the approach just described is the rotation of principals.[32] The idea again is that it is more difficult for two or more people to be corrupt than for one, even if they are not handling the agent at the same time but consecutively. For this approach to work, the officers meeting with the agents would have to have different incentives. For example, the suspect officer had the most to gain by convincing his superiors that he had come up with useful information about the loss of the agency's Russian agents. The other officer who met with the KGB officer did not have the same incentive. More generally, the officer who recruits an agent has the biggest stake in the agent's validation because the rewards for recruiting—considered the most difficult work a case officer does—are currently higher than for either handling agents or producing intelligence.[33] If the incentives for revealing fraudulent agents were as high as the incentives for recruiting, then serial monitoring or rotation would be a more valuable way of controlling agency problems. However, such a change in incentives might cause two problems. First, the changed incentive might become a perverse incentive, as in the example of the British reporting scheme. It might encourage case officers to spend more time exposing fraud than recruiting. Recruiting is the work upon which espionage depends but also the most difficult work a case office does. If the incentives or rewards for this and easier work were the same, then it is likely that case officers would spend more of their time doing the easier work. Second, raising the incentives for exposing fraud might have a bad effect on comradely feeling inside the espionage organization. This could become a significant problem, since officers already compete for recruitments and promotion.

A final way of dealing with principal-agent problems inside an espionage organization is to increase information available to managers by bringing in a third party to do the monitoring. Inspectors general serve this function in U.S. government bureaucracies,[34] as does the CIA's inspector general with regard to espionage. The idea behind inspectors general is not only that they can learn things about the organizations they inspect (they overcome knowledge asymmetry) but that they are independent and thus do not share the incentives that shape the actions of others in the organization they are monitoring. Generally speaking, there are three problems with third-party monitors such as inspectors general. The first is that the outsider status they require to ensure their independence means they might not readily understand what they are inspecting. This problem pertains particularly to the officer-agent relationship and espionage generally, because of the secrecy that surrounds it. Presumably, an espionage agency's inspector general is cleared to examine espionage, but if he has not done the work, how well will he understand what he is cleared to inspect? Second, inspectors general, like other third-party monitors, act from a distance and after the fact. This means that their monitoring does not directly affect the day-to-day business of an agency. Again, this will especially be the case in espionage because of the far-flung and contingent character of its operations. The limited impact of inspectors general also follows from the third problem with their activity: historically they have for the most part audited programs or investigated alleged wrong doing, rather than evaluated agency activities more broadly.[35] Financial auditing of espionage programs, for example, will not necessarily reveal very much about working or shirking.

The effectiveness of third-party monitoring might improve, for example, if inspectors general evaluated agency activity, a growing trend,[36] rather than simply audited accounts or investigated the specifics of alleged wrongdoing. Over time, such evaluations might affect the daily work of an organization, if followed up by investigations and audits to see if their advice and recommendations had been followed or if their advice and recommendations became congressional mandates that an agency had to follow. Because the full reports on espionage matters of CIA inspectors general are not available, it is not possible to determine how effectively they evaluate espionage programs. For the same reason, it is not possible to determine how effectively other third parties, such as special commissions or the congressional oversight staffs, evaluate these programs.[37] It is possible for third parties to deal with their lack of knowledge by hiring former members of the organization that the third party wants to monitor. At least one CIA inspector general reportedly was a former case officer.[38] Congress also hires former case officers to work on the staffs that oversee U.S. human intelligence operations.[39] But hiring those who have worked for the organizations that the third party wants to monitor may mean hiring people who have prejudices or loyalties that make them less effective monitors.[40] Even if they are knowledgeable and their work is not diminished by prejudices and loyalties, third-party monitors will still be distant from the day-to-day activities of those they monitor. In the case of espionage, they may be able to detect violations of rules, but they will be no better placed than anyone else to make judgments about the quality of the agents that the espionage organization has recruited or the worth of the information they provide. The media and interest groups are also third-party monitors, but because of the secrecy of espionage their monitoring is limited. At best, the media and interest groups serve as the so-called fire alarms that let other official third-party monitors know there might be a problem they need to address.[41] The evidence, such as it is, suggests that third-party monitoring in espionage, like other kinds of monitoring, has limited effectiveness. Two people directly involved in the Ames case have faulted the inspector general's investigation of it.[42]

Because of its pervasive secrecy, which aggravates knowledge asymmetry, espionage presents particular challenges to monitoring the principal-agent relationship in order to prevent shirking. But in any activity where this relationship obtains, monitoring is difficult. The literature on these relationships has identified, therefore, other ways to deal with principal-agent problems. One such way would be to leave in place the kinds of monitoring that occur now but to increase the sanctions for any problems that are discovered.[43] In espionage operations, where direct monitoring is more or less impossible and indirect monitoring difficult, the greatest benefit may come not from putting more effort into doing something that is inherently difficult or impossible, but from punishing the cases of shirking and fraud that are uncovered and extending the punishment from the case officer through his supervisors. This approach would be similar to the tradition in the Navy that gives discretion to the captains of its ships (they were once difficult to communicate with and monitor) but holds them accountable for anything that goes wrong, whether it might reasonably be said to be their fault or not. However, in espionage this approach may be less useful, because it is more difficult in this case than in the case of a ship at sea to determine that something has gone wrong. Ships are big and visible; when they run into something, the damage is evident. More important, on a ship at sea, there are many witnesses. When an officer meets an agent, typically there are none. Wilson points out that in coping organizations, organizations in which both the work and effects are hard to judge, finding fault and applying sanctions will always be controversial. It will thus create situations in which managers will be either criticized by those inside the organization for not backing them up or by those outside the organization for being too lenient. Directors of Central Intelligence have experienced this over the years.[44] For our purposes, it is also important to remember that emphasizing sanctions is tacit admission that information is lacking to do anything else.

The literature on the principal-agent framework identifies another way to deal with agency problems besides monitoring and sanctions: administrative measures.[45] In the context of espionage, such measures are not "merely" administrative but seem best understood as ways of gathering information on agents as part of the process of vetting them. Reviews of such measures in the CIA refer to them as the asset validation system. Evidence exists that these procedures are not uniformly or strictly adhered to. The Commission on the Intelligence Capabilities of the United States Regarding Weapons of Mass Destruction (2005) noted that "as practiced, asset validation can sometimes become an exercise in 'checking the boxes' rather than a serious effort to vet and validate the source."[46] Of an asset validation system set up in 1989, the President's Intelligence Oversight Board reported in 1996:

> We found that the CIA showed an inadequate commitment to the asset validation
> system. Although we understand that validating assets will never take on the
> same cachet as recruiting new ones, we believe it requires greater emphasis in the
> field. Despite repeated statements by DO [Directorate of Operations, which was
> the name at this time for the organization in the CIA that carried out espionage]
> managers on the importance of asset validation, a 1994 survey by the CIA Inspector
> General found that only 9 percent of DO personnel surveyed believed that
> promotion panels rewarded quality work in asset validation.[47]

By eclipsing the validation system, strong incentives to recruit, which are entirely reasonable given the major task of an espionage organization, reinforce knowledge asymmetry. They serve to reduce the information available to managers and ultimately all those who oversee the organization.

A final way to deal with agency problems, emphasized in our information age, is transparency.[48] Entirely useless as a way to monitor secret agencies, the notion of transparency is still worth considering for a moment, if only to highlight how contrary to information age ideas such agencies are. The notion of transparency declares in effect that if principals can see what their agents are doing, if they have information on their activities, they should have more power over them and be better able to control them. For example, one way to understand certain provisions of the Bill of Rights is as means to ensure the transparency of government. The First Amendment establishes a presumption in favor of citizens getting information on their government, while the Fourth Amendment establishes a presumption against the government's getting information on its citizens. If citizens know more about the government than the government knows about them, they should be able to control the government and get it to do what they want it to do, rather than vice versa. However effective transparency may be in other circumstances, all such thinking as we noted is not applicable to espionage organizations, which are supposed to be opaque, as a condition for existing at all.

Principal-agent problems are always difficult to deal with. Knowledge asymmetry and differences of interest are serious difficulties in every agency relationship. They appear to be worse in the case of human intelligence collection, however.[49] In this case, the typical ways of dealing with agency problems do not seem to work at all, or as well as they do in other cases. The need for secrecy increases the information asymmetry in every relationship involved in human intelligence, from the officer and agent to the president and director of national intelligence. This systemic information asymmetry, along with different interests, explains why there is shirking in espionage, and, hence, wasted effort— that is, effort by the agent spent on what is in his interest rather than what is in the principals' interest. The officer reporting a penetration of the CIA in the example that opened this chapter was expending a great deal of time and effort on his fabrications rather than on recruiting useful sources of information. He was also causing his superiors to waste time checking on his reports. The fabrication was easier than developing and recruiting and served his interests just as well, he might have reasoned, since it was so hard to reveal his fabrications. According to Bearden's account, he had been getting away with it for a while, which suggests how difficult it is to establish shirking in espionage. None of the ways we have discussed to detect or control shirking is sufficient. Applied together, they may be thought of as a defense in depth against shirking. Even so, they allow espionage agencies at best merely to cope with a persistent because inherent problem.

An Alternative Approach?

The discussion of shirking so far has emphasized that it occurs because managers have too little information to stop it and because those they manage have incentives to do it. In considering these incentives, the emphasis has been on such things as pay, promotions, and other material encouragements and the fact that these rewards are linked in a quid pro quo fashion to performance indicators that are not necessarily connected to the outcomes that the espionage organization is supposed to achieve. If it is so difficult to increase the information that managers of espionage organizations have on their employees, is it possible to address the other part of the shirking problem and change the incentives of the employees? Is there an alternative motivational scheme that might encourage working rather than shirking? The reason to take up this question, again, is not to outline a thorough and practical reform of espionage but to continue exploring the consequences of organizational self-knowledge and its lack.

To begin to discuss alternative motivations, we should note that intelligence officers, like all bureaucrats, work for rewards that are not simply material. Bureaucrats like their work or believe in it and do it for that reason. They also care about the opinions of their peers and work in order to be well thought of by them. Relationships with superiors are important too. These kinds of motives are evident in Bearden's account. Bearden did not like the counterintelligence officer who came to him with the news of the reported penetration, but he never questioned his commitment to the agency's work. In fact, the root of his dislike of the officer was that the officer disagreed with Bearden on a matter of agency policy and took the disagreement with grim seriousness because he was so committed to the agency's work. The officer sent to meet the reputed KGB source of the information about the penetration was considered one of the best officers of his generation. The incentive to gain and hold that reputation must have been powerful. Research also shows that bureaucratic agents appear to work better for superiors who respect them. Finally, bureaucrats may work because they take pride in being part of an organization that has the respect of the public.[50] For all these reasons, a motivational scheme that does not rely on material and directly quid pro quo incentives has something to build on.

To explore this possibility, consider a reform of the FBI, an organization that used a reward system similar to the CIA's in an operating environment that in a key way resembles the CIA's. During the reign of J. Edgar Hoover, the FBI rewarded its special agents with promotions and pay based on quantifiable activities, such as the number of stolen cars they recovered or the number of arrests they made. Consequently, FBI agents arrested a lot of deserters and recovered a lot of stolen cars. The arrests were fairly easy to make; most often the deserters were at home. To increase their car recoveries, FBI agents went to local police departments, got information on already recovered cars, and then took credit for this work. In short, FBI special agents, for whom, like intelligence officers, there exist "few good measures of what [they] are doing or how much of any given goal they are accomplishing,"[51] were playing the numbers game that intelligence officers are accused of playing. In the case of the FBI, however, there was at least one authoritative measure of the quality of its work. By the 1970s, federal prosecutors were taking only about 40 percent of the FBI's cases, often because the cases were not significant enough given everything else that was going on in their jurisdictions.[52] In other words, the incentives under which FBI agents worked led to shirking, emphasis on easy but unimportant cases (arrests in minor criminal matters), and fraud (falsely claimed recoveries). After Hoover died, the new director, Clarence Kelley, changed the rules and incentives under which FBI agents worked and the way that work was organized and assessed. Among other things, promotions came to depend less on "the numbers" (arrests and recoveries) a special agent accumulated. Greater emphasis was given to the number of cases accepted by prosecutors, a change from quantity (any arrest) to quality (an arrest in a case that a prosecutor deemed important). The change reflected a judgment of worth or quality other than what was good for the FBI special agent (promotion) or the FBI itself (autonomy and budget).[53] Following this reform, the number of interstate car thieves arrested by the FBI declined. Kelley's reforms "'eliminated the charades.' The pressure on agents to keep up a certain caseload for statistical purposes was lessened and accordingly the paperwork and diversion of energy necessary to process 'junk' cases became smaller."[54] These reforms not only made FBI agents responsive to their principals; it also made the entire FBI organization more useful to the U.S. government, less likely to "drift" bureaucratically. Insofar as federal prosecutors prosecuted cases following the policies of the Justice

Department, which policies in turn followed the lead of the president and the laws passed by Congress, the reform that made FBI agents more responsive to prosecutors made the FBI more responsive to its principals, the president and Congress. The reform induced the FBI to work more and shirk less.

The changes that Director Kelley instituted were known as the "Quality over Quantity" program,[55] the exact opposite of what the Commission on the Intelligence Capabilities of the United States Regarding Weapons of Mass Destruction found in the case of U.S. espionage, where it said, in effect, that a quantity over quality program prevailed. One way to introduce a "quality over quantity" reform in espionage would be to reward case officers not for the number of recruitments they make, but for the quality of the intelligence they produce. (A former intelligence officer reports that a review like this takes place during assessments of candidates to senior positions in the CIA.)[56] The result of this change would probably be fewer new recruitments and greater efforts to get better information from those recruits already on the books. The decrease in new recruitments would probably not be a great loss, since one "old hand" has suggested that if every case officer recruited one good source of information on every tour, the analysts would be overwhelmed.[57] The real problem with this approach would be judging the quality of the information that the case officer produced. As we have noted, this is a significant problem. In addition to the problem discussed above (good intelligence going bad through no fault of the source or the officer), there is the issue of who could reliably judge the quality of the intelligence. The so-called consumers of intelligence, the policy-makers and their staffs, have political biases or preferences that would make them suspect as judges of what was good intelligence. Intelligence, after all, unlike the practices of prosecutors, is not supposed to follow policy but lead or at least inform it. Would policy-makers find intelligence that contradicted them valuable? If the collectors understood this issue, would that affect what they collected and reported? Alternatively, analysts might judge the quality of reports. But how reliable are the analysts? Would the problem of bias and shaping collection to fit bias (not necessarily political bias) not appear here as well, at least to some degree? Beyond such questions, it seems likely that it would be hard in many cases to come up with an unambiguous judgment about the quality or importance of an intelligence report.

There is a way to emphasize quality over quantity or working over shirking in espionage besides focusing on the quality of reporting. One interpretation of what happened in the case of the FBI is that once the connection between "numbers" and rewards was reduced or changed, other incentives or motivations came to the fore. These alternative motivations, as noted above, include doing what is right, the intrinsic satisfaction of doing the job, earning the esteem of peers and the respect of a supervisor, or a feeling of reciprocity with the supervisor (that is, if the supervisor treats me well, I will not shirk). Both empirical and experimental evidence suggest that such motivations do affect workers, especially in the absence of strong quantitative or material incentives. Strong quantitative incentives "crowd-out" qualitative motivations.[58] In the case of the FBI, one can speculate that when the numbers-promotion/raise quid pro quo declined in importance, qualitative motivations became more important. Such motivations are intrinsic to the worker (morality, intrinsic satisfaction in a job well done) or partly intrinsic (peer esteem). Intrinsic motivations are more useful in activities that are more difficult to monitor and evaluate. It is difficult to offer extrinsic incentives to workers that accord accurately with valuable contributions to what the agency should be doing when, as in the case of espionage, what is being done is not visible and is inherently hard to judge. If effective, intrinsic motivations would mitigate the monitoring problem at the core of principal-agent relationships because they would amount to self-monitoring by agents. If intrinsic motivation dominated intelligence officers, they would focus on quality, not quantity, on doing good, rather than on doing well, as the "crowding-out" literature puts it,[59] and bureaucratic drift would be less of a problem and monitoring less necessary to correct it. Managers would be no better informed about what their employees were doing, but it would matter less because the employees would be more likely to do good. In discussing irregular warfare, we noted that more information makes it easier to act morally (killing only combatants). In the espionage business, more morality would make information on the activities of intelligence officers less important.

The crowding-out phenomenon suggests that to decrease shirking and fraud among officers and their agents, intelligence agencies should move from the current motivational model (largely a money for quantity of recruitment/information quid quo pro) to a new one in which intrinsic motivations dominate. When a principal cannot effectively monitor, his task is to create the environment in which self-monitoring will flourish. Creating the right environment is critical because the desire for the esteem of one's peers, for example, is not sufficient. If one desires the esteem of one's peers and one's peers esteem rule bending, if not breaking, and an ability to connive and get their way, then one will have to act as they act to earn their esteem. If, on the other hand, one's peers esteem rule compliance and selfless service, then peer esteem will come from respecting rules and acting selflessly. Norms of behavior in an organization, organizational culture, are critical to the success of self-monitoring. "FBI agents behaved as if J. Edgar Hoover were looking over their shoulders in part because the agents believed that was the right way to behave."[60] And they believed that it was the right way to behave because everything about J. Edgar Hoover's FBI—standards of dress and demeanor, the crimes its special agents investigated and the way they investigated them, the punishments meted out for misbehavior—told them that that was how they were supposed to act. Hoover created these organizational norms in transforming the old Justice Department Bureau of Investigation, which had become a disgrace and a byword for partisan and illegal activities, into the new and respected Federal Bureau of Investigation.[61] As we have noted, the new FBI, Hoover's FBI, later developed problems with shirking, but it overcame these problems by changing incentives and building on standards of integrity and professional performance instilled by Hoover.

Acknowledging that there is already more to both officer and agent motivation than extrinsic monetary incentives, the argument offered here amounts to a call for emphasizing intrinsic incentives. Increasing self-monitoring in this way would require, as we have just argued, an organizational culture that prized rule compliance and self-sacrifice, so that individuals would come to emulate that behavior. It is hard to make any general judgment, of course, but while there is certainly evidence of self-sacrifice among the CIA's employees, there is also evidence that rule compliance does not necessarily always prevail.[62] This may not be a surprise in an espionage organization, since in carrying out espionage overseas its officers violate the laws of other countries and need to think and act "outside the box" in order to succeed. In this latter way, it is like the old military special operations forces that had reputations for roguery that were matters of pride to the special operators and of concern to their superiors in the conventional armed forces.[63] Special Operations Forces (SOF) have moved beyond that now, for the most part, and pride themselves on being quiet professionals. This transformation has occurred in part because of the greater integration of SOF with the conventional military and its professional ethos. That ethos rests on a moral code enforced by military law and tradition. For example, adultery is a punishable offense in the military, as it no longer is in society at large. The military reasons that if someone cannot remain faithful to their marriage vows, there is reason to suspect that they will not remain faithful to their other duties. Whatever this reasoning may lack as a logical argument, it aims for a certain moral seriousness that is appropriate for personnel in an organization with such power. It would be no less important in an espionage organization, which may have less power but is harder to supervise.

One might plausibly object to the analogy drawn here between espionage organizations and the military. Militaries are not supposed to act outside the law at home or abroad. Nor is espionage really like law enforcement, in which, presumably, respect for the law without exception is important. Unlike military and law enforcement officers, intelligence officers must do things that are illegal and even immoral from the conventional perspective. They cannot be rule-bound goody two-shoes. In response, one would point out that rule compliance is not the same thing as saintliness. It depends on the rules. Enhanced interrogation, for example, was once within the rules. However inexact these analogies, the point remains that in a coping organization like the CIA, an important way to cope is to encourage high moral standards, compliance with which makes up for limited oversight by principals—supervisors, the president, Congress, and, ultimately, the American people. One former high ranking CIA official, without acknowledging the knowledge asymmetry inherent in espionage organizations, has emphasized the importance of morality for those who work in them. He quoted with approval a former CIA general counsel who said that the agency must employ "that extraordinary rare individual who has the talent to deal in the deceptive and manipulative and keep his or her moral ballast."[64] Neither the former officer nor general counsel commented, however, on the effect applying this standard might have on the number of people who work in espionage organizations.

What we might call the trade-off in espionage organizations between information and morality points to a more fundamental issue too little remarked on in discussions of the information age and indeed in discussions of the information revolution that we may say began in the early seventeenth century in the writings of Francis Bacon. Prior to that revolution, an acceptance of the limits of human information, knowledge, and wisdom was also an acceptance of the power of chance in human life. Accepting that "chance plays so large a role in the outcome of our actions," men of superior virtue, dimly figured in the rare individuals the general counsel spoke of, have always believed "in a standard of goodness or badness beyond results."[65] This view was "crowded out" as the influence of the early modern information revolution spread and deepened.

In appealing to such a standard in our discussion of espionage organizations, we conclude that these paradigmatic organizations of our information age can be saved only by an understanding of the relation of knowledge, chance, and morality characteristic of an older information age.

Conclusion

Our discussion of the role of intelligence in warfare led to the conclusion that organizational self-knowledge was of great importance. Our discussion of espionage as an organized activity suggests that there are limits to self-knowledge. Certainly, the limits to self-knowledge are less severe in military than in espionage organizations. For one thing, the former are more open than the latter. For another, combat provides a public test of the quality of a military force. Yet, if intelligence organizations and their espionage components are the paradigmatic organizations of the information age, as military organizations may have been in the industrial age, we should conclude that in recognizing the limits of self-knowledge in espionage organizations we are again recognizing the limits to the power of information. This in turn leads to the paradox that the unavoidable desire for information manifest in the existence of intelligence organizations creates power that knowledge may not be able to control.

Conclusion

This study has examined espionage, and intelligence more generally, as a way of examining the fate of state power in the information age. We have concluded that even in the current age of transparency, secrecy will survive. The information revolution may change the cost/benefit analysis of clandestine and covert action, making some traditional espionage activities obsolete or more difficult, but it does not put an end to espionage or covert action. On the contrary, the revolution appears to have opened up new possibilities for these venerable practices, both with regard to what is done and which agencies of government do it. These possibilities are appearing as the need for espionage and covert action to counter newly empowered nonstate actors increases. While these actors are empowered by the information revolution, states seem to be gaining more from it. This is evident from our examination of irregular warfare. In this case, we argued, advances in information technology so far appear to favor the state more than its opponents, because the principal task of the state in this kind of warfare is to increase its intelligence on the insurgents, and information technology aids the state in this regard more than it aids the insurgents in their principal task, which is to increase their resources. Bin Laden's fate is indicative of this result. In regular warfare, we argued that uncertainty remains a dominant factor. Information superiority over an enemy does not provide information superiority over chance. Neither does it reduce the importance of skill in the conduct of battle. It may even increase it. We noted in our examination of espionage organizations that information does not even dominate here. Institutional self-knowledge in this case remains elusive, as does effective net-assessment in military matters. Finally, we argued that acknowledging the limitations of our knowledge heightens the role of chance and recalls to us the importance of "a standard of goodness or badness beyond results."

In developing the framework for our assessment, we argued that the current information age is part of an information or knowledge revolution begun in early modern Europe that ultimately produced what Sherman Kent referred to as the liberal tradition. That tradition included what we called a modern understanding of intelligence, within which espionage, essentially an ancient practice, sat uneasily. Modern intelligence shared with the liberal tradition aspirations for a better, more peaceful, and prosperous world that are foreign to espionage. The liberal tradition therefore tended to deemphasize espionage, considering it a concession to the dark forces in human life that the spread of enlightenment would dissipate. Espionage was destined in this view to become redundant. An implication of the argument presented here, however, is that if any aspect of institutionalized intelligence has become redundant, it is not espionage, but analysis, the heart of intelligence, according to Kent, that has become so.

In truth, the redundancy results not from forces unleashed by the current information age. It results, rather, from the failure of social science, upon which modern intelligence relies, to live up to Kent's hopes for it. Kent's emphasis on analysis at the expense of espionage has little or no warrant. Estimative analysis—analysis designed to foretell the future with a high degree of reliability—is the critical test of the ability to overcome the power of chance in human life and thus the critical test for the claims of modern intelligence. Analysis fails this test. So, we noted, may the intuition or judgment of the statesman. But, or so we argued, when not trying to predict the future, when determining rather what to do in a given situation, the judgment of the statesman is likely to be superior to the judgment of the analyst. Analysts therefore cannot replace or substitute for the seasoned statesman. Espionage remains important because it provides some of the information that the statesman needs to use power well. Kent argued that all intelligence, including collection, relies on analysis, and that is true, as we have seen. But there are different kinds of analysis. We have argued, for example, that it is possible to think of those who practice espionage as capable of reliable expert intuitive judgment, while it is difficult to grant that reliability to the judgment of intelligence analysts, especially those involved in intelligence estimates of the future. All humans, whether analysts, collectors, or statesmen, are subject to the same mistaken ways of thinking. Social science methodology may help avoid such mistakes.[1] All should avail themselves of its help, therefore. But the effectiveness of social science methodology does not alter the conclusion that judgment in espionage is more reliable than judgment in analysis because ultimately there are more regularities in the business of espionage than in the business of predicting or estimating the future and better opportunities to understand them. The process of developing a human agent creates the chance to form hypotheses about how a possible agent will act and to test them. Developing an agent for recruitment thus creates reliable intuitive judgment about the likelihood of a successful and productive recruitment. There is no similar possibility in the process of estimating future events.

One result of the argument presented here, then, is the suggestion that we could do with a lot less estimative intelligence analysis. If that suggestion were followed, it would leave an intelligence capability more focused on espionage and other means of collection, altered as we have argued they have been and will be by the current information revolution. In addition, they should be altered by greater recognition than there has apparently been so far of the consequences for our information gathering of the fact that the growing power of the state is likely to compel its nonstate enemies to adopt low-tech approaches, as we argued in Chapter Five was already happening. History is a help in this regard. During the nineteenth century, when espionage was relatively less important in Europe, Europeans were deeply involved outside of Europe. This led them to develop information gathering techniques effective against low-tech or no-tech opponents. These differed from the traditional practices of espionage.[2] It would be difficult in our more bureaucratic age to duplicate these techniques, perhaps even to find the people able and willing to apply them. If we could recover the practice of such techniques, they would be focused on what is essentially open information, and therefore would not replace traditional espionage but rather work with it.[3]

All such suggestions about intelligence gathering assume that this activity can be improved. Improving espionage will be difficult for the reasons we discussed in Chapter Six. Related to these are additional difficulties noted by the most astute analyst of the problems surrounding the intelligence assessment of Saddam Hussein's weapons program, the kind of critical issue we are likely to face in the future. Based on the results of espionage in this case, he has written of espionage generally that "the quality of information is more important than its quantity"; genuine sources of information on important things in closed societies are likely to be few; and vetting "will remain more an art than a science," producing both false positives and false negatives. And he notes, the failures of human intelligence in the case of Iraq were not just American. "No national service did much better than the others in cultivating human sources or separating truth from fiction." In offering this sobering account of espionage, the analyst notes that in the face of these failures, there was a call for more human intelligence. This calls "to mind," he continues, "Woody Allen's famous line, 'Such bad food, and small portions, too.'"[4]

Calling for more espionage in the face of its failure in the Iraq weapons case suggests a reliance on espionage as a kind of magic charm to deal with the uncertainty of human life. In England shortly after Bacon lived, and as Colbert augmented the power of the French state through his mastery of information, "knowledge was [seen as] power, so secret knowledge was seen as a source of secret power."[5] The belief in secret power seems to have persisted. It is difficult to read about William Donovan's insistence on the effectiveness of operations behind enemy lines, despite all the evidence to the contrary, for example, and not believe he was in the grip of some belief that intelligence had occult power. Nor can one read about later hopes for the activities Donovan promoted and espionage generally without feeling that the belief may have outlived Wild Bill. Whatever may be true of those who practice espionage, it seems that those who command it may be as guilty of wishful thinking as all humans are.

We have argued that espionage is not a secret power. More than luck, though less than science, it is art, as the analyst of the Iraq intelligence failure and a former practitioner claim.[6] Furthermore, we have suggested that this art or skill is similar to the art of the general, as displayed, for example, by Caesar as he surveyed his legions in combat, and to the art of the statesman. In speaking of the art of the statesman, we might, for better reasons than word play, recall Churchill's light-hearted essay, "Painting as a Pastime."[7] Churchill compared painting to battle. It required an "all-embracing view," attentiveness to detail, and acknowledgement of luck. "The mind's eye," an expression similar to one that Aristotle used in his discussion of prudence,[8] finds the patterns and regularities amid the detail and composes the whole scene, weighing the relative importance and proper place of every element. The skill depicted by Churchill is not in predicting the future but in assessing, based on attentiveness and hard-won experience, what is immediately before one. It is the same skill, we have suggested, that is present at each step, from the intelligence officer confronting an agent, to the general commanding thousands, to the statesman leading multitudes. The difference with each step is a correspondingly larger sense implied in doing the right thing, weighing the proper place of each thing, recognizing danger and opportunity, harm and benefit. If the successful conduct of espionage requires moral ballast in its practitioners, all the more so should we assume that the art of the statesman will require virtue to the fullest degree. How else would one be able to determine what was truly dangerous and truly beneficial? In light of our examination of the information revolution and the power of the state, a field for the exercise of this virtue opens up. Both clandestine nonstate actors and private citizens seem more at risk from the power of information than does the state. Composing how to harm the former, while protecting the latter, will require careful judgment, the sort of political wisdom that both espionage and information technology may only assist.

Appendices

Appendix A

Surprise and the Importance of an Information Advantage

A surprise attack occurs because the attacker knows something the defender does not: when and where the attack will occur. A surprise attack occurs, therefore, only when one side has an information advantage over the other. What is this information advantage worth? Michael Handel downplayed its significance, noting that those who carry out surprise attacks tend to lose, at least in the long run.[1] Table A1 provides some data on the outcomes of surprise attacks. Some of the attacks started wars and others occurred in the midst of them. One could dispute the designation of the attacks as a surprise and, in some cases, the assessment of whether they succeeded or failed. This is particularly true when assessing their long-term effect. Most of these examples are drawn from standard works on surprise attack, which offer analysis of what constitutes surprise and the connection between surprise and success or failure.[2]

These historical cases suggest that surprise attack—evidence of information superiority on the part of the attacker—produces an advantage initially but not in the long term. As the literature on surprise attack suggests, this result occurs because attackers often resort to surprise because they are weaker. In the long term, it appears, this weakness most often proves fatal, even after initial success.

What do these outcomes suggest? They substantiate Handel's claim that those who carry out surprise attacks tend to lose in the long term but do not tell us much about the importance of information versus the other factors that affect the outcome of battles or wars. Often in the cases listed in Table A1, the side that had information superiority (successful surprise) also had material superiority, often as a consequence of attacking an unprepared or weak defense. More useful as a test of the value of information superiority are the special operations discussed in Chapter Four, since in those cases the attacking force was not superior in numbers or other material factors. In these cases, as noted in the chapter, surprise (information superiority) was not always essential for success.

TABLE A1. *Outcomes of Surprise Attacks*

		Immediate outcome	Long-term outcome
1776	Battle of Trenton	S	S
1904	Battle of Port Arthur	S	S
1940	The Battle of France	S	F
1941	The Japanese attack on Pearl Harbor	S	F
1941	German attack on Soviet Union in 1941	S	F
1944	German attack in the Ardennes (Battle of the Bulge)	S	F
1950	North Korean attack on South Korea	S	F
1950	Chinese intervention in Korean War	S	F
1956	Sinai campaign	S	S
1967	The Six Day War	S	S
1973	Egyptian attack on Israel	S	F
1980	Iraq attack on Iran	S	F
1982	Falklands War	S	F
1990	Iraq attack on Kuwait	S	F
2001	September 11 attacks	S	F
TOTALS			
	Success	15	4
	Failures	0	11

Appendix B

Information and the Power
of Nonstate Actors

It is remarkable how often those claiming that the information age has empowered nonstate actors fail to provide any evidence for this claim. Bruce Hoffman, for example, touts the media savvy and effectiveness of terrorist groups that exploit the new media of the information age but does not offer any evidence that their savvy actually is effective.[1] The groups that he cited as examples of information age prowess either subsequently failed (the Tamil Tigers, the Zapatistas) or suffer from low or declining approval ratings (Hamas, Hizbollah, al Qaeda).[2] Perhaps one might argue that without their media prowess, these groups would have even lower ratings. Still, some presentation and discussion of evidence would be useful. If it is true, as analysts claim,[3] that the information age has given significant advantages to nonstate actors because it improves their ability to mobilize support, recruit, raise money, gather intelligence, communicate, plan, and influence directly state populations and leaders, then nonstate actors should succeed more often against states during the information age than before it. What does the data show?

Nonstate actors have never fared well in their confrontations with states. In his modestly titled "epic history of guerrilla warfare," Max Boot reports that prior to 1945, guerrillas won only 20 percent of the time. Post 1945, they won only 39 percent of the time.[4] In their study of 648 terrorist groups that existed between 1968 and 2006, Seth Jones and Martin Libicki reported that only in 10 percent of cases did terrorism end because the terrorists achieved their goals. (Forty-three percent of terrorist organizations end their activities by adopting nonviolent political means. These cases cannot be counted as victories for nonstate violence, since they are instances in which violence was given up.) Jones and Libicki also note that if a terrorist organization becomes part of an insurgency, it achieves victory about 25 percent of the time, a result similar to the one that Boot found.[5] Audrey Cronin reports that only 6.4 percent of the 457 terrorist organizations she examined active since 1968 achieved their strategic goals in full or substantially.[6] (Cronin also reports that negotiations do not increase the likelihood of a terrorist group fully achieving its objectives, although negotiations do increase the likelihood of a terrorist group partially achieving its objectives.)[7]

Has the information age given nonstate actors the means to improve on their dismal record against states? To answer this question, we need to determine two things: when did the information age start, and what is success or failure in nonstate campaigns against states? The first of these tasks is easier than the second. We may say that the information age started in 1990 or 1991, when the worldwide web first became accessible. Shortly after this, nonstate actors started to take advantage of its possibilities, according to some analysts.[8] If we are going to assess the effect of the information age, therefore, we should look at conflicts from 1990 to the present. How should we determine success and failure in these conflicts? Some might argue that achieving objectives is too high a standard. The fact that nonstate actors can organize and fight represents an achievement in itself. But what do we mean by organize and fight? If Subcomandante Marcos of the Zapatistas has a website or e-mails journalists, is that organizing to fight? The subcommandante's activities may well indicate that the information age has lowered the entry costs to engaging the state and thus increased the number of nonstate actors who do so. Engaging the state, however, is not the same as challenging or threatening it. It is only the latter that would show some significant increase or transfer of power to nonstate actors. To prove that the information age increases the power of nonstate actors to challenge the state, one would need to show that it gives nonstate actors greater power than they had to achieve their objectives, when the state opposes their doing so. Achieving objectives, then, must be a criterion of success. In addition, the nonstate actors should have achieved these objectives without state support, if we are to have a measure of how the information age has empowered them. Of course, state support and success come in degrees, which further complicates the assessment.

With these qualifications in mind, we may turn to the data. Boot lists sixty-seven guerrilla conflicts from 1990 to 2012. Most of these he judged to be ongoing (53 percent). Of those that had ended, he determined that 19 percent ended with a guerrilla victory, 14 percent in an incumbent victory, and 11 percent in a draw. From his list of guerrilla wins, we should deduct the case of the military junta in Guinea Bissau. When the junta took power, it was not a nonstate actor as customarily understood, but a part of the state. Arguably, we should also remove from the win column perhaps as many as six cases in which the guerrillas had significant state support (for example, the Northern Alliance against the Taliban). This would reduce the percentage of guerrilla wins in the information age to 8 percent. At the same time, a number of cases that Boot lists as ongoing are unlikely to result in the guerrillas achieving any of their objectives (for example, the Continuity Irish Republican Army and the Chechen insurgents). Perhaps eight of the cases listed as ongoing could be moved to the incumbent or government column. This would mean that government "wins" would amount to 26 percent. The ratio of government to guerrilla wins (3 to 1) in the information age would then be about the ratio that Boot found in the larger post-1945 sample. It does not show a shift of power to nonstate actors in the information age.

Of the 648 cases in Jones's and Libicki's data set, 307, or 47 percent, began in 1990 or later. In only 0.02 percent of these cases did Jones and Libicki find that the terrorists won. In 15 percent of the post-1990 cases, Jones and Libicki found that the terrorism campaign ended through the adoption of nonviolent political means. The rest of the cases are ongoing. Again, these figures do not show any surge of power, or at least power to achieve their objectives, to nonstate groups in the information age. If anything, they suggest the contrary, as did our analysis in Chapter Five of the effect of information technology on the power of states and nonstate actors. The pre- and post-1990 data does show something interesting, however. Forty-seven percent of Jones's and Libicki's cases occurred in the sixteen years between 1990 and 2006, the year their data ends. Fifty-three percent occurred in the twenty-two years between 1968, when their data starts, and 1990. On average fifteen terrorist groups started each year between 1968 and 1990, while nineteen started each year on average between 1990 and 2006. That is a 26 percent difference during what we are calling the information age. Perhaps this is evidence of the previously mentioned lower entry costs for nonstate organizations, which results in more of them. This is something analysts have claimed.[9] Yet, as also previously mentioned, lower entry costs do not mean greater success.

It is true, as those who compiled it note, that the data we have been analyzing and its categorization are questionable. But if we do not use this data to discuss nonstate actors, what data do we use? What data beside anecdote do those offer who claim that the information age is empowering nonstate actors in ways that allow them to challenge states as never before? In conclusion, we might note that it should not surprise us that nonstate actors seldom achieve their objectives. They pursue coercive strategies.[10] Coercion is harder than deterrence. They want to coerce us; we want to deter them. Nonstate actors have the harder job and less to do it with.

Notes

Introduction

1. Eric Schmidt and Jared Cohen, *The New Digital Age: Reshaping the Future of People, Nations and Business* (New York: Alfred A. Knopf, 2013); Luciano Floridi, *Information: A Very Short Introduction* (New York: Oxford University Press, 2010), 3–18.

2. Michael E. Hobart and Zachary S. Schiffman, *Information Ages: Literacy, Numeracy, and the Computer Revolution* (Baltimore, MD: Johns Hopkins University Press, 1998).

3. "Has the Ideas Machine Broken Down?" *Economist*, January 12, 2013.

4. "Intelligence Agencies and the Cyber World," *Strategic Survey* 112, 1 (2012): 33.

5. Elizabeth Williamson, "Buying 'Political Intelligence' Can Pay off Big for Wall Street," *Wall Street Journal*, January 18, 2013, A1.

6. Gregory F. Treverton, *Intelligence for an Age of Terror* (Cambridge: Cambridge University Press, 2009), is representative.

7. Amy Zegart, *Spying Blind: The CIA, the FBI, and the Origins of 9/11* (Princeton: Princeton University Press, 2007) 5, 67, 75, 77, 80, 90.

8. Richard Betts, *Enemies of Intelligence: Knowledge and Power in American National Security* (New York: Columbia University Press, 2009); Robert L. Jervis, *Why Intelligence Fails: Lessons from the Iranian Revolution and the Iraq War* (Ithaca, NY: Cornell University Press, 2011).

9. Priya Satia, *Spies in Arabia: The Great War and the Cultural Foundations of Britain's Covert Empire in the Middle East* (New York: Oxford University Press, 2008), 11.

Chapter 1

1. Jacob Soll, *The Information Minister: Jean-Baptiste Colbert's Secret State Intelligence System* (Ann Arbor: University of Michigan Press, 2009), 140–52.

2. William Blackstone, *Commentaries on the Laws of England,* quoted in John Brewer, *The Sinews of Power: War, Money and the English State, 1688–1783* (New York: Alfred A. Knopf, 1989), 113. This paragraph is based on Brewer's account.

3. Caesar, *Gallic Wars*, Book 4, sections 20–21; 24–26.

4. N. J. E. Austin and N. B. Rankov, *Exploratio: Military and Political Intelligence in the Roman World from the Second Punic War to the Battle of Adrianople* (New York: Routledge, 1998), 13, 182–84.

5. Christian Tripodi, "Peacemaking through Bribes or Cultural Empathy: The Political Officer and Britain's Strategy towards the North-West Frontier, 1901–1945," *Journal of Strategic Studies* 31, 1 (February 2008): 138–39.

6. Keith Jeffrey, *MI6: The History of the Secret Intelligence Service, 1909–1949* (London: Bloomsbury, 2010), 467–68.

7. Janet Morgan, *The Secrets of Rue St. Roch: Hope and Heroism Behind Enemy Lines in the First World War* (New York: Penguin Books, 2005).

8. Mark Kramer, "The Kukliński Files and the Polish Crisis of 1980–1981: An Analysis of the Newly Released CIA Documents on Ryszard Kukliński," Cold War International History Project, Working Paper 59 (Washington, DC: Cold War International History Project, March 2009); Kramer, "A Look Back . . . A Cold War Hero: Colonel Ryszard Kukliński," www.cia.gov/news-information/featured-story-archive/2010-featured-story-archive/colonel-ryszard-kuklinski.html; Benjamin B. Fischer, "The Vilification and Vindication of Colonel Kukliński," www.cia.gov/library/center-for-the-study-of-intelligence/kent csi/vol44no3/html/v44i3a03 htm#fnr41; Benjamin Weiser, *A Secret Life: The Polish Officer, His Covert Mission, and the Price He Paid to Save His Country* (New York: Public Affairs, 2005).

9. Mark Kramer, "US Intelligence Performance and US Policy during the Polish Crisis of 1980–81: Revelations from the Kukliński Files," *Intelligence and National Security* 26, 2–3 (April–June 2011): 325–27.

10. Richard K. Betts, *Enemies of Intelligence: Knowledge and Power in American National Security* (New York: Columbia University Press, 2009), 19–52; John Diamond, *The CIA and the Culture of Failure: U.S. Intelligence from the End of the Cold War to the Invasion of Iraq* (Stanford: Stanford University Press, 2008).

11. Arther Ferrill, "Roman Military Intelligence," in *Go Spy the Land: Military Intelligence in History*, ed. Keith Neilson and B. J. C. McKercher (Westport, CT: Praeger, 1992), 24.

12. Numbers 13:1–20; Joshua 2:1–2.

13. Ira Meistrich, "War's Cradle," *MHQ: The Quarterly Journal of Military History* 17, 3 (Spring 2005): 84–93; Lawrence H. Keeley, *War before Civilization: The Myth of the Peaceful Savage* (New York: Oxford University Press, 1996); Chester G. Starr, *Political Intelligence in Classical Greece* (Leiden: E. J. Brill, 1974), 8–28; Arther Ferrill, *The Origins of War: From the Stone Age to Alexander the Great* (Boulder, CO: Westview Press, 1991), 182.

14. Thucydides, *The Peloponnesian War*, 1.5, 1.8.

15. Margaret Jacobs, *Scientific Culture and the Making of the Industrial West* (New York: Oxford University Press, 1997), 191.

16. For example, Martha Crenshaw, "Theories of Terrorism: Instrumental and Organizational Approaches," in *Inside Terrorist Organizations*, ed. David C. Rapoport (New York: Columbia University Press, 1988), 15.

17. James Madison, *The Federalist 51*, edited, with an introduction and notes, by Jacob Cooke (Middletown, CT: Wesleyan University Press, 1961), 349.

18. Rose Mary Sheldon, *Intelligence Activities in Ancient Rome: Trust in the Gods, but Verify* (New York: Frank Cass, 2005), 14.

19. Sun Tzu, *The Art of War*, translated and with an introduction by Samuel Griffith (New York: Oxford University Press, 1963), 63, 149, 66, 101, 106, 137, 138, 145, 148, 149.

20. Plato, *Laws*, 625e–26a, cited by Starr, *Political Intelligence in Classical Greece*, 2. The translation quoted here is Thomas Pangle's, *The Laws of Plato, Translated, with Notes and an Interpretive Essay* (New York: Basic Books, 1980), 4.

21. Starr, *Political Intelligence in Classical Greece,* 2–3, 15.

22. For realism, see for example, John J. Mearsheimer, *The Tragedy of Great Power Politics* (New York: W. W. Norton and Company, 2001), 35–37, 46–48, 408–9, n. 35.

23. Alexander Orlov, *Handbook of Intelligence and Guerrilla Warfare* (Ann Arbor: University of Michigan Press, 1963), 5, 9, 10, 12–13.

24. Sherman Kent, *Strategic Intelligence for American World Policy* (Princeton: Princeton University Press, 1966, with a new introduction; 1949).

25. Philip E. Tetlock, *Expert Political Judgment: How Good Is It? How Can We Know?* (Princeton: Princeton University Press, 2005), 17 n. 29, 143 n. 22, 238 n. 22.

26. Kent, *Strategic Intelligence for American World Policy*, 177.

27. Kent, *Strategic Intelligence for American World Policy*, 7.

28. Kent, *Strategic Intelligence for American World Policy*, 3.

29. Kent, *Strategic Intelligence for American World Policy*, 156.

30. Kent presents the steps on pages 157–58 and discusses them on pages 159–79.

31. Kent, *Strategic Intelligence for American World Policy*, viii, xxi–xxii, 152. In discussing the kinds of things intelligence needs to find out, Kent mentions secrets only in military matters, 32–37.

32. Kent, *Strategic Intelligence for American World Policy*, 155.

33. Kent, *Strategic Intelligence for American World Policy*, 155.

34. Luciano Floridi, *Information: A Very Short Introduction* (New York: Oxford University Press, 2010), 22–25.

35. Kent, *Strategic Intelligence for American World Policy*, 157–58, 174.

36. Robert L. Jervis, *Why Intelligence Fails: Lessons from the Iranian Revolution and the Iraq War* (Ithaca, NY: Cornell University Press, 2010), 130–31.

37. Kent, *Strategic Intelligence for American World Policy*, 160.

38. Kent, *Strategic Intelligence for American World Policy*, 174, 160–61. Emphasis not in original.

39.   Kent, *Strategic Intelligence for American World Policy*, 206.

40.   Kent, *Strategic Intelligence for American World Policy*, 60–61.

41.   Kent, *Strategic Intelligence for American World Policy*, 175.

42.   Kent, *Strategic Intelligence for American World Policy*, 60, 206, 160, 175; Abram Shulsky and Gary E. Schmitt, *Silent Warfare: Understanding the World of Intelligence*, 3rd ed. (Washington, DC: Brassey's, 2002), 173–75. Tetlock, *Expert Political Judgment*, found experts worse at predicting the future than algorithms.

43.   Sheldon, *Intelligence Activities in Ancient Rome*, 92, 129–30.

44.   James C. Scott, *Seeing Like a State: How Certain Schemes to Improve the Human Condition Have Failed* (New Haven: Yale University Press, 1998).

45.   Michael Mann, "The Autonomous Power of the State," in *States in History*, ed. John A. Hall (New York: Basil Blackwell, 1987), 113–15.

46.   Soll, *The Information Minister*, 17–19.

47.   Peter Burke, "Tacitism, Skepticism, and Reason of State," in *The Cambridge History of Political Thought 1450–1700*, ed. J. H. Burns and Mark Goldie (Cambridge: Cambridge University Press, 1991), 484–90.

48.   Burke, "Tacitism, Skepticism, and Reason of State," 479.

49.   Burke, "Tacitism, Skepticism, and Reason of State," 480.

50.   Burke, "Tacitism, Skepticism, and Reason of State," 480–81, 483.

51.   Stephen Budiansky, *Her Majesty's Spymaster: Elizabeth I, Sir Francis Walsingham, and the Birth of Modern Espionage* (New York: Penguin Group, 2005); Diego Navarro Bonilla, "'Secret Intelligences' in European Military, Political and Diplomatic Theory: An Essential Factor in the Defense of the Modern State (Sixteenth and Seventeenth Centuries)," *Intelligence and National Security* 27, 2 (2012): 283–301.

52.   David Tucker, "Jefferson and the Practice of Empire," in *Natural Right and Political Right: Essays in Honor of Harry V. Jaffa*, ed. Thomas B. Silver and Peter W. Schramm (Durham, NC: Carolina Academic Press, 1984), 27–43.

53.   Kent, *Strategic Intelligence for American World Policy*, 155.

54.   Kent, *Strategic Intelligence for American World Policy*, 155, 39, 4–5.

55.   Kent, *Strategic Intelligence for American World Policy*, 4–5.

56.   Edward A. Shils, *The Torment of Secrecy* (Chicago: Ivan R. Dee, 1996; 1956), 11.

57.   Burke, "Tacitism, Skepticism, and Reason of State," 482.

58.   Burke, "Tacitism, Skepticism, and Reason of State," 487.

59.   Jeffrey, *MI6*, 12, 24, 62, 63, 72, 78, 151, 163.

60.   Morgan, *The Secrets of Rue St. Roch*, 51, 53, 56–57.

61.   Carlo Ginzburg, "High and Low: The Theme of Forbidden Knowledge in the Sixteenth and Seventeenth Centuries," *Past and Present* 73 (November 1976): 28–41.

62.   This was one view, not universally accepted. See Joseph Canning, *Ideas of*

Power in the Late Middle Ages, 1279–1417 (Cambridge: Cambridge University Press, 2011).

63. Paul J. Bagley, "On the Practice of Esotericism," *Journal of the History of Ideas* 53, 2 (April–June 1992): 231–47.

64. William Eamon, *Science and the Secrets of Nature: Books of Secrets in Medieval and Early Modern Culture* (Princeton: Princeton University Press, 1996), 15–37, esp. 22.

65. Canning, *Ideas of Power in the Late Middle Ages*, 11–59.

66. "When Does Research Enhance Security, and When Does It Diminish It?" *Economist*, December 31, 2011.

67. "Modern science, which is a by-product and an essential part of the people's revolution." Henry Wallace, "The Price of Free World Victory," a speech delivered to the Free World Association, New York City, May 8, 1942, http:/newdeal.feri.org/Wallace/haw17.htm#15.

68. Shils, *The Torment of Secrecy*, 26; consider also 201.

69. Robert O'Harrow, Jr., *No Place to Hide* (New York: Free Press, 2005).

70. Alane Kochems, "No More Secrets: National Security Strategies for a Transparent World," workshop report, American Bar Association Standing Committee on Law and National Security, March 2011; Gregory Treverton, *Intelligence for an Age of Terror* (Cambridge: Cambridge University Press, 2009), 4, 31, 220.

71. David Tucker, *Enlightened Republicanism: A Study of Jefferson's Notes on the State of Virginia* (Lanham, MD: Lexington Books, 2008).

72. Soll, *The Information Minister*, 80; Daniel R. Headrick, *When Information Came of Age: Technologies of Knowledge in the Age of Reason and Revolution, 1700–1850* (New York: Oxford University Press, 2000), 69.

73. Thomas Hobbes, *Leviathan*, ed. Richard Tuck (Cambridge: Cambridge University Press, 1991), 62. I use standard orthography.

74. Hobbes, *Leviathan*, 90.

75. Michael Herman, *Intelligence Power in Peace and War* (Cambridge: Cambridge University Press, 1996), 2, quoting Lawrence Freedman, "Strategic Studies and the Problem of Power," in *War, Strategy and International Politics*, ed. Lawrence Freedman, Paul Hayes, and Robert O'Neill (Oxford: Clarendon Press, 1992), 291.

76. "Leviathan" is a reference to the monster of the deep in Job, 41:1, 33–34: "Upon earth there is not his like, who is made without fear. He beholdeth all high things: he is a king over all the children of pride."

77. Chester Bowles, *Promises to Keep: My Years in Public Life, 1941–1969* (New York: Harper and Row, 1971), 1.

78. Hobbes, *Leviathan*, 35–36.

79. Francis Bacon, *The New Organon and Related Writings*, ed. Fulton H. Anderson (Indianapolis: Bobbs-Merrill Company, 1960), 39.

80. Vannevar Bush, "Science, The Endless Frontier: A Report to the President on a Program for Postwar Scientific Research," Office of Scientific Research and Development, July 5, 1945 (Washington, DC,: National Science Foundation, 1960).

81. Julian Martin, *Francis Bacon, the State, and the Reform of Natural philosophy* (Cambridge: Cambridge University Press, 1992), 35, 70–71, 165–66; Peter Pesic, "Wrestling with Proteus: Francis Bacon and the 'Torture' of Nature," *Isis* 90, 1 (March 1999): 81–94.

82. Eamon, *Science and the Secrets of Nature*, 61.

83. Bacon, *The New Organon and Related Writings*, 113–14.

84. Martin, *Francis Bacon, the State, and the Reform of Natural philosophy*, 66.

85. Bacon, *The New Organon and Related Writings*, 33–34.

86. Hobbes, *Leviathan*, 14, emphasis in original.

87. S. Marc Cohen, "Aristotle on Thinking (*Noêsis*)," *faculty.washington.edu/ smcohen/433/AristotleThinking.pdf*.

88. David Freeberg, *The Eye of the Lynx: Galileo, His Friends and the Beginnings of Modern Natural History* (Chicago: Chicago University Press, 2003).

89. Bacon was also more skeptical of hypotheses than later scientists because, as noted in our discussion of Kent's method, forming hypotheses may insert a bias into the collection of data.

90. Michael E. Hobart and Zachary S. Schiffman, *Information Ages: Literacy, Numeracy, and the Computer Revolution* (Baltimore, MD: Johns Hopkins University Press, 1998), 6, 159–60, 177–78; Eugene Wigner, "The Unreasonable Effectiveness of Mathematics in the Natural Sciences," *Communications on Pure and Applied Mathematics* 23 (1960): 1–14.

91. Wallace, "The Price of Free World Victory."

92. Vannevar Bush, *Modern Arms and Free Men: A Discussion of the Role of Science in Preserving Democracy* (New York: Simon and Schuster, 1949), 9, 137, 262, 135.

93. Bacon, *The New Organon and Related Writings*, 267–68; Bush, *Modern Arms and Free Men*, 263.

94. Jervis, *Why Intelligence Fails*, 150. Jervis cites Betts, *Enemies of Intelligence*.

95. Jervis, *Why Intelligence Fails*, 150–53, makes a good case for the utility of social science approaches.

96. Bacon, *The New Organon and Related Writings*, 115–16.

97. Peter L. Bernstein, *Against the Gods: The Remarkable Story of Risk* (New York: John Wiley and Sons, 1996), 232.

Chapter 2

1. Charles Howard Carter, *The Secret Diplomacy of the Habsburgs, 1598–1625* (New York: Columbia University Press, 1962), 137.

2. In addition to the sources cited in this chapter, its presentation of espionage

draws on Alan Marshall, *Intelligence and Espionage in the Reign of Charles II, 1660–1685* (Cambridge: Cambridge University Press, 1994); Christopher Andrew and Vasili Mitrokhin, *The Sword and the Shield: The Mitrokhin Archive and the Secret History of the KGB* (New York: Basic Books, 1999); John Earl Haynes, Harvey Klehr, and Alexander Vassiliev, *Spies: The Rise and Fall of the KGB in America* (New Haven: Yale University Press, 2009); David Atlee Phillips, *The Night Watch* (New York: Atheneum, 1977); Frank S. Russell, *Intelligence Gathering in Classical Greece* (Ann Arbor: University of Michigan Press, 1999); Rose Mary Sheldon, *Intelligence Activities in Ancient Rome: Trust in the Gods, but Verify* (New York: Routledge, 2005); Martin Thomas, *Empires of Intelligence: Security Services and Colonial Disorder after 1914* (Berkeley: University of California Press, 2008); Simon Kitson, *The Hunt for Nazi Spies: Fighting Espionage in Vichy France* (Chicago: University of Chicago Press, 2008).

3. Niccolo Machiavelli, *The Prince*, translated, with an introduction, by Harvey C. Mansfield (Chicago: University of Chicago Press, 1985), 101.

4. Victor Cherkashin, with Gregory Feifer, *Spy Handler: Memoir of a KGB Officer* (New York: Basic Books, 2005), 49–51, 122–29.

5. Christopher Felix, *A Short Course in the Secret War* (Lanham, MD: Madison Books, 1963, 2001), 55–56.

6. Duane R. Clarridge, with Digby Diehls, *A Spy for All Seasons: My Life in the CIA* (New York: Scribner, 1997), 81–82.

7. Clarridge, *A Spy for All Seasons*, 123–48.

8. Felix, *A Short Course in the Secret War*, 56.

9. Peter Taylor, *Beating the Terrorists?: Interrogation in Omagh, Gough and Castlereagh* (London: Penguin Books, 1980).

10. Benjamin Weiser, *A Secret Life: The Polish Officer, His Covert Mission, and the Price He Paid to Save His Country* (New York: Public Affairs, 2005).

11. Clarridge, *A Spy for All Seasons*, 146. For a useful discussion of motivations in espionage, which this chapter draws on, see Randy Burkett, "An Alternative Framework for Agent Recruitment: From MICE to RASCALS," *Studies in Intelligence* 57, 1 (Extracts, March 2013), 7–17. Also useful is Felix, *A Short Course in the Secret War*, 54–61.

12. For example, see Gregory Treverton, *Intelligence for an Age of Terror* (New York: Cambridge University Press, 2009), 9; Amy Zegart, *Spying Blind: The CIA, the FBI, and the Origins of 9/11* (Princeton: Princeton University Press, 2007), 5.

13. Henry A. Crumpton, *The Art of Intelligence: Lessons from a Life in the CIA's Clandestine Service* (New York: Penguin Press, 2012), 135; Burton Gerber, "Managing HUMINT: The Need for a New Approach," in *Transforming U.S. Intelligence*, ed. Jennifer E. Sims and Burton Gerber (Washington, DC: Georgetown University Press, 2005), 184–85; Treverton, *Intelligence for an Age of Terror*.

14. Michael Freeman, David Tucker, and Steffen Merten, "Finding Patterns Prior to an Attack," *Journal of Policing, Intelligence and Counter Terrorism* 5, 1 (November 2010): 75–85.

15. *CTX*, Special Issue, "Intelligence and Terrorism," ed. David Tucker, 3, 4 (2014).

16. For examples of this, see Eamon Collins with Mick McGovern, *Killing Rage* (London: Granta Books, 1997). Collins was an intelligence officer in the IRA. See also Vernon Loeb, "Clan, Family Ties Called Key to Army's Capture of Hussein," *Washington Post*, December 16, 2003, 27; Steven Emerson, "The Inside Story behind the Awlaki Assassination," Investigative Project on Terrorism, September 30, 2011, www.investigativeproject.org/3210/exclusive-the-inside-story-behind-the-awlaki.

17. On this point, see David Tucker, *Illuminating the Dark Arts of War: Terrorism, Sabotage, and Subversion in Homeland Security and the New Conflict* (New York: Continuum, 2012), 49–76; and Frank Kitson, *Low-Intensity Operations: Subversion, Insurgency, Peacekeeping* (Harrisburg, PA: Stackpole Books, 1971), 127.

18. Frances D'Emilio and Colleen Barry, "Italy CIA Rendition Trial: Court Upholds American Convictions," Associated Press, September 9, 2012.

19. Felix, *A Short Course in the Secret War*, 26–28, 104.

20. Crumpton, *The Art of Intelligence*, 78–81.

21. Allen M. Hornblum, *The Invisible Harry Gold: The Man Who Gave the Soviets the Bomb* (New Haven: Yale University Press, 2010).

22. Felix, *A Short Course in the Secret War*, 54. For other comments relevant to issues raised in the paragraph, see 50–51, 113.

23. For chance in espionage, see, for example, Janet Morgan, *The Secrets of Rue St. Roch: Hope and Heroism behind Enemy Lines in the First World War* (London: Penguin Books, 2005), 53; Clarridge, *A Spy for All Seasons*, 123, 128, 134, 138, 144; and Cherkashin, *Spy Handler*, 4, 30.

24. Crumpton, *The Art of Intelligence*, 63.

25. Daniel Kahneman and Gary Klein, "Conditions for Intuitive Expertise: A Failure to Disagree," *American Psychologist* (September 2009): 515–26.

26. This formulation is taken from Daniel Kahneman, *Thinking, Fast and Slow* (New York: Farrar, Straus and Giroux, 2011), 240, summarizing Kahneman and Klein, "Conditions for Intuitive Expertise," 522.

27. Kahneman and Klein, "Conditions for Intuitive Expertise," 522.

28. Crumpton, *The Art of Intelligence*, 63.

29. Kahneman, *Thinking, Fast and Slow*, 9, 14, 207 fn. 23.

30. Kahneman and Klein, "Conditions for Intuitive Expertise," 520, 524.

31. Julius Caesar, *The Gallic War*, 6.30.

32. Kahneman and Klein, "Conditions for Intuitive Expertise," 516.

33. Crumpton, *The Art of Intelligence*, 63–64. Like Crumpton, Kahneman argues that expert judgment is a matter of practice, *Thinking, Fast and Slow*, 11–12.

34. Colin McColl, *Preface*, in Morgan, *The Secrets of Rue St. Roch*, xvii–xviii.

35. Douglas Waller, *Wild Bill Donovan: The Spymaster Who Created the OSS and Modern American Espionage* (New York: Free Press, 2011), 51–53.

36. Eric Schmitt and Thom Shanker, *Counterstrike: The Untold Story of America's Secret Campaign against al Qaeda* (New York: Times Books, 2011), 38–39.

37. Crumpton, *The Art of Intelligence*, 113.

38. Robert L. Jervis, *Why Intelligence Fails: Lessons from the Iranian Revolution and the Iraq War* (Ithaca, NY: Cornell University Press, 2010), 142. Treverton, *Intelligence for an Age of Terror*, 17–18, 43, 105–6.

39. Major General Michael T. Flynn, USA, Captain Matt Pottinger, USMC, and Paul D. Batchelor, DIA, "Fixing Intel: A Blueprint for Making Intelligence Relevant in Afghanistan," Center for a New American Security, Voices from the Field, January 2010, 9, 17, 23; Elaine M. Grossman, "Brave Thinkers, Interview with Michael T. Flynn," *Atlantic Magazine*, November 2010, www.theatlantic.com/magazine/archive/2010/11/michael-t-flynn/8271/.

Chapter 3

1. Stephen Grey, *Ghost Plane: The True Story of the CIA Torture Program* (New York: St. Martin's Press, 2006), 211; Steve Hendricks, *A Kidnapping in Milan: The CIA on Trial* (New York: W. W Norton, 2011). Both sources must be used with caution; Hendricks is particularly tendentious.

2. Information on the assassination comes from Danna Harman, "Dubai Assassination Spotlights Top Cop Skills in a Modern-day Casablanca," *Christian Science Monitor*, March 19, 2010; and Duncan Gardham, "Dubai Hamas Assassination: How It Was Planned," *Telegraph*, February 17, 2010.

3. David Atlee Phillips, *The Night Watch* (New York: Atheneum, 1977); and Stuart Herrington (COL, USA Ret), *Traitors among Us: Untold Stories of Cold War Espionage* (New York: Harcourt, 1999) are useful accounts of covert action and counterintelligence, respectively, before the current information revolution.

4. Joel Brenner, *America the Vulnerable: Inside the New Threat Matrix of Digital Espionage, Crime and Warfare* (New York: Penguin Press, 2011), 163.

5. Grey, *Ghost Plane*.

6. Robert Jervis, "Intelligence, Counterintelligence, Perception, and Deception," in *Vaults, Masks and Mirrors: Rediscovering U.S. Counterintelligence*, ed. Jennifer Sims and Burton Gerber (Washington, DC: Georgetown University Press, 2009), 71–73, briefly and clearly offers an account of counterintelligence that makes clear how the wilderness comes about.

7. Duane R. Clarridge, with Digby Diehls, *A Spy for All Seasons: My Life in the CIA* (New York: Scribner, 1997), 138–39; Victor Cherkashin, with Gregory Feifer, *Spy Handler: Memoir of a KGB Officer* (New York: Basic Books, 2005), 21.

8. William R. Johnson, *Thwarting Enemies at Home and Abroad: How To Be a*

Counterintelligence Officer (Washington, DC: Georgetown University Press, 2009; originally published Bethesda, MD: Stone Trail Press, 1987), 144.

9. Christopher Felix, *A Short Course in the Secret War* (Lanham, MD: Madison Books, 2001), 115–16.

10. Herrington, *Traitors among Us*, 94.

11. Evgeny Morozov, *The Net Delusion: The Dark Side of Internet Freedom* (New York: Public Affairs, 2011), 143–78.

12. Kenneth Conboy and Dale Andradé, *Spies and Commandos: How America Lost the Secret War in North Vietnam* (Lawrence: University Press of Kansas, 2000).

13. Liam Collins, "The Abbottabad Documents: Bin Laden's Security Measures," *CTC Sentinel* 5, 5 (May 2012): 1–4; Aki Peritz and Eric Rosenbach, *Find, Fix, Finish: Inside the Counterterrorism Campaigns that Killed bin Laden and Devastated al Qaeda* (New York: Public Affairs, 2012), 210–11, 216–17.

14. Pew Research, "On Anniversary of bin Laden's Death, Little Backing of al Qaeda. Before His Death in 2011, Support for bin Laden Himself Had Waned," April 30, 2012, www.pewglobal.org/2012/04/30/on-anniversary-of-bin-ladens-death-little-backing-of-al-qaeda.

15. Mark Bowden, *The Finish: The Killing of Osama bin Laden* (New York: Atlantic Monthly Press, 2012), 123–24, 130, 136.

16. Robert O'Harrow, *No Place to Hide* (New York: Free Press, 2006), 49, 215.

17. "Intelligence Agencies and the Cyber World," *Strategic Survey* 112, 1 (2012): 45–46.

18. Scott Wilson and Zachary A. Goldfarb, "Obama Announces Proposals to Reform NSA Surveillance," *Washington* Post, August 9, 2013.

19. David Tucker and Christopher J. Lamb, "Restructuring Special Operations Forces for Emerging Threats," Strategic Forum, no. 219, Institute for National Strategic Studies, National Defense University, Washington, DC, 2006.

20. Johnson, *Thwarting Enemies at Home and Abroad*, 202; Jervis, "Intelligence, Counterintelligence, Perception, and Deception," 71.

21. Michelle K. Van Cleave, "Counterintelligence and National Strategy," National Defense University Press, Washington, DC, April 2007.

22. J. C. Masterman, *The Double-Cross System in the War of 1939 to 1945* (New Haven: Yale University Press, 1972), 104.

23. Johnson, *Thwarting Enemies at Home and Abroad*, 205–6.

24. "Intelligence Agencies and the Cyber World," 40.

25. David Tucker, *Illuminating the Dark Arts of War: Terrorism, Sabotage, and Subversion in Homeland Security and the New Conflict* (New York: Continuum, 2012), 95–133.

26. For example, John Arquilla and David Ronfeldt, "Cyberwar Is Coming," in *In Athena's Camp: Preparing for Conflict in the Information Age*, ed. Arquilla and Ronfeldt (Santa Monica, CA: RAND, 1997), 23–60.

27. "National Security Council Directive on Office of Special Projects," Washington, June 18, 1948, *Foreign Relations of the United States, 1945–1950, Retrospective Volume, Emergence of the Intelligence Establishment,* Document 292, http://history.state.gov/historicaldocuments/frus1945–50Intel/d292.

28. Gregory Treverton, *Intelligence for an Age of Terror* (Cambridge: Cambridge University Press, 2009), 207–34.

29. Felix, *A Short Course in the Secret War,* 39.

30. Harman, "Dubai Assassination Spotlights Top Cop Skills in a Modern-day Casablanca."

31. Keith Jeffrey, *MI6: The History of the Secret Intelligence Service, 1909–1949* (London: Bloomsbury, 2010), 177, 351–58, 606–7; John Ranleagh, *The Agency: The Rise and Decline of the CIA* (New York: Simon and Schuster, 1986), 220–24.

32. Felix, *A Short Course in the Secret War,* 144.

33. Joanne Omang and George C. Wilson, "Questions about Plane's Origins Grow," *Washington Post,* October 9, 1986, A1, A32.

34. "Hasenfus Tempers Comments on the CIA," *New York Times,* November 3, 1986, www.nytimes.com/1986/11/03/world/hasenfus-tempers-comments-on-cia.html; Theodore Draper, *A Very Thin Line: The Iran-Contra Affairs* (New York: Hill and Wang, 1991), 352–54, 362–63.

35. Steve Coll, *Ghost Wars: The Secret History of the CIA, Afghanistan, and bin Laden, from the Soviet Invasion to September 10, 2001* (New York: Penguin Books, 2005), 378–79, 393–95.

36. Felix, *A Short Course in the Secret War,* 145.

37. Henry A. Crumpton, *The Art of Intelligence: Lessons from a Life in the CIA's Clandestine Service* (New York: Penguin Press, 2012), 125.

38. Mark Mazzetti, *The Way of the Knife: The CIA, a Secret Army, and a War at the Ends of the Earth* (New York: Penguin Press, 2013), 81.

39. David Tucker, *Skirmishes at the Edge of Empire: The United States and International Terrorism* (Westport, CT: Praeger, 1997), 41–42.

40. Coll, *Ghost Wars,* 470–71.

41. Crumpton, *The Art of Intelligence,* 206, 227, 184.

42. Barton Gellman, "Secret Unit Expands Rumsfeld's Domain; New Espionage Branch Delving into CIA Territory," *Washington Post,* January 23, 2005, A1; "McCain Expects Hearings on Defense Intelligence Unit; Pentagon Disputes Some of Post Report," *Washington Post,* January 24, 2005; Douglas Jehl and Eric Schmitt, "Reports on Pentagon's New Spy Units Set Off Questions in Congress," *New York Times,* January 25, 2005, A6.

43. Jack Goldsmith, "The Remarkably Open Syrian Covert Action," *Lawfare,* July 23, 2013, www.lawfareblog.com/2013/07/the-remarkably-open-syrian-covert-action.

44. The ability of computer forensics to identify the authors of cyber opera-

tions is subject of debate. Erik Gartzke, "The Myth of Cyberwar: Bringing War in Cyberspace Back Down to Earth," *International Security* 38, 4 (Fall 2013): 70–71; "Intelligence Agencies and the Cyber World," 41.

45. Treverton, *Intelligence for an Age of Terror*, 221–23, 228.

46. "Putin Signs NGO 'Foreign Agents' Law," Radio Free Europe Documents and Publications, July 21, 2012.

Chapter 4

1. Martin Van Creveld, *The Rise and Decline of the State* (Cambridge: Cambridge University Press, 1999), esp. 336–54, 377–94.

2. Carl Von Clausewitz, *On War*, edited and translated by Michael Howard and Peter Paret (Princeton: Princeton University Press, 1976), 117.

3. Clausewitz, *On War*, 101.

4. Clausewitz, *On War*, 85, 139, 149, 89, 120, 102, 106, 194, 210, 102, 622. Katherine L. Herbig, "Chance and Uncertainty in *On War*," in *Clausewitz and Modern Strategy*, ed. Michael I. Handel (London: Frank Cass, 1986), 95–116; Alan Beyerchen, "Clausewitz, Nonlinearity, and the Unpredictability of War," *International Security* 17, 3 (Winter 1991/92): 59–90.

5. Martin Van Creveld, *Command in War* (Cambridge: Harvard University Press, 1985), 264–68.

6. Peter L. Bernstein, *Against the Gods: The Remarkable Story of Risk* (New York: John Wiley and Sons, 1996), 232.

7. Michael I. Handel, *Intelligence and Military Operations* (London: Frank Cass and Company, 1990), 60; Henry A. Crumpton, *The Art of Intelligence: Lessons from a Life in the CIA's Clandestine Service* (New York: Penguin Press, 2012), 63–65.

8. Clausewitz, *On War*, 117. For contemporary statements of this view, see John Keegan, *Intelligence in War: Knowledge of the Enemy from Napoleon to al-Qaeda* (New York: Alfred A. Knopf, 2003); Handel, *Intelligence and Military Operations*; and David Kahn, "An Historical Theory of Intelligence," in *Intelligence Theory: Key Questions and Debates*, ed. Peter Gill, Stephen Marrin, and Mark Pythian (New York: Routledge, 2009).

9. Michael I. Handel, *War, Strategy and Intelligence* (London: Frank Cass and Company, 1989), 230, 132 (Handel provides no data to support his claim that surprise seldom succeeds; evidence for it is in Appendix A); David Tucker, *Illuminating the Dark Arts of War: Terrorism, Sabotage, and Subversion in Homeland Security and the New Conflict* (New York: Continuum, 2012), 59–62.

10. Sun Tzu, *The Art of War*, translated and with an introduction by Samuel B. Griffith (New York: Oxford University Press, 1963), 84, 138, 145, 149.

11. Sun Tzu, *The Art of War*, 72.

12. Sun Tzu, *The Art of War*, 92–93.

13. Sun Tzu, *The Art of War*, 77, 79.

14. Quoted in Aaron Friedberg, *In the Shadow of the Garrison State: America's Anti-Statism and Its Cold War Grand Strategy* (Princeton: Princeton University Press, 2000), 338.

15. Andrew F. Krepinevich, "Cavalry to Computers: The Pattern of Military Revolutions," *National Interest,* no. 37 (September 1994): 30–42.

16. The remark about perfect knowledge is quoted in Michael Herman, *Intelligence Services in the Information Age* (London: Frank Cass, 2002), 29; William A. Owens and Ed Offley, *Lifting the Fog of War* (Baltimore, MD: Johns Hopkins University Press, 2001).

17. Richard B. Andres, Craig Wills, and Thomas E. Griffith, Jr., "Winning with Allies: The Strategic Value of the Afghan Model," *International Security* 30, 3 (Winter 2005/6): 135, 139.

18. Andres, Wills, and Griffith, "Winning with Allies," 141–44.

19. Lt. Gen. Paul K. Van Riper, USMC, "Information Superiority," *Marine Corps Gazette* 81, 6 (June 1997): 54–62.

20. Handel, *Intelligence and Military Operations*, 22.

21. Stephen Biddle, *Military Power: Explaining Victory and Defeat in Modern Battle* (Princeton: Princeton University Press, 2004).

22. Biddle, *Military Power*, 62–66.

23. William Rosenau, *Special Operations Forces and Elusive Enemy Ground Targets: Lessons from Vietnam and the Persian Gulf War* (Santa Monica, CA: RAND, 2001), 43; Owens and Offley, *Lifting the Fog of War*, 179.

24. Adam Entous, Julian E. Barnes, and Siobhan Gorman, "U.S. Scurries to Shore Up Spying on Russia," *Wall Street Journal*, March 24, 2014, A1.

25. One authority on deception has argued that it is always less costly to deceive than to detect deception. Barton Whaley and Jeffrey Busby, "Detecting Deception: Practice, Practitioners, and Theory," in *Strategic Denial and Deception: The Twenty-First Century Challenge*, ed. Roy Godson and James J. Wirtz (New Brunswick, NJ: Transaction Publishers, 2001), 185–86.

26. Richard A. Clarke and Robert K. Knake, *Cyber War: The Next Threat to National Security and What to Do about It* (New York: Ecco, 2010), 5–9; David E. Sanger, *Confront and Conceal: Obama's Secret Wars and Surprising Use of American Power* (New York: Crown Publishers, 2012), 199; Jim Wolf, "U.S. Code-cracking Agency Works as if Compromised," *Reuters,* December 16, 2010, www.reuters.com/article/idUSTRE6BZ20101216.

27. The intelligence cycle: policy-makers request information, which leads the intelligence community to collect, analyze, and disseminate intelligence that leads policy-makers to make new requests for information.

28. Richard Ned Lebow, *Between War and Peace: The Nature of International*

Crisis (Baltimore, MD: Johns Hopkins University Press, 1984), 154–64, 172–84; Thomas G. Mahnken, *Uncovering Ways of War: U.S. Intelligence and Foreign Military Innovation, 1918–1941* (Ithaca, NY: Cornell University Press, 2002), 82–85; Robert Jervis, *Why Intelligence Fails: Lessons from the Iranian Revolution and the Iraq War* (Ithaca, NY: Cornell University Press, 2010), 139.

29. Biddle, *Military Power*, 66.

30. Biddle, *Military Power*, 62; Stephen Biddle, "Allies, Airpower, and Modern Warfare: The Afghan Model in Afghanistan and Iraq," *International Security* 30, 3 (Winter 2005/6): 164–67.

31. Biddle, "Allies, Airpower, and Modern Warfare," 168–69; and Stephen Biddle, "Iraq, Afghanistan, and American Military Transformation," in *Strategy in the Contemporary World*, ed. John Bayliss, James Wirtz, Colin S. Gray, and Eliot Cohen (New York: Oxford University Press, 2007), 274–94.

32. The description of special operations in this paragraph draws on William H. McRaven, *Spec Ops: Case Studies in Special Operations Warfare: Theory and Practice* (Novato, CA: Presidio Press, 1995).

33. For more on SOF, see David Tucker and Christopher J. Lamb, *United States Special Operations Forces* (New York: Columbia University Press, 2007).

34. Biddle, *Military Power*, 42, 60–61, 69; McRaven, *Spec Ops*, 3–23.

35. This assumes opposing forces of more or less equal skill. A numerically inferior force can overcome a numerically superior force if the numerically inferior force is more skilled tactically than the superior force, Biddle, *Military Power*, 69.

36. McRaven, *Spec Ops*, 4–8.

37. McRaven, *Spec Ops*, 155. For surprise in the Saint Nazaire and Mussolini operations, 154–55, 190–92, 195, 197, 327.

38. McRaven, *Spec Ops*, 19.

39. McRaven, *Spec Ops*, 273.

40. Biddle, "Allies, Airpower, and Modern Warfare," 161–62; Biddle, "Military Power: A Reply," *Journal of Strategic Studies* 28, 3 (June 2005): 461–62.

41. For example, Eliot Cohen, "Stephen Biddle on Military Power," *Journal of Strategic Studies* 28, 3 (June 2005): 413–24; Michael Horowitz and Stephen Rosen, "Evolution or Revolution," *Journal of Strategic Studies* 28, 3 (June 2005): 437–48.

42. Handel, *Intelligence and Military Operations*, 2, 14, 21, 54, 65–66.

43. Keegan, *Intelligence in War*, 6, 18, 334; 243–44, 248, 256–57; 81, 97; 332.

44. Ralph Bennett, "Intelligence and Strategy: Some observations on the War in the Mediterranean, 1941–1942," in Handel, *Intelligence and Military Operations*, 445.

45. Handel, *Intelligence and Military Operations*, 38, 58; Keegan, *Intelligence in War*, 218–19.

46. Kahn, "An Historical Theory of Intelligence," 6, 9–10; Keegan, *Intelligence in War*, 174, 179–80, 66.

47. Caesar, *Gallic Wars*, 8:18.

48. "Kahn, "An Historical Theory of Intelligence," 9. For a contrary view, see Bennett, "Intelligence and Strategy," 456.

49. Clausewitz, *On War*, 119.

50. Janet Morgan, *The Secrets of Rue St. Roch: Hope and Heroism behind Enemy Lines in the First World War* (London: Penguin Books, 2005); Keith Jeffrey, *MI6: The History of the Secret Intelligence Service, 1909–1949* (London: Bloomsbury Publishing, 2010), 747.

51. Bennett, "Intelligence and Strategy," 82–83.

52. Bennett, "Intelligence and Strategy," 75; Stephen Ambrose, *Ike's Spies: Eisenhower and the Espionage Establishment* (New York: Anchor Books, 1981), 40.

53. Handel, *Intelligence and Military Operations*, 22.

54. Bennett, "Intelligence and Strategy," 75; Keegan, *Intelligence in War*, 321–22.

55. Bennett, "Intelligence and Strategy," 89.

56. Sir Harry Hinsley, "Thirty-First Harmon Memorial Lecture: World War II: An Intelligence Revolution," in *The Intelligence Revolution: A Historical Perspective*, Proceedings of the Thirteenth Military History Symposium, U.S. Air Force Academy, October 1988 (Washington, DC: Office of Air Force History, 1991), 10; Gerhard L. Weinberg, *A World at Arms: A Global History of World War II* (New York: Cambridge University Press, 1994), 547–57.

57. Richard A. Woytak, *On the Border of War and Peace: Polish Intelligence and the Diplomacy in 1937–1939 and the Origins of the Ultra Secret* (Boulder, CO: Eastern European Quarterly, 1979), 8–9; Gustave Bertrand, *Enigma ou la Plus Grande Enigme de la Guerre 1939–1945* (Paris: Librairie Plon, 1973), 24.

58. Quoted in Bruce Hoffman, *Inside Terrorism* (New York: Columbia University Press, 2006), 219.

59. Mahnken, *Uncovering Ways of War*, 44, 75, 121, 140; Robert J. Young, "French Military Intelligence and Nazi Germany, 1938–1939," in *Knowing One's Enemies: Intelligence Assessment before the Two World Wars*, ed. Ernest R. May (Princeton: Princeton University Press, 1984), 276.

60. May, *Knowing One's Enemies*, 69–70, 210.

61. Young, "French Military Intelligence and Nazi Germany, 1938–1939," 276.

62. Norman Stone, "Austria-Hungary," in May, *Knowing One's Enemies*, 46, 49.

63. May, *Knowing One's Enemies*, 42–43; Mahnken, *Uncovering Ways of War*, 37; Jeffrey, *MI6*, 504–5.

64. May, *Knowing One's Enemies*, 42–43; Mahnken, *Uncovering Ways of War*, 37; Jeffrey, *MI6*, 504–5; Benjamin Weiser, *A Secret Life: The Polish Officer, His Covert Mission, and the Price He Paid to Save His Country* (New York: PublicAffairs, 2005), 328.

65. Jeffrey, *MI6*, 185; Jervis, *Why Intelligence Fails*, 136–38, 140–42; May, *Knowing One's Enemies*, 133, 262–63.

66. May, *Knowing One's Enemies*, 50, 145, 399, 519, 537; Mahnken, *Uncovering Ways of War*, 83–85, 177–78; Richard K. Betts, *Enemies of Intelligence: Knowledge and Power in American National Security* (New York: Columbia University Press, 2007), 24, 46; Jervis, *Why Intelligence Fails*; Richards J. Heuer, Jr., *The Psychology of Intelligence Analysis*, www.cia.gov/library/center-for-the-study-of-intelligence/csi-publications/books-and-monographs/psychology-of-intelligence-analysis/art5.html.

67. Mahnken, *Uncovering Ways of War*, 83, 93.

68. Jeffrey, *MI6*, 351–58; 590.

69. Ambrose, *Ike's Spies*, 31–32.

70. Thomas L. Ahern, Jr., "The Way We Do Things: Black Entry Operations into North Vietnam," Center for the Study of Intelligence, Central Intelligence Agency, May 2005, 4.

71. On the effects of the resistance, see M. R. D. Foot, *SOE in France: An Account of the Work of the British Special Operations Executive in France, 1940–1944* (London: Frank Cass, 2004), 381–86; M. R. D. Foot, *Resistance: European Resistance to Nazism, 1940–1945* (New York: McGraw-Hill, 1977), 313–14; M. R. D. Foot, "What Good Did Resistance Do?," in *Resistance in Europe* (London: Allen Lane, 1975), 204–20; Alan S. Milward, "The Economic and Strategic Effectiveness of Resistance," in *Resistance in Europe*, 186–203; Williamson Murray and Allan R. Millett, *A War to Be Won: Fighting the Second World War* (Cambridge: Belknap Press of Harvard University Press, 2000), 405–9; John Keegan, *The Second World War* (New York: Viking, 1989), 483–96; Keegan, *Intelligence in War*, 339–49; Douglas Porch, *The French Secret Services: A History of French Intelligence from the Dreyfus Affair to the Gulf War* (New York: Farrar, Straus and Giroux, 1995), 260–64; Max Hastings, *Inferno: The World at War, 1939–1945* (New York: Alfred A. Knopf, 2011), 394–95; Max Hastings, *Das Reich: The March of the 2nd SS Panzer Division through France* (New York: Holt, Rinehart and Winston, 1981), 41, 44–45, 76–79.

72. For the claim and an analysis of the utility and effectiveness of sabotage, see Tucker, *Illuminating the Dark Arts of War*, 153, 135–66.

73. Murray and Millett, *A War to Be Won*, 406–7.

74. Hastings, *Das Reich*, 183–84; Hastings, *Inferno*, 395.

75. Keegan, *The Second World War*, 488; Martin Gilbert, *The Second World War: A Complete History* (New York: Henry Holt and Company, 1989), 527.

76. Ambrose, *Ike's Spies*, 68–71.

77. Douglas Waller, *Wild Bill Donovan: The Spymaster Who Created the OSS and Modern American Espionage* (New York: Free Press, 2011), 268–71, 370.

78. Ahern, "The Way We Do Things," provides details, esp. 15, 18, 22.

79. Ahern, "The Way We Do Things," 61–62.

80. An argument made to the author in defense of their craft by specialists in military deception.

81. On the deception campaign and its effects, see Kenneth Conboy and Dale Andradé, *Spies and Commandos: How America Lost the Secret War in North Vietnam* (Lawrence: University Press of Kansas, 2000), 194–95, 211, 219–20.

82. See, for example, Ambrose, *Ike's Spies*, 132, 143; Murray and Millett, *A War to Be Won*, 408–9.

Chapter 5

1. John Keegan, *Intelligence in War: Knowledge of the Enemy from Napoleon to al-Qaeda* (New York: Alfred A. Knopf, 2003), 334.

2. Keegan, *Intelligence in War*, 15.

3. John Grenier, *The First Way of War: American War Making on the Frontier* (Cambridge: Cambridge University Press, 2005).

4. Caesar, *The Gallic War*, 6.6; C. E. Callwell, *Small Wars: Their Principles and Practice*, ed. Douglas Porch (Lincoln: University of Nebraska Press, 1996), 40; Priya Satia, *Spies in Arabia: The Great War and the Cultural Foundations of Britain's Covert Empire in the Middle East* (New York: Oxford University Press, 2008), 163.

5. Major C. B. Dening, "Modern Problems of Guerilla Warfare," *Army Quarterly and Defence Journal* 13 (1926): 347–54; Caroline Elkins, *Imperial Reckoning: The Untold Story of Britain's Gulag in Kenya* (New York: Henry Holt, 2004). Ivan Arreguin-Toft, *How the Weak Win Wars: A Theory of Asymmetric Conflict* (Cambridge: Cambridge University Press, 2005), explores the consequences of moral constraint on counterguerrilla strategy.

6. N. J. E. Austin and N. B. Rankov, *Exploratio: Military and Political Intelligence in the Roman World from the Second Punic War to the Battle of Adrianople* (New York: Routledge, 1998), 13, 184.

7. David Kahn, "An Historical Theory of Intelligence," in *Intelligence Theory: Key Questions and Debates*, ed. Peter Gill, Stephen Marrin, and Mark Pythian (New York: Routledge, 2008), 10.

8. Eamon Collins, *Killing Rage* (London: Granta Publications, 1997), provides numerous similar examples. Collins was an intelligence officer in the IRA who cooperated with the authorities, and subsequently retracted his cooperation. He was killed in 1999, presumably by the IRA or some of its members.

9. Frank Kitson, *Low-Intensity Operations: Subversion, Insurgency, Peacekeeping* (Harrisburg, PA: Stackpole Books, 1971), 102–22. Kitson's account is the *locus classicus* for understanding irregular warfare as a contest between hiders and finders.

10. Kitson, *Low-Intensity Operations*, 127–29.

11. Bradley W. C. Bamford, "The Role and Effectiveness of Intelligence in Northern Ireland," *Intelligence and National Security* 20, 4 (December 2005): 581–607.

12. Kitson, *Low-Intensity Operations*, 117; Eric Schmitt and Thom Shanker, *Counterstrike: The Untold Story of America's Secret Campaign against Al Qaeda* (New York: Times Books, 2011), 40, 77.

13. G. H. McCormick and G. Owen, "Security and Coordination in a Clandestine Organization," *Mathematical and Computer Modeling* 31 (2000): 175–92.

14. Sir David Omand, Jamie Bartlett, and Carl Miller, "Introducing Social Media Intelligence (SOCMINT)," *Intelligence and National Security* 27, 6 (2012): 801–23.

15. Christopher J. Lamb and Evan Munsing, "Secret Weapon: High-value Target Teams as an Organizational Innovation," Strategic Perspectives 4, Institute for National Strategic Studies, National Defense University, Washington, DC, March 2011; Dale Andradé, *Ashes to Ashes: The Phoenix Program and the Vietnam War* (Lanham, MD: Lexington Books, 1990), 188–91.

16. For example, see Colonel Stuart A. Herrington (Ret.), *Traitors among Us: Inside the Spy Catcher's World* (New York: Harcourt, 1999).

17. Again Collins, *Killing Rage*, provides numerous similar examples.

18. For example, Peter Taylor, *Beating the Terrorists? Interrogation in Omagh, Gough and Castlereagh* (London: Penguin Books, 1980); Alistair Horne, *Savage War of Peace: Algeria, 1954–1962* (New York: Penguin Books, 1987), 204–7.

19. Vernon Loeb, "Clan, Family Ties Called Key to Army's Capture of Hussein," *Washington Post*, December 16, 2003, 27; Steven Emerson, "The Inside Story behind the Awlaki Assassination," Investigative Project on Terrorism, September 30, 2011, http://www.investigativeproject.org/3210/exclusive-the-inside-story-behind-the-awlaki.

20. Michael J. Schroeder, "Intelligence Capacities of the U.S. Military in the Sandino Rebellion, Las Segovias, Nicaragua, 1927–1932: Successes, Failures, Lessons," unpublished manuscript.

21. For further details on and some exceptions to some of the generalizations in this paragraph, see Blake W. Mobley, *Terrorism and Counterintelligence: How Terrorist Groups Elude Detection* (New York: Columbia University Press, 2012).

22. Mobley, *Terrorism and Counterintelligence*, 242–43.

23. Max Boot, *Invisible Armies: An Epic History of Guerrilla Warfare from Ancient Times to the Present* (New York: Liveright Publishing Corporation, 2013), 503–4.

24. http://www.fbi.gov/stats-services/publications/ten-most-wanted-fugitives-60th-anniversary-1950–2010/fbi_ten_most_wanted_fugitives_program; Joseph Mark Calvert, "Public Enemies: A Demographic Analysis of Federal Fugitive Wanted Posters," MA thesis, Auburn University, 2012, 1–2.

25. Thomas J. Miles, "Estimating the Effect of *America's Most Wanted*: A Duration Analysis of Wanted Fugitives," *Journal of Law and Economics*, 48 (April 2005): 281–306, discusses some of the variables that affect hiding duration.

26. Liam Collins, "The Abbottabad Documents: Bin Laden's Security Measures," *CTC Sentinel* 5, 5 (May 2012): 1–4.

27. Osama bin Laden letter, April 26, 2011, SOCOM-2012–0000010-HT, http://www.ctc.usma.edu/posts/socom-2012–0000010-english, 8.

28. David Tucker, *Illuminating the Dark Arts of War: Terrorism, Sabotage, and Subversion in Homeland Security and the New Conflict* (New York: Continuum, 2012), 219–40.

29. Lamb and Munsing, "Secret Weapon," 49–53; Bin Laden letter, 8; Joby Warrick, *Triple Agent: The al Qaeda Mole Who Infiltrated the CIA* (New York: Doubleday, 2011).

30. Andradé, *Ashes to Ashes*, 188–91; Mark Urban, *Task Force Black: The Explosive True Story of the Secret Special Forces War in Iraq* (New York: Little, Brown, 2011).

31. Stanley McChrystal, *My Share of the Task: A Memoir* (New York: Portfolio Publishing, 2013), 161, 259.

32. Carter Malkasian, "Toward a Better Understanding of Attrition: The Korean and Vietnam Wars," *Journal of Military History*, 68 (July 2004): 911–42.

33. Flavia Krause-Jackson and Hans Nichols, "Obama Poised to Step up Criticism of Mubarak if Crackdown Is Intensified," Bloomberg, January 26, 2011.

34. For a typical debate, see Daniel Byman, "Why Drones Work," *Foreign Affairs* 92, 4 (July/August 2013): 32–43; and Audrey Kurth Cronin, "Why Drones Fail," *Foreign Affairs* 92, 4 (July/August 2013): 44–54.

35. Robert C. Toth, "Preemptive Anti-terrorist Raids Allowed," *Washington Post*, April 16, 1984, A19; Abraham McLaughlin, "How Far Americans Would Go to Fight Terror," *Christian Science Monitor*, November 14, 2001, 1.

36. Warrick, *Triple Agent*, 90; "Nigeria's Most Wanted Man, Dead or Alive," *Economist*, August 24, 2103.

37. For different accounts of the effectiveness of leadership targeting, see Jenna Jordan, "When Heads Roll: Assessing the Effectiveness of Leadership Decapitation," *Security Studies* 18 (2009): 719–55; Patrick B. Johnson, "Does Decapitation Work? Assessing the Effectiveness of Leadership Targeting in Counterinsurgency Campaigns," *International Security* 36, 4 (Spring 2012): 47–79; Bryan C. Price, "Targeting Top Terrorists: How Leadership Decapitation Contributes to Counterterrorism," *International Security* 36, 4 (Spring 2012): 9–46; Stephanie Carvin, "The Trouble with Targeted Killing," *Security Studies* 21, 3 (2012): 529–55.

38. Nancy Roberts and Sean Everton, "Strategies for Combating Dark Networks," *Journal of Social Structure* 12, 2 (2011): 1–32.

39. Daniel Kahneman and Gary Klein, "Conditions for Intuitive Expertise: A Failure to Disagree," *American Psychologist* 64, 6 (September 2009): 515–26.

40. Bonnie H. Erickson, "Secret Societies and Social Structure," *Social Forces*

60 (September 1981): 193, 195–97. John Earl Haynes, Harvey Klehr, and Alexander Vasiliev, *Spies: The Rise and Fall of the KGB in America* (New Haven: Yale University Press, 2011), provide numerous examples of "inside" nodes linked to "outside" nodes and the fatal problems this caused for Soviet espionage.

41. Some network analysts recognize this problem. See, for example, Roberts and Everton, "Strategies for Combating Dark Networks," 11, and the sources cited there.

42. Andradé, *Ashes to Ashes*, 37–39.

43. In addition to the studies cited in Footnote 36, see Edward H. Kaplan, Alex Mintz, Shaul Mishal, and Claudio Samban, "What Happened to Suicide Bombings in Israel: Insights from a Terrorist Stock Model," *Studies in Conflict and Terrorism* 28 (2005): 225–35; and Andrew W. Boyden, Philip Menard, and Robert Ramirez, "Making the Case: What Is the Problem with Targeted Killing?" thesis, Naval Postgraduate School, December 2009.

44. Riley Sunderland, "Antiguerrilla Intelligence in Malaya, 1948–1960," Memorandum RM-4172 ISA, September 1964 (Santa Monica, CA: RAND, 1964). For a complementary though not entirely corroborative account, see Karl Hack, "British Intelligence and Counter-Insurgency in the Era of Decolonisation: The Example of Malaya," *Intelligence and National Security* 14, 2 (1999): 124–55. According to Hack, intelligence "was the essential core of operations by 1952–53."

45. Sunderland, "Antiguerrilla Intelligence in Malaya, 1948–1960," 31.

46. Schmitt and Shanker, *Counterstrike*, 83.

47. Sunderland, "Antiguerrilla Intelligence in Malaya, 1948–1960," 54, 46.

48. Keegan, *Intelligence in War*, 219.

49. David Tucker, *Skirmishes at the Edge of Empire: The United States and International Terrorism* (Westport, CT: Praeger Publishers, 1997), 40–41, 104, citing newspaper reports; and Duane R. Clarridge with Digby Diehl, *A Spy for All Seasons: My Life in the CIA* (New York: Scribner, 1997), 336, who offer similar yet different accounts of the operation against the ANO; Mobley, *Terrorism and Counterintelligence*, 20–62.

50. David Cunningham, *There's Something Happening Here: The New Left, the Klan, and FBI Counterintelligence* (Berkeley: University of California Press, 2004), 50–51; John Drabble, "The FBI, COINTELPRO-WHITE HATE, and the Decline of the Ku Klux Klan Organizations in Alabama," *Alabama Review* 61 (January 2008): 3–47.

51. Manuel R. Torres Soriano, "The Vulnerabilities of Online Terrorism," *Studies in Conflict and Terrorism* 35 (2012): 263–77.

52. Sunderland, "Antiguerrilla Intelligence in Malaya, 1948–1960," 42.

53. Keegan, *Intelligence in War*, 97.

54. Kitson, *Low-Intensity Operations*, 97.

55. Major General Michael Flynn, USA, Captain Matt Pottinger, USMC, and Paul D. Batchelor, DIA, "Fixing Intel: A Blueprint for Making Intelligence Relevant in Afghanistan," Voices from the Field, Center for a New American Security, January 2011.

56. For details, see Tucker, *Illuminating the Dark Arts of War*, 95–107.

57. For some evidence on the fate of nonstate actors in the information age, see Appendix B.

Chapter 6

1. Milt Bearden and James Risen, *The Main Enemy: the Inside Story of the CIA's Final Showdown with the KGB* (New York: Random House, 2003), 477.

2. Bearden and Risen, *The Main Enemy*, 479.

3. Bearden and Risen, *The Main Enemy*, 481.

4. Bearden and Risen, *The Main Enemy*, 477, 479.

5. Edgar Kiser, "Comparing Varieties of Agency Theory in Economics, Political Science, and Sociology: An Illustration from State Policy Implementation," *Sociological Theory* 17 (July 1999): 146.

6. Peter D. Feaver, *Armed Servants: Agency, Oversight, and Civil-Military Relations* (Cambridge: Harvard University Press, 2003), 68.

7. On the residual effect of these origins, consider Burton Gerber, "Managing Humint: The Need for a New Approach," in *Transforming U.S. Intelligence*, ed. Jennifer E. Sims and Burton Gerber (Washington, DC: Georgetown University Press, 2005), 189.

8. For this perspective, see in addition to Feaver, *Armed Servants*; and John Brehm and Scott Gates, *Working, Shirking and Sabotage: Bureaucratic Response to a Democratic Public* (Ann Arbor: University of Michigan Press, 1999); Jan-Erik Lane, *Public Administration and Public Management: The Principal-Agent Perspective* (New York: Routledge, 2005).

9. Kiser, "Comparing Varieties of Agency Theory in Economics, Political Science, and Sociology," 154. For an example of "bureaucratic drift," consider William Heisel, "HUD's Dollar Homes Falls Short of Mission," Los Angeles Times, April 12, 2009, http://www.latimes.com/news/nationworld/nation/la-fi-dollarhome12–2009apr12,0,641747.story?page=1.

"HUD officials said that because the Dollar Homes program was mandated by Congress, it does not receive the same type of attention and follow-up as programs created by HUD itself. 'You have to keep in mind that this program wasn't created for success,' said Vance Morris, the director of HUD's office of single-family asset management, which oversees the Dollar Homes program. 'Sometimes you have programs created for success and others that were created to be compliant with the law. In this case, we are just complying with the law.'"

10. John MacGaffin, "Clandestine Human Intelligence: Spies, Counterspies, and Covert Action," in *Transforming U.S. Intelligence*, 94–95.

11. David Tucker, *Confronting the Unconventional: Innovation and Transformation in Military Affairs* (Carlisle, PA: U.S. Army War College, 2006); Amy B. Zegart, *Spying Blind: The CIA, the FBI, and the Origins of 9/11* (Princeton: Princeton University Press, 2007), 120–68.

12. James Q. Wilson, *Bureaucracy: What Government Agencies Do and Why They Do It* (New York: Basic Books, 1989), 154–75.

13. I am indebted to Christopher J. Lamb for pointing this out.

14. Robert Jervis, "Intelligence, Counterintelligence, Perception, and Deception," in *Vaults, Masks and Mirrors: Rediscovering U.S. Counterintelligence*, ed. Jennifer Sims and Burton Gerber (Washington, DC: Georgetown University Press, 2009), 73.

15. Jervis, "Intelligence, Counterintelligence, Perception, and Deception," 73.

16. The Commission on the Intelligence Capabilities of the United States Regarding Weapons of Mass Destruction, Report to the President of the United States, March 31, 2005, http://govinfo.library.unt.edu/wmd/about.html, 159.

17. Francis Fukuyama, *State-Building: Government and World Order in the 21st Century* (Ithaca, NY: Cornell University Press, 2004), 43–45.

18. Wilson, *Bureaucracy*, 155.

19. On this point, see also Gerber, "Managing HUMINT," 190–91.

20. See Lane, *Public Administration and Public Management*, 63–76. Feaver discusses budgeting as a way of encouraging efficiency in the military and the problems with this approach, *Armed Servants*, 77–78.

21. MacGaffin, "Clandestine Human Intelligence," 94.

22. The Commission on the Intelligence Capabilities of the United States Regarding Weapons of Mass Destruction, 367; Sandy Grimes and Jeanne Vertefeuille, *Circle of Treason: A CIA Account of Traitor Aldrich Ames and the Men He Betrayed* (Annapolis, MD: Naval Institute Press, 2012), 126, 136, 186.

23. For the comments of a case officer on the polygraph, see Duane R. Clarridge, *A Spy for All Seasons: My Life in the CIA* (New York: Scribner, 1997), 146.

24. For example, Feaver, *Armed Servants*, 72–75.

25. Clarridge, *A Spy for All Seasons*, 80–81; Gerber, "Managing HUMINT," 189.

26. Grimes and Vertefeuille, *Circle of Treason*, 135.

27. MacGaffin, "Clandestine Human Intelligence," 80, 86, insists on this point.

28. Alan Marshall, *Intelligence and Espionage in the Reign of Charles II, 1660–1685* (Cambridge: Cambridge University Press, 1994), 26, 120.

29. Keith Jeffery, *MI6: The History of the Secret Intelligence Service, 1909–1949* (London: Bloomsbury, 2010), 633.

30. The Commission on the Intelligence Capabilities of the United States Regarding Weapons of Mass Destruction, 159.

31. Grimes and Vertefeuille, *Circle of Treason*, 42, 73; Henry A. Crumpton, *The Art of Intelligence: Lessons from a Life in the CIA's Clandestine Service* (New York: Penguin Press, 2012), 113.

32. Kiser, "Comparing Varieties of Agency Theory in Economics, Political Science, and Sociology," 152.

33. On this point, consider Gerber, "Managing HUMINT," 190–91; Crumpton, *The Art of Intelligence*, 65.

34. On U.S. government inspectors general, see Kathryn Newcomer and George Grob, "Federal Offices of the Inspector General: Thriving on Chaos?" *American Review of Public Administration* 34, 3 (September 2004): 235–51.

35. Newcomer and Grob, "Federal Offices of the Inspector General," 240.

36. Newcomer and Grob, "Federal Offices of the Inspector General," 240–43.

37. "CIA-U.S. Senate Spat Complicates Spying Oversight," March 19, 2014, www.azcentral.com/story/news/politics/2014/03/19/cia-us-senate-spat-complicates-spying-oversight/6628881/.

38. Liane Hansen, "Interview: Frederick Hitz Discusses His Book 'The Great Game: The Myth and Reality of Espionage,'" National Public Radio, Weekend Edition, May 16, 2004.

39. On the monitoring or oversight of intelligence organizations by Congress, see Loch K. Johnson, "Governing in the Absence of Angels: On the Practice of Intelligence Accountability in the United States," in *Who's Watching the Spies? Establishing Intelligence Service Accountability*, ed. Hans Born, Loch K. Johnson, and Ian Leigh (Washington, DC: Potomac Books, 2005), 57–78; and Amy Zegart, *Eyes on Spies: Congress and the United States Intelligence Community* (Stanford: Hoover Institution Press, 2011).

40. On this issue, see Angelo M. Codevilla and Frederick Hitz, "Symposium: Q: Is New Leadership Needed to Restore the Central Intelligence Agency?" *Insight on the News* 18, 13 (April 15, 2002): 40–44, which discusses and illustrates a host of prejudices. Consider also James Risen, "Reason Cited for Ousting of Terror Inquiry's Director," *New York Times*, May 9, 2002, A34; and Greg Miller, "Leader of 9/11 Probe Resigns Suddenly; Terror: Ex-CIA Official Was Hired to Investigate Why Spy Agencies Failed to Halt Attacks. Some Feared He Would Go Easy on Ex-employer," *Los Angeles Times*, April 30, 2002, A1, which recount the personal connections and activities of a former CIA inspector general.

41. On fire alarms, see Johnson, "Governing in the Absence of Angels," 59–60; and Kiser, "Comparing Varieties of Agency Theory in Economics, Political Science, and Sociology," 155.

42. Grimes and Vertefeuille, *Circle of Treason*, 151–52, 159.

43. For an example of this, see Wilson, *The Investigators: Managing FBI and Narcotics Agents* (New York: Basic Books, 1978), 194.

44. Wilson, *Bureaucracy*, 169–70; David Ignatius, "Danger Point in Spy Reform," *Washington Post*, October 21, 2005, A23, and "How the CIA Came Unglued," *Washington Post*, May 12, 2006, A21. See also John Diamond, *The CIA and the Culture of Failure: U.S. Intelligence from the End of the Cold War to the Invasion of Iraq* (Stanford: Stanford University Press, 2008), 224–25.

45. Kiser, "Comparing Varieties of Agency Theory in Economics, Political Science, and Sociology," 155; and Wilson, *Bureaucracy*, 163–64.

46. The Commission on the Intelligence Capabilities of the United States Regarding Weapons of Mass Destruction, 160.

47. "Report on the Guatemala Review," June 28, 1996, President's Intelligence Oversight Board, www.ciponline.org/iob.htm#ASSET.

48. Fukuyama, *State-Building*, 50.

49. Wilson, *Bureaucracy*, 168–71, discusses other organizations like HUMINT organizations, in which monitoring is particularly difficult.

50. On these points, see Wilson, *Bureaucracy*, 156–57; Brehm and Gates, *Working, Shirking, and Sabotage*, 3, 75–92, 107–8. Consider also David Dickinson and Marie-Claire Villeval, "Does Monitoring Decrease Work Effort? The Complementarity between Agency and Crowding-out Theories," *Games and Economic Behavior* 63 (2008): 56–76; and Torre Ellingsen and Magnus Johannesson, "Pride and Prejudice: The Human Side of Incentive Theory," *American Economic Review* 98, 3 (2008): 990–1008.

51. Wilson, *The Investigators*, 161.

52. Wilson, *Bureaucracy*, 162; Wilson, *The Investigators*, 126–47, provides an extended discussion.

53. On what was important to the FBI, see Wilson, *The Investigators*, 165–72.

54. Wilson, *The Investigators*, 131, 144.

55. Wilson, *The Investigators*, 131.

56. Crumpton, *The Art of Intelligence*, 100.

57. Clarridge, *A Spy for All Seasons*, 82. According to one intelligence officer (interviewed by the author), the standard of one significant recruitment a tour was actually promulgated at one time in the CIA or at least in one of its divisions.

58. Lanse Minkler, "Shirking and Motivations in Firms: Survey Evidence on Worker Attitudes," *International Journal of Industrial Organization* 22 (2004): 863–84. See also Torre Ellingsen and Magnus Johannesson, "Pride and Prejudice: The Human Side of Incentive Theory," *American Economic Review* 98, 3 (2008): 990–1008; David Dickinson and Marie-Claire Villeval, "Does Monitoring Decrease Work Effort?: The Complementarity between Agency and Crowding-Out Theories," *Games and Economic Behavior* 63 (2008): 56–76; Dirk Sliwka, "Trust as a Signal of a Social Norm and the Hidden Costs of Incentive Schemes," *American Economic Review* 97 (June 2007): 999–1012; and Michael C. Jensen, "Self-Interest, Altruism,

Incentives and Agency Theory," in *Foundations of Organizational Strategy*, ed. Michael C. Jensen (Cambridge: Harvard University Press, 1998).

59. For example, *Dan Ariely, Anat Bracha,* and *Stephan Meier*, "Doing Good or Doing Well? Image Motivation and Monetary Incentives in Behaving Prosocially," *American Economic Review* 99 (March 2009): 544–55.

60. Wilson, *Bureaucracy*, 110.

61. Wilson, *Bureaucracy*, 97–98; Wilson, *The Investigators*, 166–68, 171.

62. R. Jeffrey Smith, "Files Unsealed before Sentencing Detail Rule-Breaker's Rise at CIA," *Washington Post*, February 26, 2009, A3, reports that "CIA officer Kyle 'Dusty' Foggo, who pleaded guilty in September to wire fraud, rose steadily through the agency's ranks to become its third-highest-ranking official despite a record of misconduct and warnings in his personnel file that he was willing to disregard or break the agency's rules, according to Justice Department documents unsealed yesterday in preparation for Foggo's sentencing today in Alexandria." Consider also Joby Warrick and R. Jeffrey Smith, "Latest CIA Scandal Puts Focus on How Agency Polices Self," *Washington Post*, March 20, 2009, A1. This article does not refer to the Foggo scandal.

63. For details, see David Tucker and Christopher J. Lamb, *United States Special Operations Forces* (New York: Columbia University Press, 2007), 69–106.

64. Gerber, "Managing HUMINT," 192.

65. Harry V. Jaffa, "Can There Be Another Winston Churchill?" in *Statesmanship: Essays in Honor of Sir Winston Churchill*, ed. Harry V. Jaffa (Durham, NC: Carolina Academic Press, 1981), 32.

Conclusion

1. Robert Jervis, *Why Intelligence Fails: Lessons from the Iranian Revolution and the Iraq War* (Ithaca, NY: Cornell University Press, 2010), 187, 189–93; Philip E. Tetlock, *Expert Political Judgment: How Good Is It? How Can We Know?* (Princeton: Princeton University Press, 2005).

2. C. A. Bayly, *Empire and Information: Intelligence Gathering and Social Communication in India, 1780–1870* (Cambridge: Cambridge University Press, 1996); Martin Thomas, *Empires of Intelligence: Security Services and Colonial Disorder after 1914* (Berkeley: University of California Press, 2008); Priya Satia, *Spies in Arabia: The Great War and the Cultural Foundations of Britain's Covert Empire in the Middle East* (New York: Oxford University Press, 2008).

3. For some suggestions along these lines, see Christopher J. Lamb and David Tucker, "Restructuring Special Operations Forces for Emerging Threats," *Strategic Forum* no. 219, Institute for National Strategic Studies, National Defense University, January 2006.

4. Jervis, *Why Intelligence Fails*, 140, 142.

5. Alan Marshall, *Intelligence and Espionage in the Reign of Charles II, 1660–1685* (Cambridge: Cambridge University Press, 1994), 120.

6. Henry A. Crumpton, *The Art of Intelligence: Lessons from a Life in the CIA's Clandestine Service* (New York: Penguin Press, 2012).

7. Winston S. Churchill, *Amid These Storms: Thoughts and Adventures* (New York: Charles Scribner's Sons, 1932), 305–20.

8. Aristotle, *Nicomachean Ethics*, 1143b13–14; 1144a11–12.

Appendix A

1. Michael I. Handel, *War, Strategy and Intelligence* (London: Frank Cass and Company, 1989), 230, 132.

2. Richard K. Betts, *Surprise Attack: Lessons for Defense Planning* (Washington, DC: Brookings Institution, 1982); Ephraim Kam, *Surprise Attack: The Victim's Perspective* (Cambridge: Harvard University Press, 1988, 2004); Scott Helfstein, "Backfire: Behavioral Decision Making and the Strategic Risks of Successful Surprise," *Foreign Policy Analysis* 8 (2012): 275–92.

Appendix B

1. Bruce Hoffman, *Inside Terrorism* (New York: Columbia University Press, 2006), 197–228.

2. "Views of Extremism," Pew Research, Global Attitudes Project, www.pewglobal.org/2012/07/10/chapter-5-views-of-extremism-2/; "Osama bin Laden Largely Discredited among Muslim Publics in Recent Years," Pew Research, Global Attitudes Project, www.pewglobal.org/2011/05/02/osama-bin-laden-largely-discredited-among-muslim-publics-in-recent-years/.

3. Hoffman, *Inside Terrorism*, 197–228; Thomas X. Hammes, "War Evolves into the Fourth Generation," *Contemporary Security Policy* 26, 2 (August 2005): 189–221; John Arquilla, *Aspects of Netwar and the Conflict with al Qaeda* (Monterey, CA: Information Operations Center, 2009).

4. Max Boot, *Invisible Armies: An Epic History of Guerrilla Warfare from Ancient Times to the Present* (New York: Liveright Publishing Corporation, 2013), Appendix, Summary of Database.

5. Seth G. Jones and Martin C. Libicki, *How Terrorist Groups End: Lessons for Countering al Qa'ida* (Santa Monica, CA: RAND, 2008), xiv, 100–101.

6. Audrey Kurth Cronin, *How Terrorism Ends: Understanding the Decline and Demise of Terrorist Campaigns* (Princeton: Princeton University Press, 2009), 215.

7. Cronin, *How Terrorism Ends,* 216–17.

8. David Ronfeldt, John Arquilla, Graham E. Fuller, and Melissa Fuller, *The Zapatista Social Netwar in Mexico* (Santa Monica, CA: RAND, 1998).

9. John Ferris, "Generations at War?" *Contemporary Security Policy* 26, 2 (August 2005): 252.

10. Hammes, "War Evolves into the Fourth Generation," 190.

Selected Bibliography

Ahern, Thomas L. Jr. "The Way We Do Things: Black Entry Operations into North Vietnam." Center for the Study of Intelligence, Central Intelligence Agency, May, 2005.

Ambrose, Stephen. *Ike's Spies: Eisenhower and the Espionage Establishment.* New York: Anchor Books, 1981.

Andradé, Dale. *Ashes to Ashes: The Phoenix Program and the Vietnam War.* Lanham, MD: Lexington Books, 1990.

Andres, Richard B., Craig Wills, and Thomas E. Griffith, Jr. "Winning with Allies: The Strategic Value of the Afghan Model." *International Security* 30, 3 (Winter 2005/6): 124–60.

Andrew, Christopher, and Vasili Mitrokhin. *The Sword and the Shield: The Mitrokhin Archive and the Secret History of the KGB.* New York: Basic Books, 1999.

Arquilla, John. *Aspects of Netwar and the Conflict with al Qaeda.* Monterey, CA: Information Operations Center, 2009.

Arquilla, John, and David Ronfeldt. "Cyberwar Is Coming." In *In Athena's Camp: Preparing for Conflict in the Information Age.* Edited by John Arquilla and David Ronfeldt. Santa Monica, CA: RAND, 1997.

Austin, N. J. E., and N. B. Rankov. *Exploratio: Military and Political Intelligence in the Roman World from the Second Punic War to the Battle of Adrianople.* New York: Routledge, 1998.

Bacon, Francis. *The New Organon and Related Writings.* Edited by Fulton H. Anderson. Indianapolis, IN: Bobbs-Merrill Company, 1960.

Bagley, Paul J. "On the Practice of Esotericism." *Journal of the History of Ideas* 53, 2 (April–June 1992): 231–47.

Bamford, Bradley W. C. "The Role and Effectiveness of Intelligence in Northern Ireland." *Intelligence and National Security* 20, 4 (December 2005): 581–607.

Bayly, C. A. *Empire and Information: Intelligence Gathering and Social Communication in India, 1780–1870.* Cambridge: Cambridge University Press, 1996.

Bearden, Milt, and James Risen. *The Main Enemy: The Inside Story of the CIA's Final Showdown with the KGB.* New York: Random House, 2003.

Bennett, Ralph. "Intelligence and Strategy: Some Observations on the War in the Mediterranean, 1941–1942." In *Intelligence and Military Operations.* Edited by Michael I. Handel. London: Frank Cass and Company, 1990.

Bernstein, Peter L. *Against the Gods: The Remarkable Story of Risk.* New York: John Wiley and Sons, 1996.

Bertrand, Gustave. *Enigma ou la Plus Grande Enigme de la Guerre 1939–1945.* Paris: Librairie Plon, 1973.

Betts, Richard K. *Surprise Attack: Lessons for Defense Planning.* Washington, DC: Brookings Institution, 1982.

———. *Enemies of Intelligence: Knowledge and Power in American National Security.* New York: Columbia University Press, 2009.

Beyerchen, Alan. "Clausewitz, Nonlinearity, and the Unpredictability of War." *International Security* 17, 3 (Winter 1991/92).

Biddle, Stephen. *Military Power: Explaining Victory and Defeat in Modern Battle.* Princeton: Princeton University Press, 2004.

———. "Military Power: A Reply." *Journal of Strategic Studies* 28, 3 (June 2005): 453–69.

———. "Allies, Airpower, and Modern Warfare: The Afghan Model in Afghanistan and Iraq." *International Security* 30, 3 (Winter 2005/6): 164–67.

———. "Iraq, Afghanistan, and American Military Transformation." In *Strategy in the Contemporary World.* Edited by John Bayliss, James Wirtz, Colin S. Gray, and Eliot Cohen. New York: Oxford University Press, 2007.

Bonilla, Diego Navarro. "'Secret Intelligences' in European Military, Political and Diplomatic Theory: An Essential Factor in the Defense of the Modern State (Sixteenth and Seventeenth Centuries)." *Intelligence and National Security* 27, 2 (2012): 283–301.

Bowden, Mark. *The Finish: The Killing of Osama bin Laden.* New York: Atlantic Monthly Press, 2012.

Bowles, Chester. *Promises to Keep: My Years in Public Life, 1941–1969.* New York: Harper and Row, 1971.

Boyden, Andrew W., Philip Menard, and Robert Ramirez. "Making the Case: What Is the Problem with Targeted Killing?" Thesis, Naval Postgraduate School, December 2009.

Brenner, Joel. *America the Vulnerable: Inside the New Threat Matrix of Digital Espionage, Crime and Warfare.* New York: Penguin Press, 2011.

Brewer, John. *The Sinews of Power: War, Money and the English State, 1688–1783.* New York: Alfred A. Knopf, 1989.

Budiansky, Stephen. *Her Majesty's Spymaster: Elizabeth I, Sir Francis Walsingham, and the Birth of Modern Espionage.* New York: Penguin Group, 2005.

Burke, Peter. "Tacitism, Skepticism, and Reason of State." In *The Cambridge History of Political Thought 1450–1700.* Edited by J. H. Burns and Mark Goldie. Cambridge: Cambridge University Press, 1991.

Burkett, Randy. "An Alternative Framework for Agent Recruitment: From MICE to RASCALS." *Studies in Intelligence* 57, 1 (Extracts, March 2013).

Bush, Vannevar. *Modern Arms and Free Men: A Discussion of the Role of Science in Preserving Democracy.* New York: Simon and Schuster, 1949.

———. "Science, the Endless Frontier: A Report to the President on a Program for Postwar Scientific Research." Office of Scientific Research and Development, July 5, 1945. Washington, DC,: National Science Foundation, 1960.

Callwell, C. E. *Small Wars: Their Principles and Practice.* Edited by Douglas Porch. Lincoln: University of Nebraska Press, 1996.

Canning, Joseph. *Ideas of Power in the Late Middle Ages, 1279–1417.* Cambridge: Cambridge University Press, 2011.

Carter, Charles Howard. *The Secret Diplomacy of the Habsburgs, 1598–1625.* New York: Columbia University Press, 1962.

Carvin, Stephanie. "The Trouble with Targeted Killing." *Security Studies* 21, 3 (2012): 529–55.

Cherkashin, Victor, with Gregory Feifer. *Spy Handler: Memoir of a KGB Officer.* New York: Basic Books, 2005.

Churchill, Winston S. *Amid These Storms: Thoughts and Adventures.* New York: Charles Scribner's Sons, 1932.

Clarke, Richard A., and Robert K. Knake. *Cyber War: The Next Threat to National Security and What to Do about It.* New York: Ecco, 2010.

Clarridge, Duane R., with Digby Diehls. *A Spy for All Seasons: My Life in the CIA.* New York: Scribner, 1997.

Codevilla, Angelo M., and Frederick Hitz. "Symposium: Q: Is New Leadership Needed to Restore the Central Intelligence Agency?" *Insight on the News* 18, 13 (April 15, 2002): 40–44.

Cohen, Eliot. "Stephen Biddle on Military Power." *Journal of Strategic Studies* 28, 3 (June 2005): 413–24.

Coll, Steve. *Ghost Wars: The Secret History of the CIA, Afghanistan, and bin Laden, from the Soviet Invasion to September 10, 2001.* New York: Penguin Books, 2005.

Collins, Eamon, with Mick McGovern. *Killing Rage.* London: Granta Books, 1997.

Collins, Liam. "The Abbottabad Documents: Bin Laden's Security Measures." *CTC Sentinel* 5, 5 (May 2012).

Conboy, Kenneth, and Dale Andradé. *Spies and Commandos: How America Lost the Secret War in North Vietnam.* Lawrence: University Press of Kansas, 2000.

Crenshaw, Martha. "Theories of Terrorism: Instrumental and Organizational Approaches." In *Inside Terrorist Organizations.* Edited by David C. Rapoport. New York: Columbia University Press, 1988.

Crumpton, Henry A. *The Art of Intelligence: Lessons from a Life in the CIA's Clandestine Service.* New York: Penguin Press, 2012.

Cunningham, David. *There's Something Happening Here: The New Left, the Klan, and FBI Counterintelligence.* Berkeley: University of California Press, 2004.

Dening, Major C. B. "Modern Problems of Guerilla Warfare." *Army Quarterly and Defence Journal* 13 (1926).

Diamond, John. *The CIA and the Culture of Failure: U.S. Intelligence from the End of the Cold War to the Invasion of Iraq.* Stanford: Stanford University Press, 2008.

Drabble, John. "The FBI, COINTELPRO-WHITE HATE, and the Decline of the Ku Klux Klan Organizations in Alabama." *Alabama Review* 61 (January 2008): 3–47.

Eamon, William. *Science and the Secrets of Nature: Books of Secrets in Medieval and Early Modern Culture.* Princeton: Princeton University Press, 1996.

Erickson, Bonnie H. "Secret Societies and Social Structure." *Social Forces* 60 (September 1981).

Feaver, Peter D. *Armed Servants: Agency, Oversight, and Civil-Military Relations.* Cambridge: Harvard University Press, 2003.

Felix, Christopher. *A Short Course in the Secret War.* Lanham, MD: Madison Books, 1963, 2001.

Ferrill, Arther. *The Origins of War: From the Stone Age to Alexander the Great.* Boulder, CO: Westview Press, 1991.

———. "Roman Military Intelligence." In *Go Spy the Land: Military Intelligence in History.* Edited by Keith Neilson and B. J. C. McKercher. Westport, CT: Praeger, 1992.

Fischer, Benjamin B. "The Vilification and Vindication of Colonel Kukliński." www.cia.gov/library/center-for-the-study-of-intelligence/kent csi/vol44no3/html/v44i3a03 htm#fnr41.

Floridi, Luciano. *Information: A Very Short Introduction.* New York: Oxford University Press, 2010.

Flynn, Major General Michael, USA, Captain Matt Pottinger, USMC, and Paul D. Batchelor. "Fixing Intel: A Blueprint for Making Intelligence Relevant in Afghanistan." Voices from the Field, Center for a New American Security, January 2011.

Foot, M. R. D. "What Good Did Resistance Do?" In *Resistance in Europe, 1939–1945.* Based on the proceedings of a symposium held at the University of Salford, March 1973. Edited by Stephen Hawes and Ralph White. London: Allen Lane, 1975.

———. *Resistance: European Resistance to Nazism, 1940–1945.* New York: McGraw-Hill, 1977.

———. *SOE in France: An Account of the Work of the British Special Operations Executive in France, 1940–1944.* London: Frank Cass, 2004.

Freeberg, David. *The Eye of the Lynx: Galileo, His Friends and the Beginnings of Modern Natural History*. Chicago: Chicago University Press, 2003.

Gartzke, Erik. "The Myth of Cyberwar: Bringing War in Cyberspace Back Down to Earth." *International Security* 38, 4 (Fall 2013).

Gerber, Burton. "Managing HUMINT: The Need for a New Approach." In *Transforming U.S. Intelligence*. Edited by Jennifer E. Sims and Burton Gerber. Washington, DC: Georgetown University Press, 2005.

Gilbert, Martin. *The Second World War: A Complete History*. New York: Henry Holt and Company, 1989.

Ginzburg, Carlo. "High and Low: The Theme of Forbidden Knowledge in the Sixteenth and Seventeenth Centuries." *Past and Present* 73 (November 1976): 28–41.

Grenier, John. *The First Way of War: American War Making on the Frontier*. Cambridge: Cambridge University Press, 2005.

Grey, Stephen. *Ghost Plane: The True Story of the CIA Torture Program*. New York: St. Martin's Press, 2006.

Grimes, Sandy, and Jeanne Vertefeuille. *Circle of Treason: A CIA Account of Traitor Aldrich Ames and the Men He Betrayed*. Annapolis, MD: Naval Institute Press, 2012.

Hack, Karl. "British Intelligence and Counter-Insurgency in the Era of Decolonisation: The Example of Malaya." *Intelligence and National Security* 14, 2 (1999): 124–55.

Handel, Michael I. *War, Strategy and Intelligence*. London: Frank Cass and Company, 1989.

———. *Intelligence and Military Operations*. London: Frank Cass and Company, 1990.

Hastings, Max. *Das Reich: The March of the 2nd SS Panzer Division through France*. New York: Holt, Rinehart and Winston, 1981.

———. *Inferno: The World at War, 1939–1945*. New York: Alfred A. Knopf, 2011.

Haynes, John Earl, Harvey Klehr, and Alexander Vasiliev. *Spies: The Rise and Fall of the KGB in America*. New Haven: Yale University Press, 2011.

Headrick, Daniel R. *When Information Came of Age: Technologies of Knowledge in the Age of Reason and Revolution, 1700–1850*. New York: Oxford University Press, 2000.

Helfstein, Scott. "Backfire: Behavioral Decision Making and the Strategic Risks of Successful Surprise." *Foreign Policy Analysis* 8 (2012): 275–92.

Hendricks, Steve. *A Kidnapping in Milan: The CIA on Trial*. New York: W. W. Norton and Company, 2011.

Herbig, Katherine L. "Chance and Uncertainty in *On War*." In *Clausewitz and Modern Strategy*. Edited by Michael I. Handel. London: Frank Cass, 1986.

Herman, Michael. *Intelligence Power in Peace and War*. Cambridge: Cambridge University Press, 1996.

———. *Intelligence Services in the Information Age.* London: Frank Cass, 2002.

Herrington, Stuart (COL, USA Ret.). *Traitors among Us: Inside the Spy Catcher's World.* New York: Harcourt, 1999.

Heuer, Richards J., Jr. *The Psychology of Intelligence Analysis.* www.cia.gov/library/center-for-the-study-of-intelligence/csi-publications/books-and-monographs/psychology-of-intelligence-analysis/art5.html.

Hinsley, Sir Harry. "Thirty-First Harmon Memorial Lecture: World War II: An Intelligence Revolution." In *The Intelligence Revolution: A Historical Perspective,* Proceedings of the Thirteenth Military History Symposium, U.S. Air Force Academy, October 1988. Washington, DC: Office of Air Force History, 1991.

Hobart, Michael E., and Zachary S. Schiffman. *Information Ages: Literacy, Numeracy, and the Computer Revolution.* Baltimore, MD: Johns Hopkins University Press, 1998.

Hornblum, Allen M. *The Invisible Harry Gold: The Man Who Gave the Soviets the Bomb.* New Haven: Yale University Press, 2010.

Horowitz, Michael, and Stephen Rosen. "Evolution or Revolution." *Journal of Strategic Studies* 28, 3 (June 2005): 437–48.

Jacobs, Margaret. *Scientific Culture and the Making of the Industrial West.* New York: Oxford University Press, 1997.

Jaffa, Harry V. "Can There Be Another Winston Churchill?" In *Statesmanship: Essays in Honor of Sir Winston Churchill.* Edited by Harry V. Jaffa. Durham, NC: Carolina Academic Press, 1981.

Jeffrey, Keith. *MI6: The History of the Secret Intelligence Service, 1909–1949.* London: Bloomsbury, 2010.

Jervis, Robert L. "Intelligence, Counterintelligence, Perception, and Deception." In *Vaults, Masks and Mirrors: Rediscovering U.S. Counterintelligence.* Edited by Jennifer Sims and Burton Gerber. Washington, DC: Georgetown University Press, 2009.

———. *Why Intelligence Fails: Lessons from the Iranian Revolution and the Iraq War.* Ithaca, NY: Cornell University Press, 2011.

Johnson, Loch K. "Governing in the Absence of Angels: On the Practice of Intelligence Accountability in the United States." In *Who's Watching the Spies? Establishing Intelligence Service Accountability.* Edited by Hans Born, Loch K. Johnson, and Ian Leigh. Washington, DC: Potomac Books, 2005.

Johnson, Patrick B. "Does Decapitation Work? Assessing the Effectiveness of Leadership Targeting in Counterinsurgency Campaigns." *International Security* 36, 4 (Spring 2012): 47–79.

Jordan, Jenna. "When Heads Roll: Assessing the Effectiveness of Leadership Decapitation." *Security Studies* 18 (2009): 719–55.

Kahn, David. "An Historical Theory of Intelligence." In *Intelligence Theory: Key Questions and Debates.* Edited by Peter Gill, Stephen Marrin, and Mark Pythian. New York: Routledge, 2009.

Kahneman, Daniel, and Gary Klein. "Conditions for Intuitive Expertise: A Failure to Disagree." *American Psychologist* 64, 6 (September 2009): 515–26.

———. *Thinking, Fast and Slow.* New York: Farrar, Straus and Giroux, 2011.

Kam, Ephraim. *Surprise Attack: The Victim's Perspective.* Cambridge: Harvard University Press, 1988, 2004

Keegan, John. *The Second World War.* New York: Viking, 1989.

———. *Intelligence in War: Knowledge of the Enemy from Napoleon to al-Qaeda.* New York: Alfred A. Knopf, 2003.

Keeley, Lawrence H. *War before Civilization: The Myth of the Peaceful Savage.* New York: Oxford University Press, 1996.

Kent, Sherman. *Strategic Intelligence for American World Policy.* Princeton: Princeton University Press, 1949, 1966.

Kitson, Frank. *Low-Intensity Operations: Subversion, Insurgency, Peacekeeping.* Harrisburg, PA: Stackpole Books, 1971.

Kitson, Simon. *The Hunt for Nazi Spies: Fighting Espionage in Vichy France.* Chicago: University of Chicago Press, 2008.

Kochems, Alane. "No More Secrets: National Security Strategies for a Transparent World." Workshop report, American Bar Association Standing Committee on Law and National Security, March 2011.

Kramer, Mark. "The Kukliński Files and the Polish Crisis of 1980–1981: An Analysis of the Newly Released CIA Documents on Ryszard Kukliński." Cold War International History Project, working paper 59. Washington, DC, March 2009.

———. "US Intelligence Performance and US Policy during the Polish Crisis of 1980–81: Revelations from the Kukliński Files." *Intelligence and National Security* 26, 2–3 (April–June 2011): 325–27.

Krepinevich, Andrew F. "Cavalry to Computers: The Pattern of Military Revolutions." *National Interest* 37 (September 1994): 30–42.

Lamb, Christopher J., and Evan Munsing. "Secret Weapon: High-value Target Teams as an Organizational Innovation." Strategic Perspectives 4, Institute for National Strategic Studies, National Defense University, Washington, DC, March 2011.

Lebow, Richard Ned. *Between War and Peace: The Nature of International Crisis.* Baltimore, MD: Johns Hopkins University Press, 1984.

McChrystal, Stanley. *My Share of the Task: A Memoir.* New York: Portfolio Publishing, 2013.

McCormick, G. H., and G. Owen. "Security and Coordination in a Clandestine Organization." *Mathematical and Computer Modeling* 31 (2000): 175–92.

MacGaffin, John. "Clandestine Human Intelligence: Spies, Counterspies, and Covert Action." In *Transforming U.S. Intelligence*. Edited by Jennifer E. Sims and Burton Gerber. Washington, DC: Georgetown University Press, 2005.

McRaven, William H. *Spec Ops: Case Studies in Special Operations Warfare: Theory and Practice*. Novato, CA: Presidio Press, 1995.

Mahnken, Thomas G. *Uncovering Ways of War: U.S. Intelligence and Foreign Military Innovation, 1918–1941*. Ithaca, NY: Cornell University Press, 2002.

Malkasian, Carter. "Toward a Better Understanding of Attrition: The Korean and Vietnam Wars." *Journal of Military History*, 68 (July 2004): 911–42.

Mann, Michael. "The Autonomous Power of the State." In *States in History*. Edited by John A. Hall. New York: Basil Blackwell, 1987.

Marshall, Alan. *Intelligence and Espionage in the Reign of Charles II, 1660–1685*. Cambridge: Cambridge University Press, 1994.

Martin, Julian. *Francis Bacon, the State, and the Reform of Natural Philosophy*. Cambridge: Cambridge University Press, 1992.

Masterman, J. C. *The Double-Cross System in the War of 1939 to 1945*. New Haven: Yale University Press, 1972.

Mazzetti, Mark. *The Way of the Knife: The CIA, a Secret Army, and a War at the Ends of the Earth*. New York: Penguin Press, 2013.

Meistrich, Ira. "War's Cradle." *MHQ: The Quarterly Journal of Military History* 17, 3 (Spring 2005): 84–93.

Miles, Thomas J. "Estimating the Effect of *America's Most Wanted*: A Duration Analysis of Wanted Fugitives." *Journal of Law and Economics* 48 (April 2005): 281–306.

Milward, Alan S. "The Economic and Strategic Effectiveness of Resistance." In *Resistance in Europe, 1939–1945*. Based on the proceedings of a symposium held at the University of Salford, March 1973. Edited by Stephen Hawes and Ralph White. London: Allen Lane, 1975.

Mobley, Blake W. *Terrorism and Counterintelligence: How Terrorist Groups Elude Detection*. New York: Columbia University Press, 2012.

Morgan, Janet. *The Secrets of Rue St. Roch: Hope and Heroism behind Enemy Lines in the First World War*. New York: Penguin Books, 2005.

Morozov, Evgeny. *The Net Delusion: The Dark Side of Internet Freedom*. New York: Public Affairs, 2011.

Murray, Williamson, and Allan R. Millett. *A War to Be Won: Fighting the Second World War*. Cambridge: Belknap Press of Harvard University Press, 2000.

O'Harrow, Robert, Jr. *No Place to Hide*. New York: Free Press, 2005.

Omand, Sir David, Jamie Bartlett, and Carl Miller. "Introducing Social Media Intelligence (SOCMINT)." *Intelligence and National Security* 27, 6 (2012): 801–23.

Orlov, Alexander. *Handbook of Intelligence and Guerrilla Warfare*. Ann Arbor: University of Michigan Press, 1963.

Owens, William A., and Ed Offley. *Lifting the Fog of War*. Baltimore, MD: Johns Hopkins University Press, 2001.

Peritz, Aki, and Eric Rosenbach. *Find, Fix, Finish: Inside the Counterterrorism Campaigns That Killed bin Laden and Devastated al Qaeda*. New York: Public Affairs, 2012.

Pesic, Peter. "Wrestling with Proteus: Francis Bacon and the 'Torture' of Nature." *Isis* 90, 1 (March 1999): 81–94.

Phillips, David Atlee. *The Night Watch*. New York: Atheneum, 1977.

Porch, Douglas. *The French Secret Services: A History of French Intelligence from the Dreyfus Affair to the Gulf War*. New York: Farrar, Straus and Giroux, 1995.

Price, Bryan C. "Targeting Top Terrorists: How Leadership Decapitation Contributes to Counterterrorism." *International Security* 36, 4 (Spring 2012): 9–46.

Roberts, Nancy, and Sean Everton. "Strategies for Combating Dark Networks." *Journal of Social Structure* 12, 2 (2011): 1–32.

Rosenau, William. *Special Operations Forces and Elusive Enemy Ground Targets: Lessons from Vietnam and the Persian Gulf War*. Santa Monica, CA: RAND, 2001.

Russell, Frank S. *Intelligence Gathering in Classical Greece*. Ann Arbor: University of Michigan Press, 1999.

Sanger, David E. *Confront and Conceal: Obama's Secret Wars and Surprising Use of American Power*. New York: Crown Publishers, 2012.

Satia, Priya. *Spies in Arabia: The Great War and the Cultural Foundations of Britain's Covert Empire in the Middle East*. New York: Oxford University Press, 2008.

Schmidt, Eric, and Jared Cohen. *The New Digital Age: Reshaping the Future of People, Nations and* Business. New York: Alfred A. Knopf, 2013.

Schmitt, Eric, and Thom Shanker. *Counterstrike: The Untold Story of America's Secret Campaign against al Qaeda*. New York: Times Books, 2011.

Schroeder, Michael J. "Intelligence Capacities of the U.S. Military in the Sandino Rebellion, Las Segovias, Nicaragua, 1927–1932: Successes, Failures, Lessons." Unpublished manuscript.

Scott, James C. *Seeing Like a State: How Certain Schemes to Improve the Human Condition Have Failed*. New Haven: Yale University Press, 1998.

Sheldon, Rose Mary. *Intelligence Activities in Ancient Rome: Trust in the Gods, but Verify*. New York: Frank Cass, 2005.

Shulsky, Abram, and Gary E. Schmitt, *Silent Warfare: Understanding the World of Intelligence*. 3rd ed. Washington, DC: Brassey's, 2002.

Soll, Jacob. *The Information Minister: Jean-Baptiste Colbert's Secret State Intelligence System*. Ann Arbor: University of Michigan Press, 2009.

Soriano, Manuel R. Torres. "The Vulnerabilities of Online Terrorism." *Studies in Conflict and Terrorism* 35 (2012): 263–77.

Starr, Chester G. *Political Intelligence in Classical Greece.* Leiden: E. J. Brill, 1974.

Sunderland, Riley. "Antiguerrilla Intelligence in Malaya, 1948–1960." Memorandum RM-4172 ISA. Santa Monica, CA: RAND, 1964.

Taylor, Peter. *Beating the Terrorists?: Interrogation in Omagh, Gough and Castlereagh.* London: Penguin Books, 1980.

Tetlock, Philip E. *Expert Political Judgment: How Good Is It? How Can We Know?* Princeton: Princeton University Press, 2005.

Thomas, Martin. *Empires of Intelligence: Security Services and Colonial Disorder after 1914.* Berkeley: University of California Press, 2008.

Treverton, Gregory F. *Intelligence for an Age of Terror.* Cambridge: Cambridge University Press, 2009.

Tripodi, Christian. "Peacemaking through Bribes or Cultural Empathy: The Political Officer and Britain's Strategy towards the North-West Frontier, 1901–1945." *Journal of Strategic Studies* 31 (February 2008): 123–51.

Tucker, David. "Jefferson and the Practice of Empire." In *Natural Right and Political Right: Essays in Honor of Harry V. Jaffa.* Edited by Thomas B. Silver and Peter W. Schramm. Durham, NC: Carolina Academic Press, 1984.

———. *Skirmishes at the Edge of Empire: The United States and International Terrorism* (Westport, CT: Praeger, 1997), 41–42.

———. *Confronting the Unconventional: Innovation and Transformation in Military Affairs.* Carlisle, PA: U.S. Army War College, 2006.

———. *Illuminating the Dark Arts of War: Terrorism, Sabotage, and Subversion in Homeland Security and the New Conflict* (New York: Continuum, 2012).

Tucker, David, and Christopher J. lamb. "Restructuring Special Operations Forces for Emerging Threats." Strategic Forum, no. 219, **Institute for National Strategic Studies, National Defense University, Washington, DC,** 2006.

——— *United States Special Operations Forces.* New York: Columbia University Press, 2007.

Urban, Mark. *Task Force Black: The Explosive True Story of the Secret Special Forces War in Iraq.* New York: Little, Brown, 2011.

Van Cleave, Michelle K. "Counterintelligence and National Strategy." National Defense University Press, Washington, DC, April 2007.

Van Creveld, Martin. *Command in War.* Cambridge: Harvard University Press, 1985.

———. *The Rise and Decline of the State.* Cambridge: Cambridge University Press, 1999.

Waller, Douglas. *Wild Bill Donovan: The Spymaster Who Created the OSS and Modern American Espionage.* New York: Free Press, 2011.

Warrick, Joby. *Triple Agent: The al Qaeda Mole Who Infiltrated the CIA*. New York: Doubleday, 2011.

Weinberg, Gerhard L. *A World at Arms: A Global History of World War II*. New York: Cambridge University Press, 1994.

Weiser, Benjamin. *A Secret Life: The Polish Officer, His Covert Mission, and the Price He Paid to Save His Country*. New York: Public Affairs, 2005.

Wigner, Eugene. "The Unreasonable Effectiveness of Mathematics in the Natural Sciences." *Communications on Pure and Applied Mathematics* 23 (1960): 1–14.

Wilson, James Q. *Bureaucracy: What Government Agencies Do and Why They Do It*. New York: Basic Books, 1989.

Woytak, Richard A. *On the Border of War and Peace: Polish Intelligence and the Diplomacy in 1937–1939 and the Origins of the Ultra Secret*. Boulder, CO: Eastern European Quarterly, 1979.

Young, Robert J. "French Military Intelligence and Nazi Germany, 1938–1939." In *Knowing One's Enemies: Intelligence Assessment before the Two World Wars*. Edited by Ernest R. May. Princeton: Princeton University Press, 1984.

Zegart, Amy. *Spying Blind: The CIA, the FBI, and the Origins of 9/11*. Princeton: Princeton University Press, 2007.

———. *Eyes on Spies: Congress and the United States Intelligence Community*. Stanford: Hoover Institution Press, 2011.

Index